Disney · PIXAR

FINDING NEMO

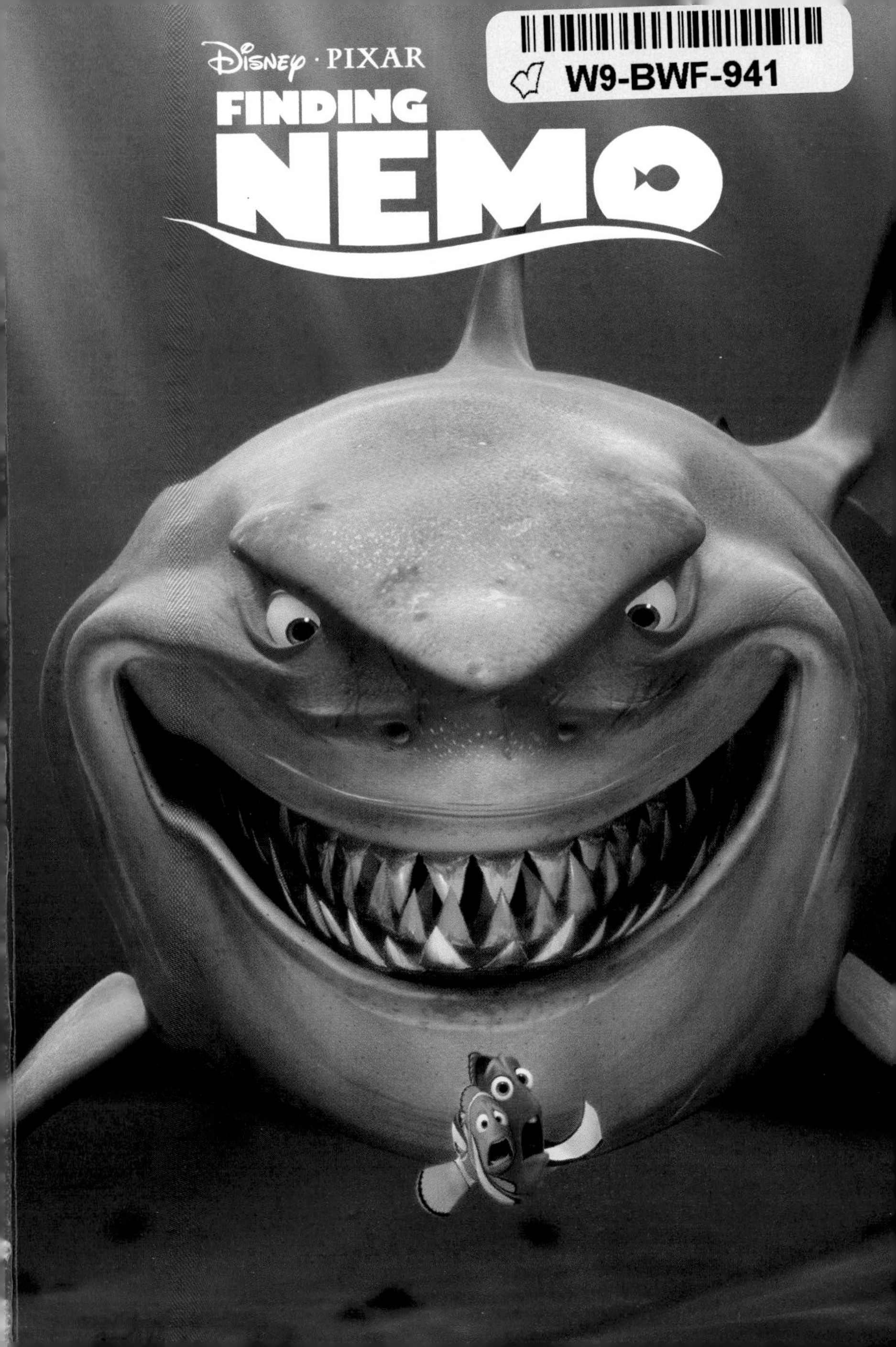

Contributing Editor - Amy Court Kaemon
Copy Editor - Paul Morrissey
Graphic Design and Lettering - Dave Snow
Cover Layout - Anna Kernbaum
Graphic Artists - Anna Kernbaum & Tomás Montalvo-Lagos

Editor - Elizabeth Hurchalla
Managing Editor - Jill Freshney
Production Coordinator - Antonio DePietro
Production Manager - Jennifer Miller
Art Director - Matt Alford
Editorial Director - Jeremy Ross
VP of Production - Ron Klamert
President & C.O.O. - John Parker
Publisher & C.E.O. - Stuart Levy

Email: editor@TOKYOPOP.com
Come visit us online at www.TOKYOPOP.com

A **TOKYOPOP**® Cine-Manga™
TOKYOPOP Inc.
5900 Wilshire Blvd., Suite 2000, Los Angeles, CA 90036

Finding Nemo

ISBN: 1-59182-758-2

First TOKYOPOP® printing: November 2003

10 9 8 7 6 5 4 3 2 1

Printed in Canada

Disney · PIXAR
FINDING NEMO

TOKYOPOP®
Los Angeles • Tokyo • London

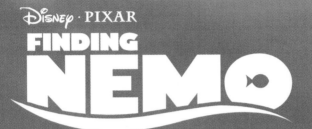

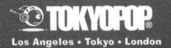

Disney · PIXAR

FINDING NEMO

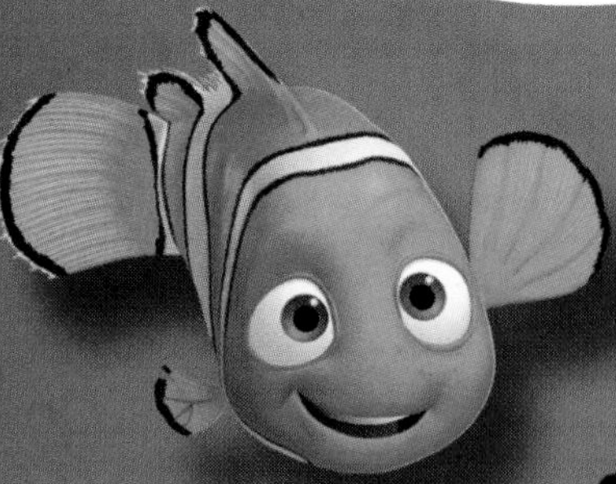

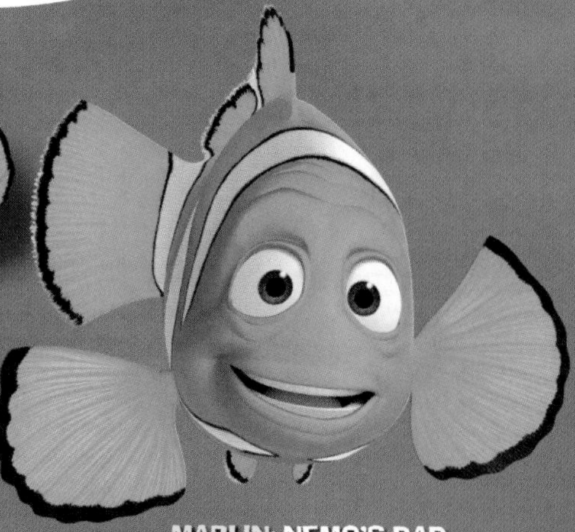

NEMO: A SPIRITED SIX-YEAR-OLD CLOWNFISH WHO LOVES TO PLAY AND CRAVES ADVENTURE.

MARLIN: NEMO'S DAD. HE CAN BE A LITTLE TOO CAUTIOUS SOMETIMES, BUT HE'D CROSS AN ENTIRE OCEAN FOR HIS SON.

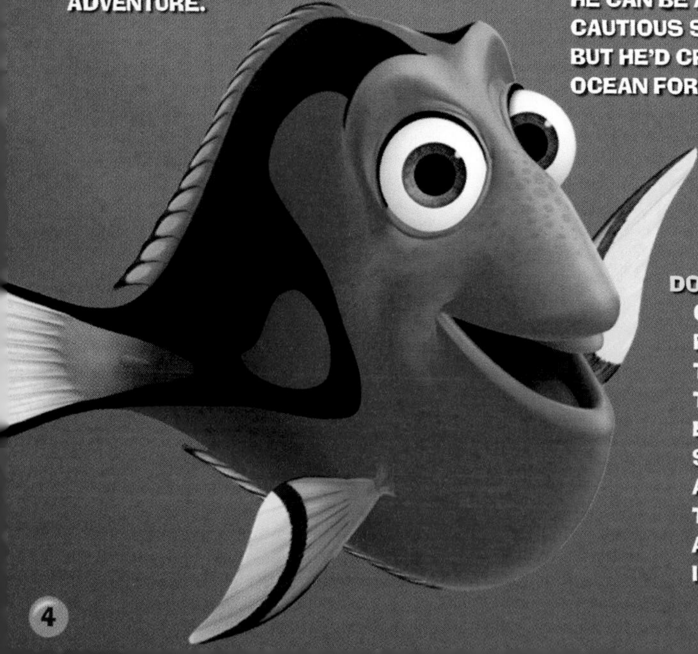

DORY: A HAPPY-GO-LUCKY REGAL BLUE TANG. TRUSTS EVERYONE SHE MEETS AND FORGETS THINGS ALMOST INSTANTLY.

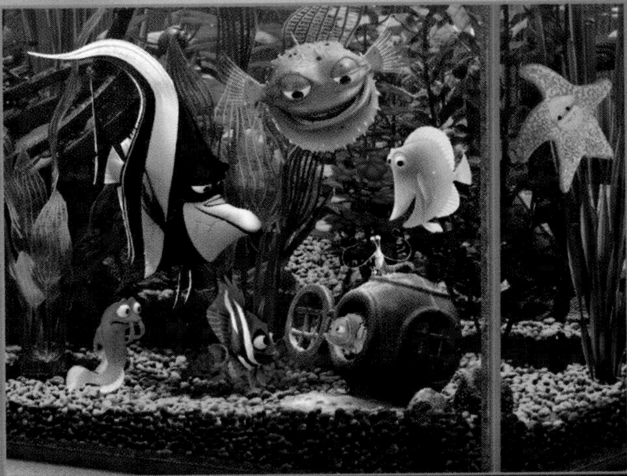

THE TANK GANG: BUBBLES, GURGLE, GILL, DEB, BLOAT, JACQUES AND PEACH ARE THE RESIDENTS OF THE SALT-WATER AQUARIUM ON WALLABY WAY.

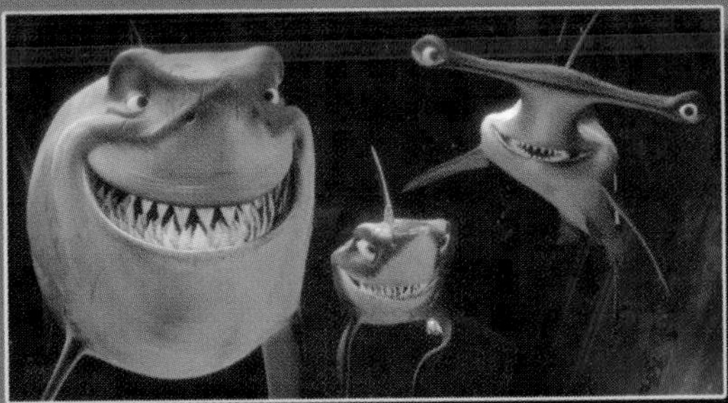

THE SHARKS: BRUCE, CHUM AND ANCHOR ARE FEROCIOUS SHARKS WHO'VE TAKEN AN OATH (TO TRY) NOT TO EAT FISH.

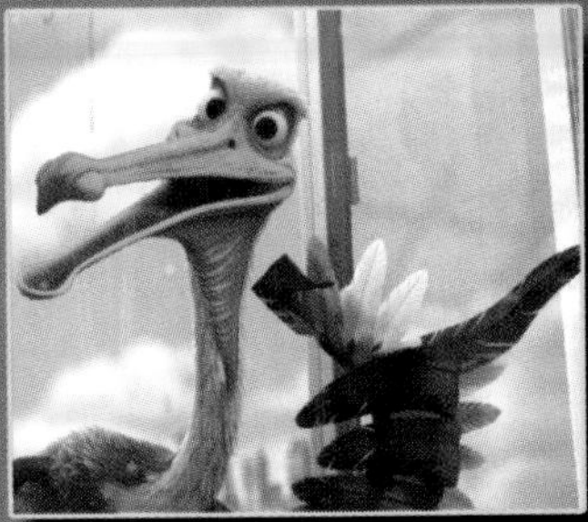

NIGEL: A PELICAN WHO LIVES IN SYDNEY HARBOR AND REGULARLY VISITS THE TANK GANG.

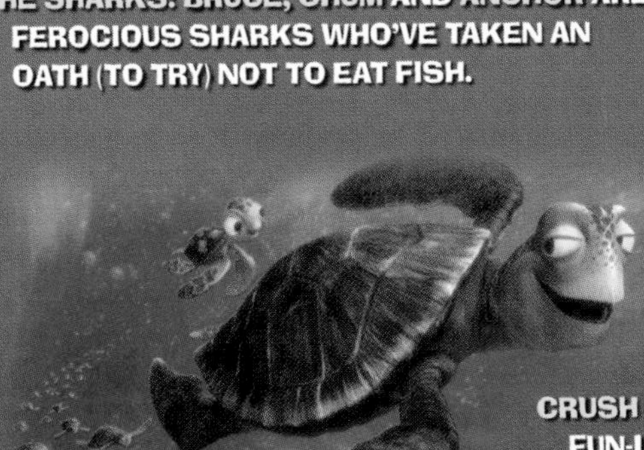

CRUSH AND SQUIRT: CRUSH IS A FUN-LOVING SEA TURTLE WHO LOVES CHASING THRILLS WITH HIS SON, SQUIRT.

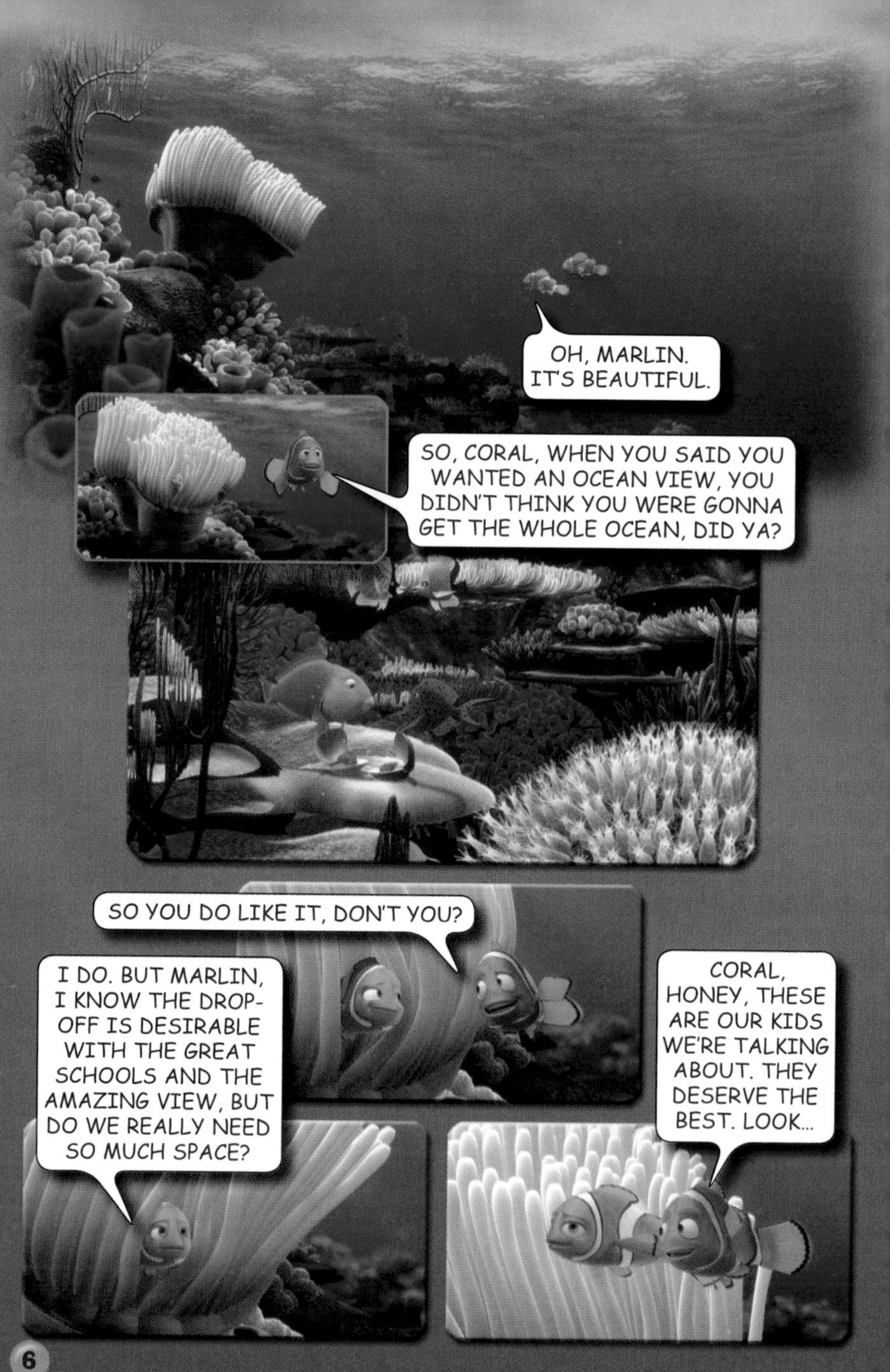
OH, MARLIN. IT'S BEAUTIFUL.
SO, CORAL, WHEN YOU SAID YOU WANTED AN OCEAN VIEW, YOU DIDN'T THINK YOU WERE GONNA GET THE WHOLE OCEAN, DID YA?
SO YOU DO LIKE IT, DON'T YOU?
I DO. BUT MARLIN, I KNOW THE DROP-OFF IS DESIRABLE WITH THE GREAT SCHOOLS AND THE AMAZING VIEW, BUT DO WE REALLY NEED SO MUCH SPACE?
CORAL, HONEY, THESE ARE OUR KIDS WE'RE TALKING ABOUT. THEY DESERVE THE BEST. LOOK...

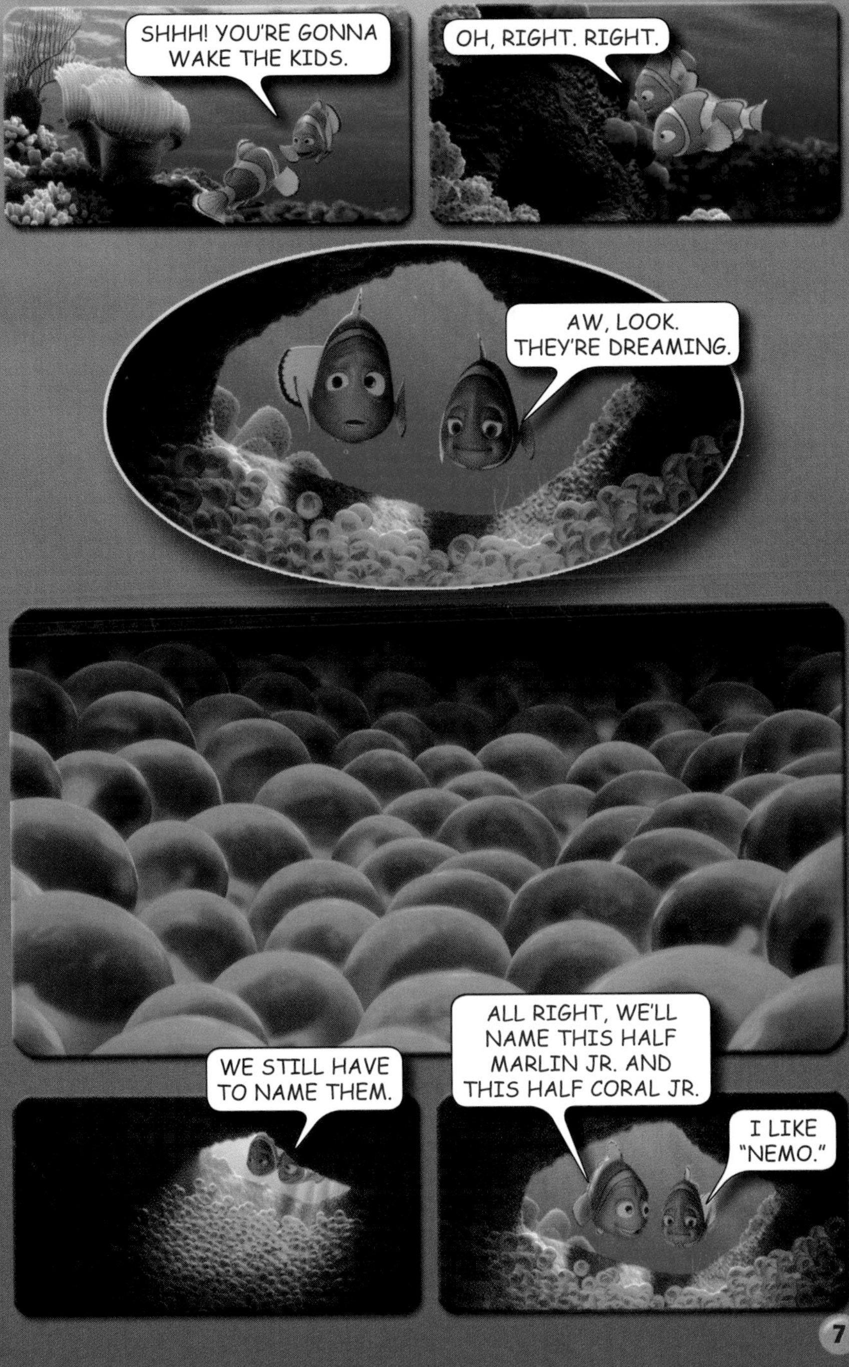
SHHH! YOU'RE GONNA WAKE THE KIDS.
OH, RIGHT. RIGHT.
AW, LOOK. THEY'RE DREAMING.
WE STILL HAVE TO NAME THEM.
ALL RIGHT, WE'LL NAME THIS HALF MARLIN JR. AND THIS HALF CORAL JR.
I LIKE "NEMO."

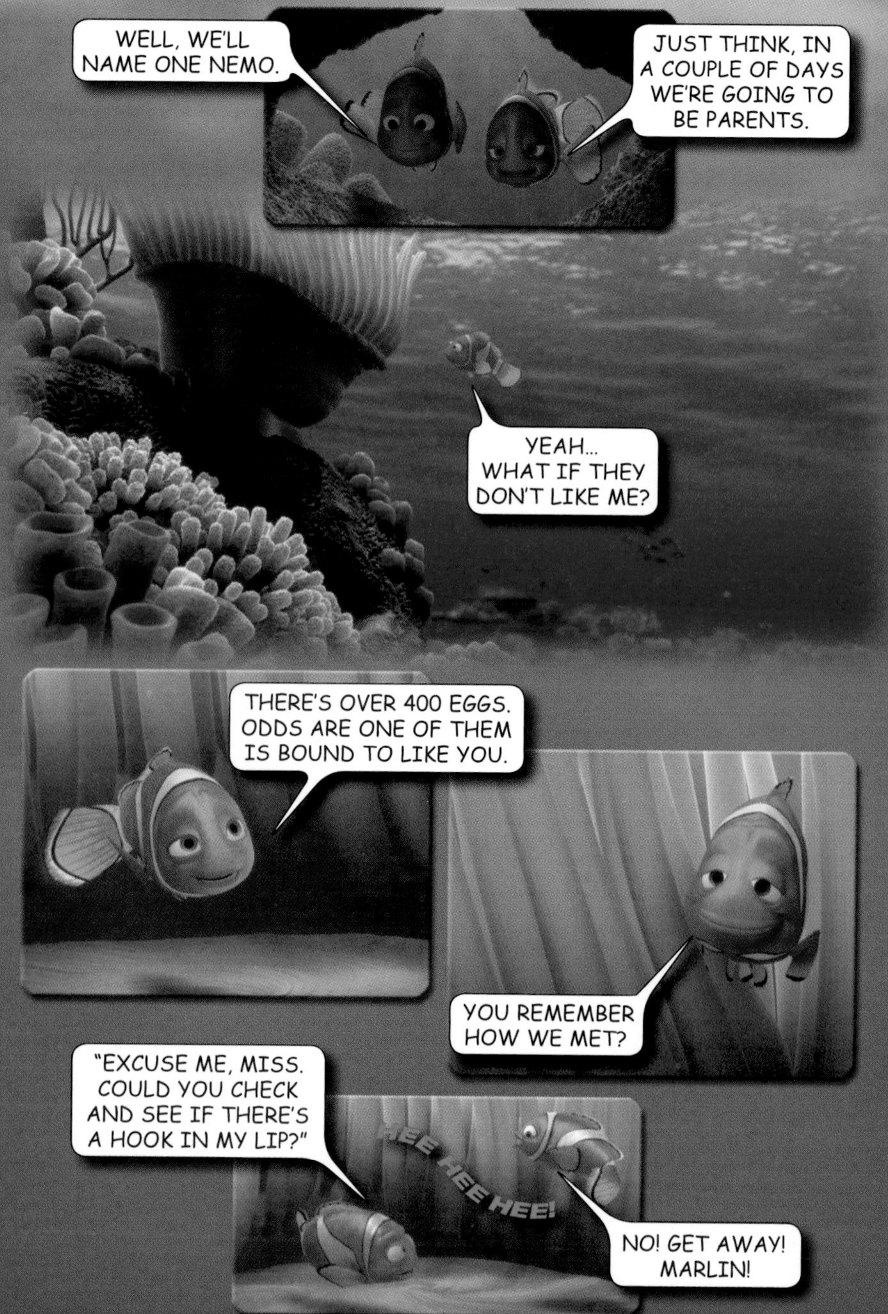
WELL, WE'LL NAME ONE NEMO.
JUST THINK, IN A COUPLE OF DAYS WE'RE GOING TO BE PARENTS.
YEAH... WHAT IF THEY DON'T LIKE ME?
THERE'S OVER 400 EGGS. ODDS ARE ONE OF THEM IS BOUND TO LIKE YOU.
YOU REMEMBER HOW WE MET?
"EXCUSE ME, MISS. COULD YOU CHECK AND SEE IF THERE'S A HOOK IN MY LIP?"
HEE HEE HEE HEE!
NO! GET AWAY! MARLIN!

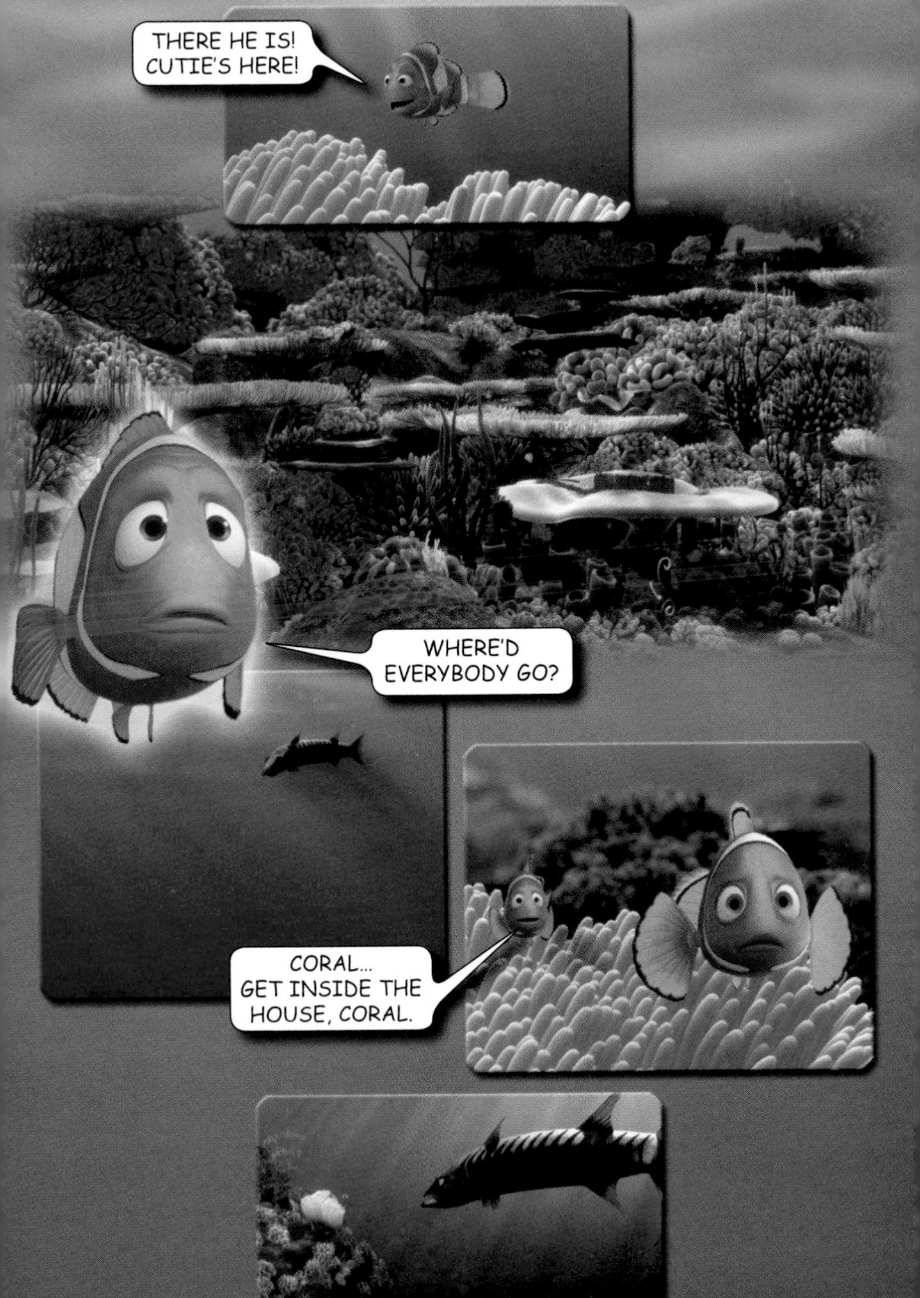
THERE HE IS! CUTIE'S HERE!
WHERE'D EVERYBODY GO?
CORAL... GET INSIDE THE HOUSE, CORAL.

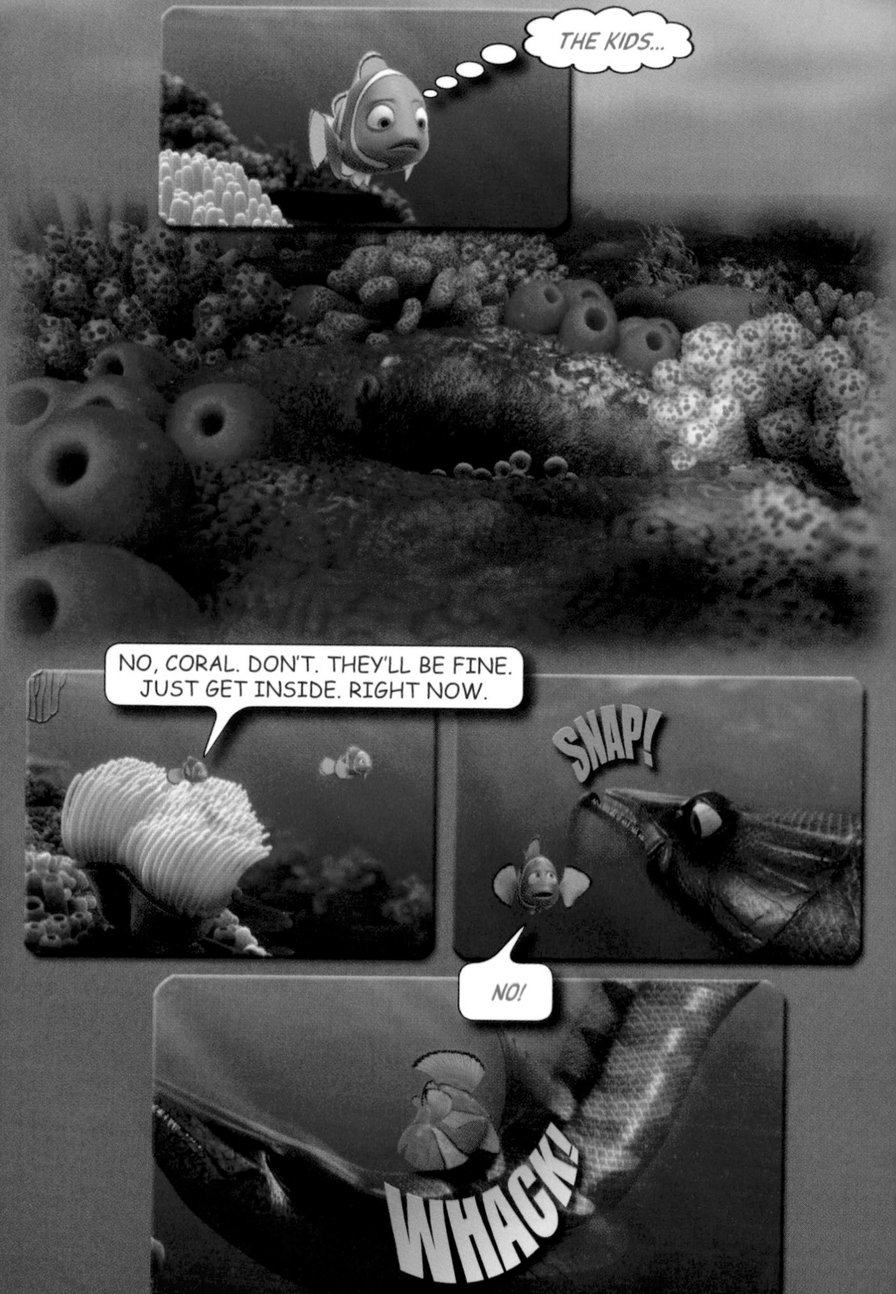
THE KIDS...
NO, CORAL. DON'T. THEY'LL BE FINE. JUST GET INSIDE. RIGHT NOW.
SNAP!
NO!
WHACK!

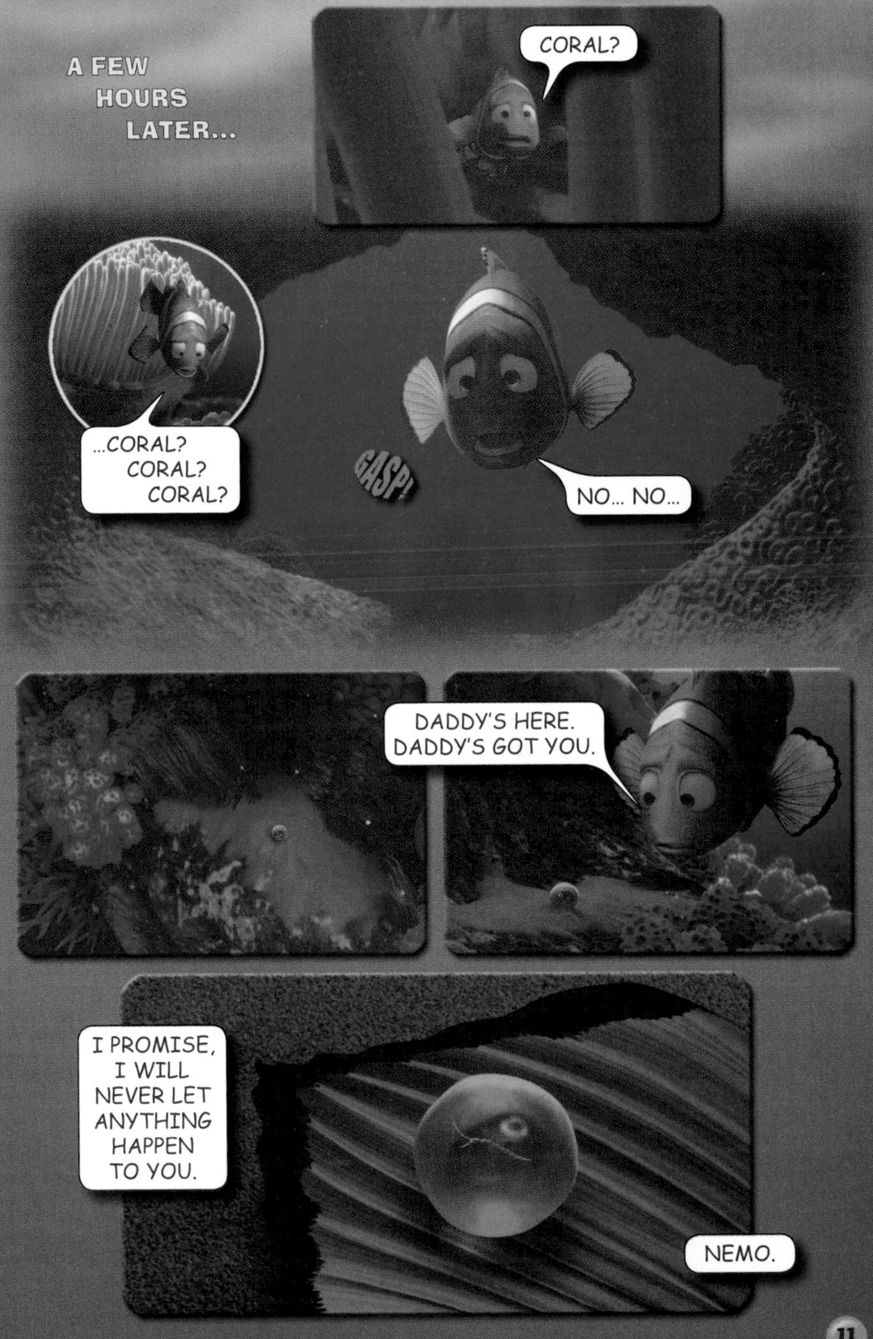
A FEW HOURS LATER...
CORAL?
...CORAL? CORAL? CORAL?
GASP!
NO... NO...
DADDY'S HERE. DADDY'S GOT YOU.
I PROMISE, I WILL NEVER LET ANYTHING HAPPEN TO YOU.
NEMO.

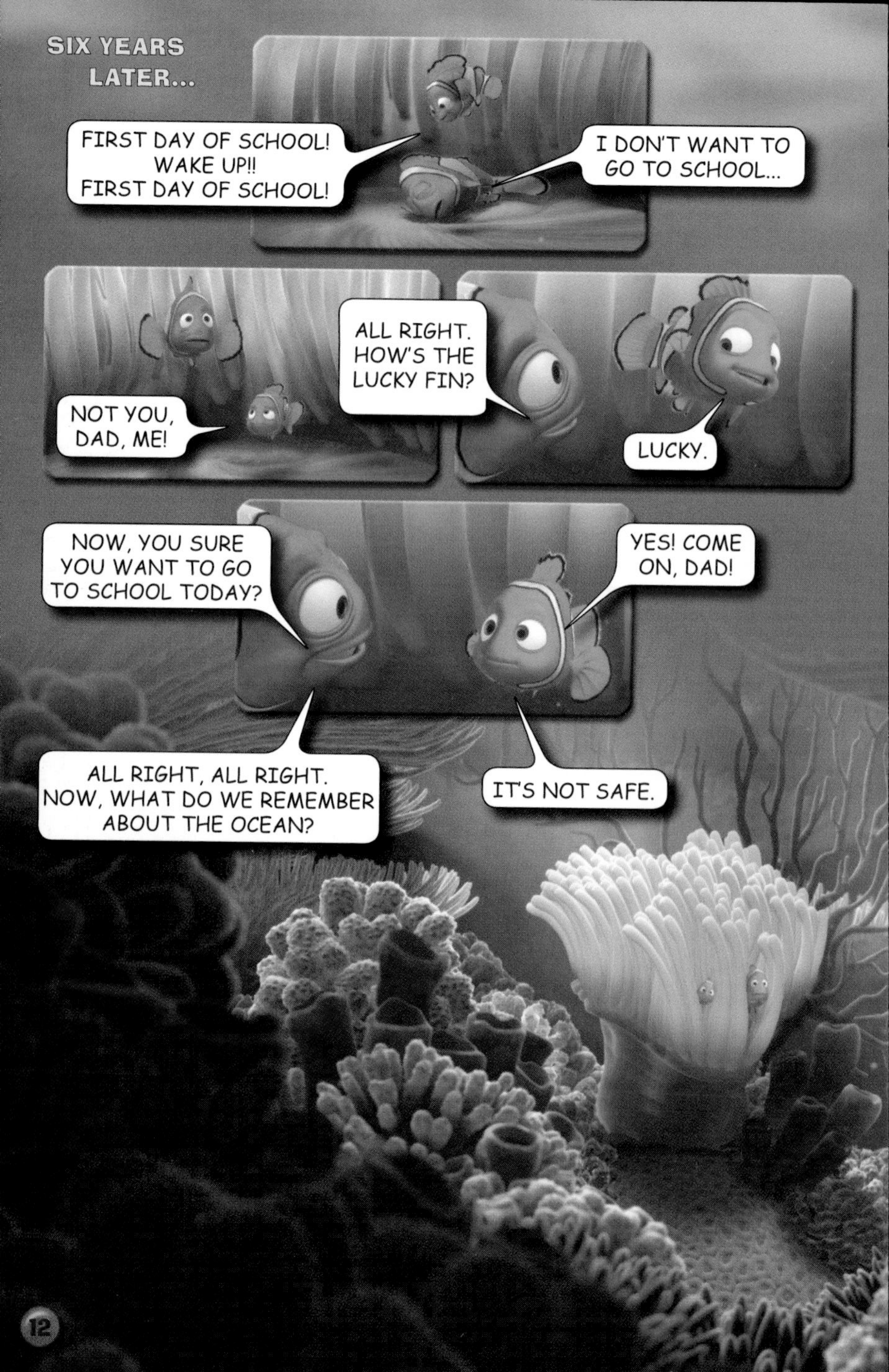
SIX YEARS LATER...
FIRST DAY OF SCHOOL! WAKE UP!! FIRST DAY OF SCHOOL!
I DON'T WANT TO GO TO SCHOOL...
NOT YOU, DAD, ME!
ALL RIGHT. HOW'S THE LUCKY FIN?
LUCKY.
NOW, YOU SURE YOU WANT TO GO TO SCHOOL TODAY?
YES! COME ON, DAD!
ALL RIGHT, ALL RIGHT. NOW, WHAT DO WE REMEMBER ABOUT THE OCEAN?
IT'S NOT SAFE.

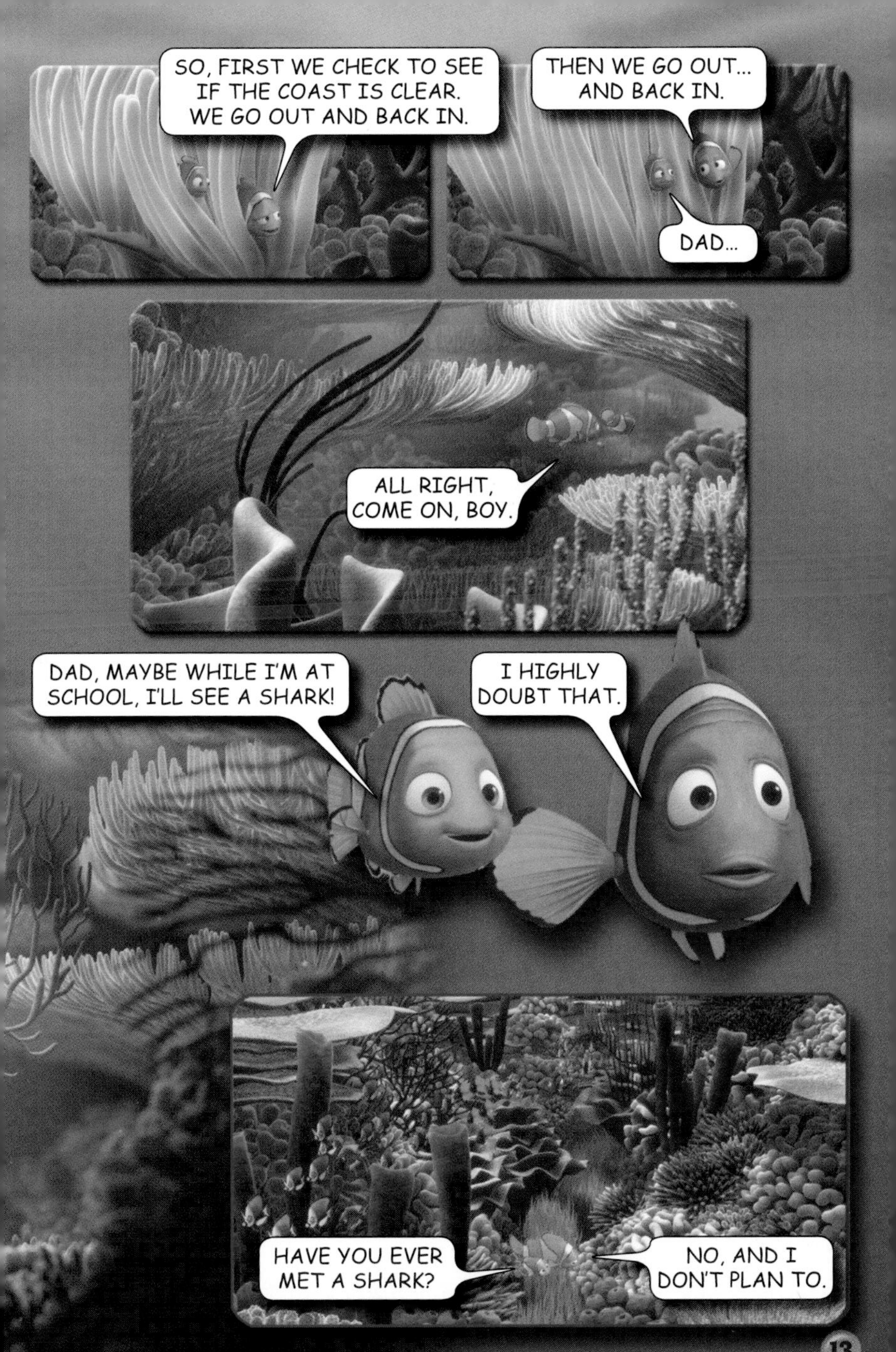
SO, FIRST WE CHECK TO SEE IF THE COAST IS CLEAR. WE GO OUT AND BACK IN.
THEN WE GO OUT... AND BACK IN.
DAD...
ALL RIGHT, COME ON, BOY.
DAD, MAYBE WHILE I'M AT SCHOOL, I'LL SEE A SHARK!
I HIGHLY DOUBT THAT.
HAVE YOU EVER MET A SHARK?
NO, AND I DON'T PLAN TO.

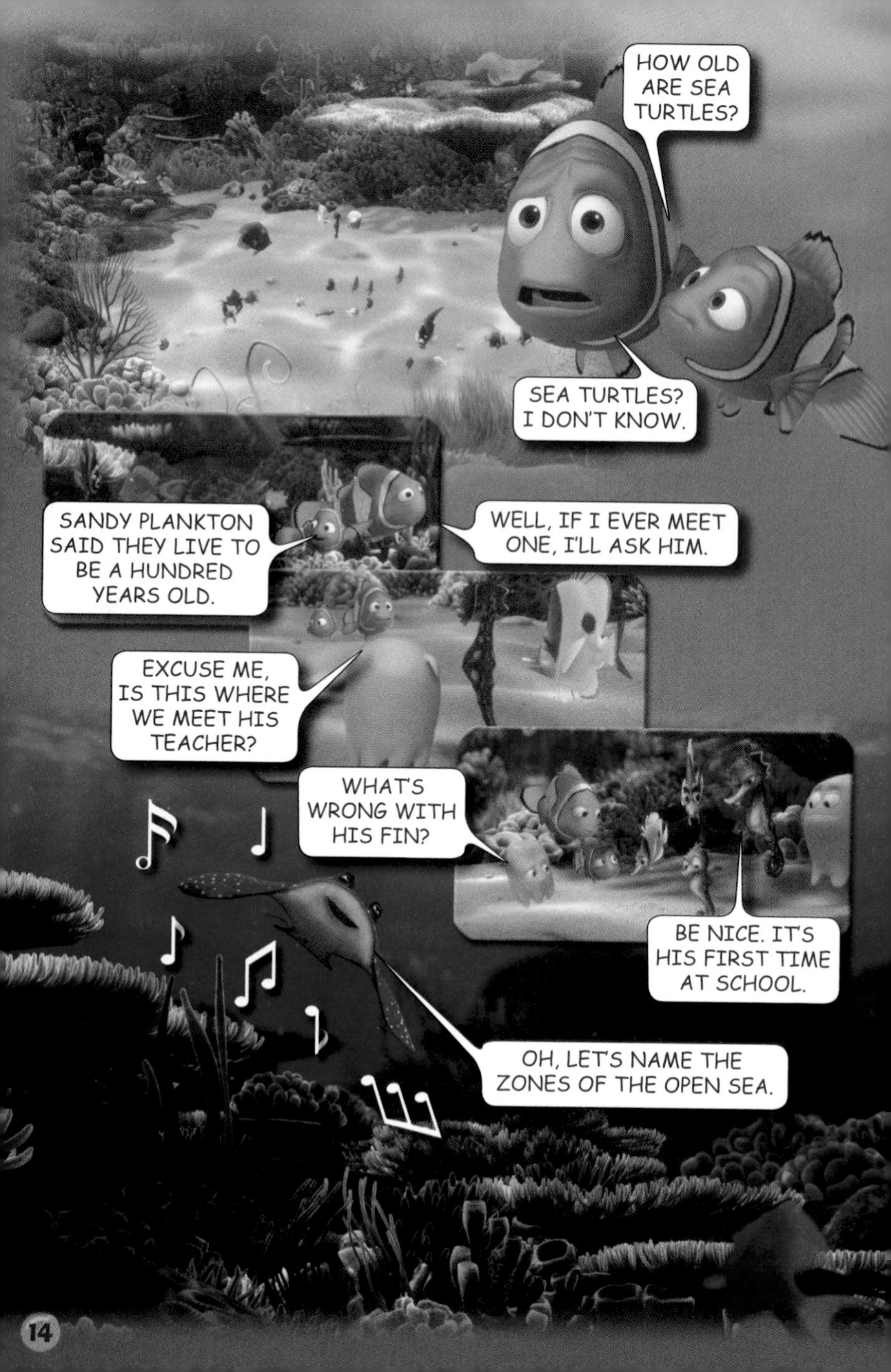
HOW OLD ARE SEA TURTLES?
SEA TURTLES? I DON'T KNOW.
SANDY PLANKTON SAID THEY LIVE TO BE A HUNDRED YEARS OLD.
WELL, IF I EVER MEET ONE, I'LL ASK HIM.
EXCUSE ME, IS THIS WHERE WE MEET HIS TEACHER?
WHAT'S WRONG WITH HIS FIN?
BE NICE. IT'S HIS FIRST TIME AT SCHOOL.
OH, LET'S NAME THE ZONES OF THE OPEN SEA.

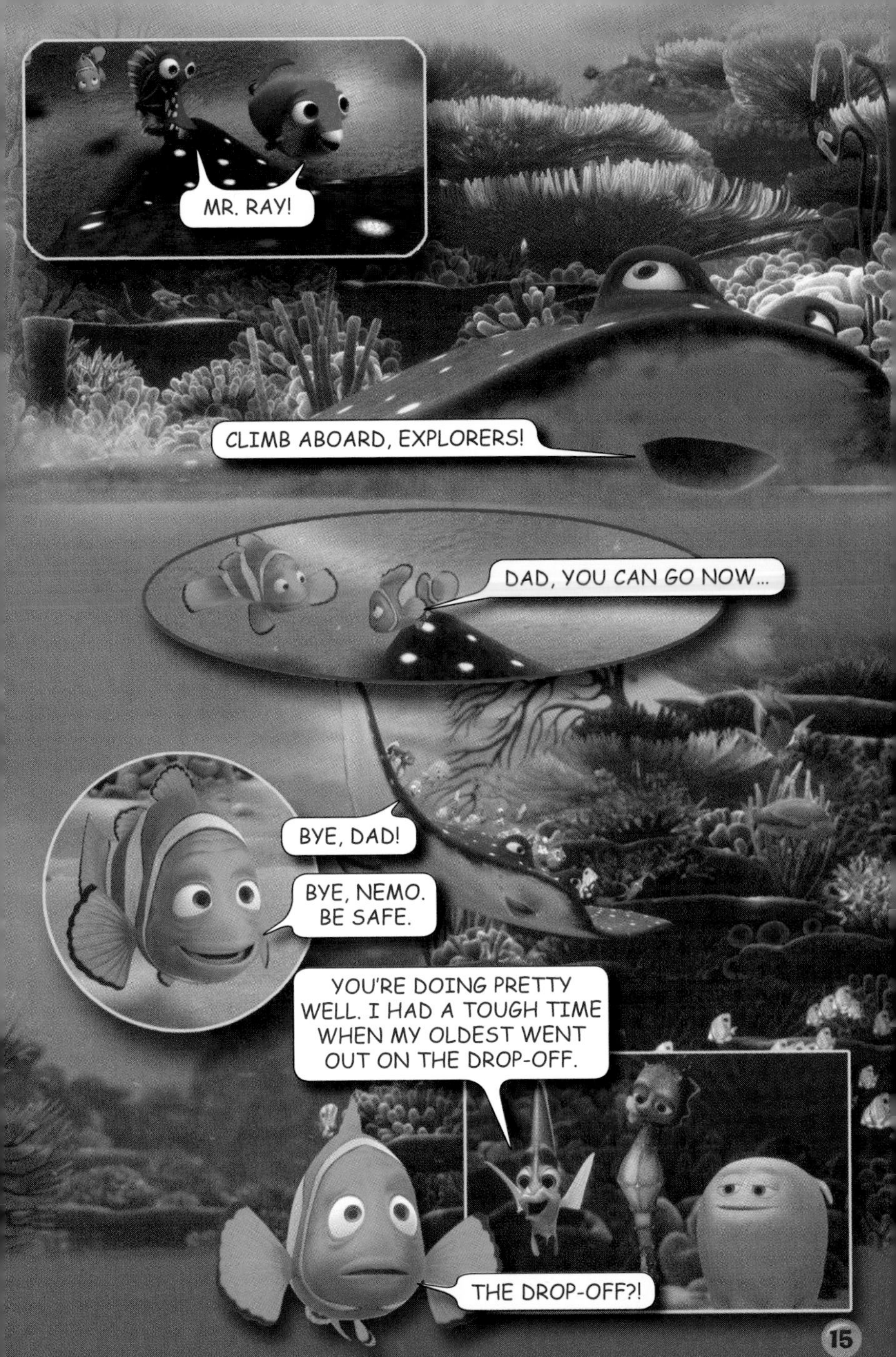
MR. RAY!
CLIMB ABOARD, EXPLORERS!
DAD, YOU CAN GO NOW...
BYE, DAD!
BYE, NEMO. BE SAFE.
YOU'RE DOING PRETTY WELL. I HAD A TOUGH TIME WHEN MY OLDEST WENT OUT ON THE DROP-OFF.
THE DROP-OFF?!

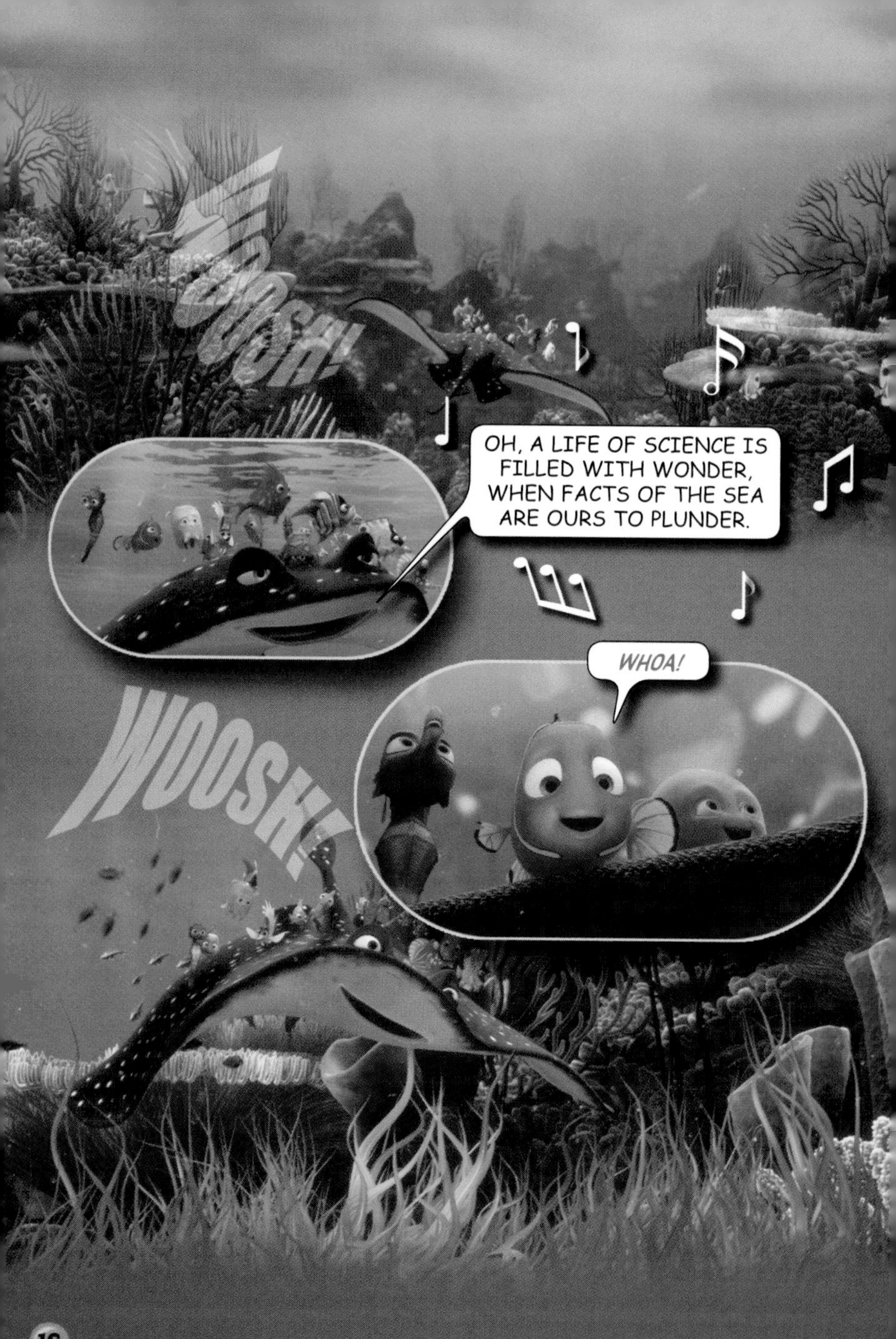
WOOSH!
OH, A LIFE OF SCIENCE IS FILLED WITH WONDER, WHEN FACTS OF THE SEA ARE OURS TO PLUNDER.
WHOA!
WOOSH!

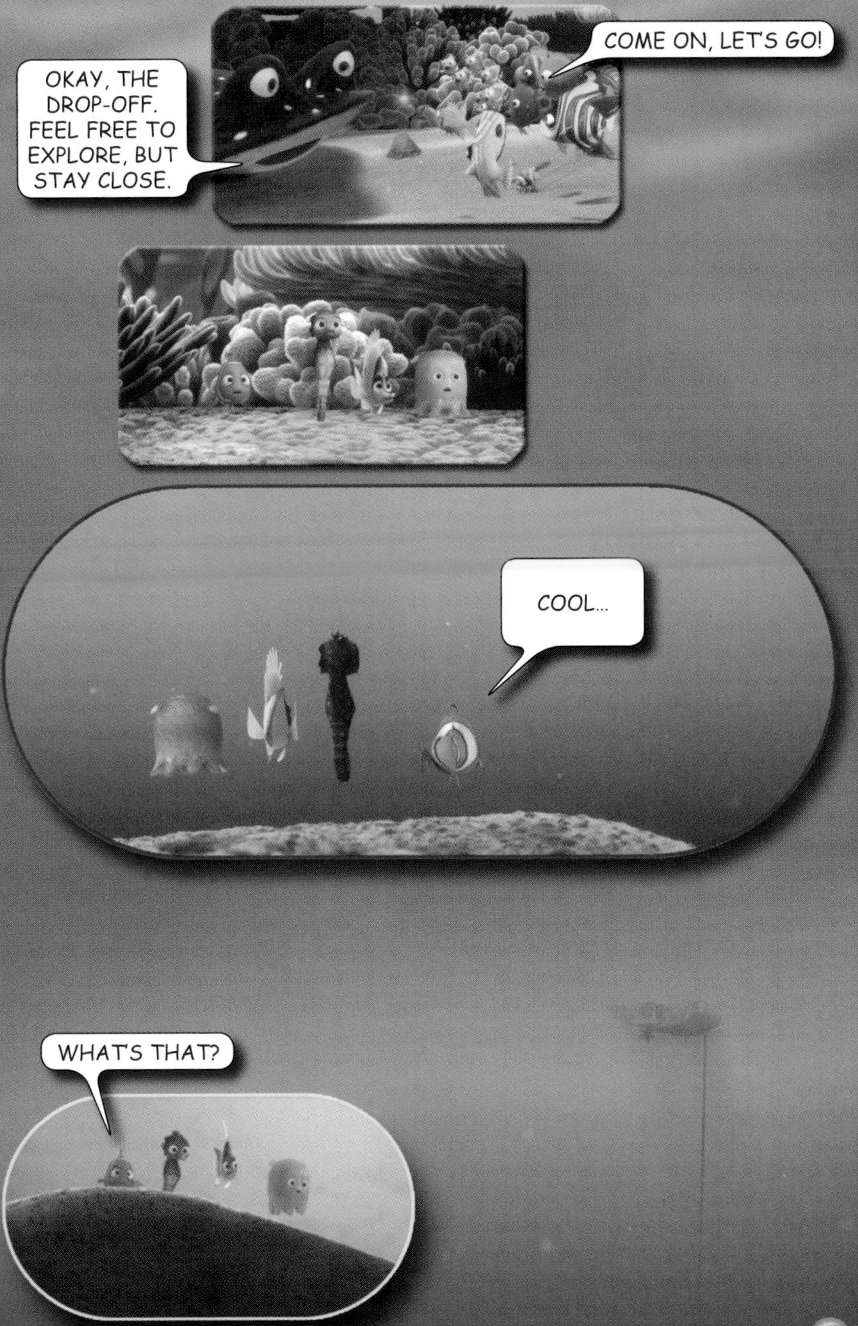
OKAY, THE DROP-OFF. FEEL FREE TO EXPLORE, BUT STAY CLOSE.
COME ON, LET'S GO!
COOL...
WHAT'S THAT?

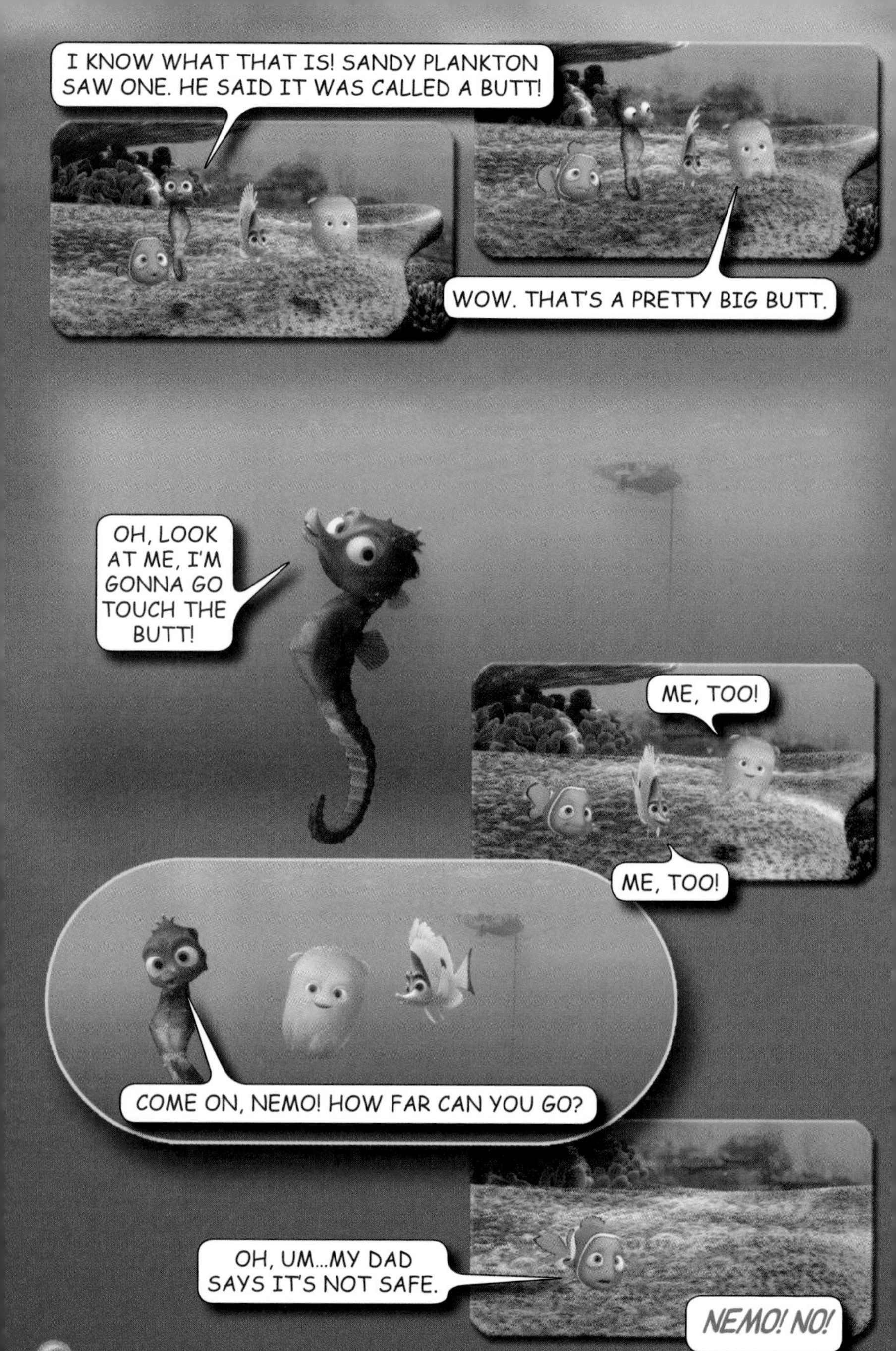
I KNOW WHAT THAT IS! SANDY PLANKTON SAW ONE. HE SAID IT WAS CALLED A BUTT!
WOW. THAT'S A PRETTY BIG BUTT.
OH, LOOK AT ME, I'M GONNA GO TOUCH THE BUTT!
ME, TOO!
ME, TOO!
COME ON, NEMO! HOW FAR CAN YOU GO?
OH, UM...MY DAD SAYS IT'S NOT SAFE.
NEMO! NO!

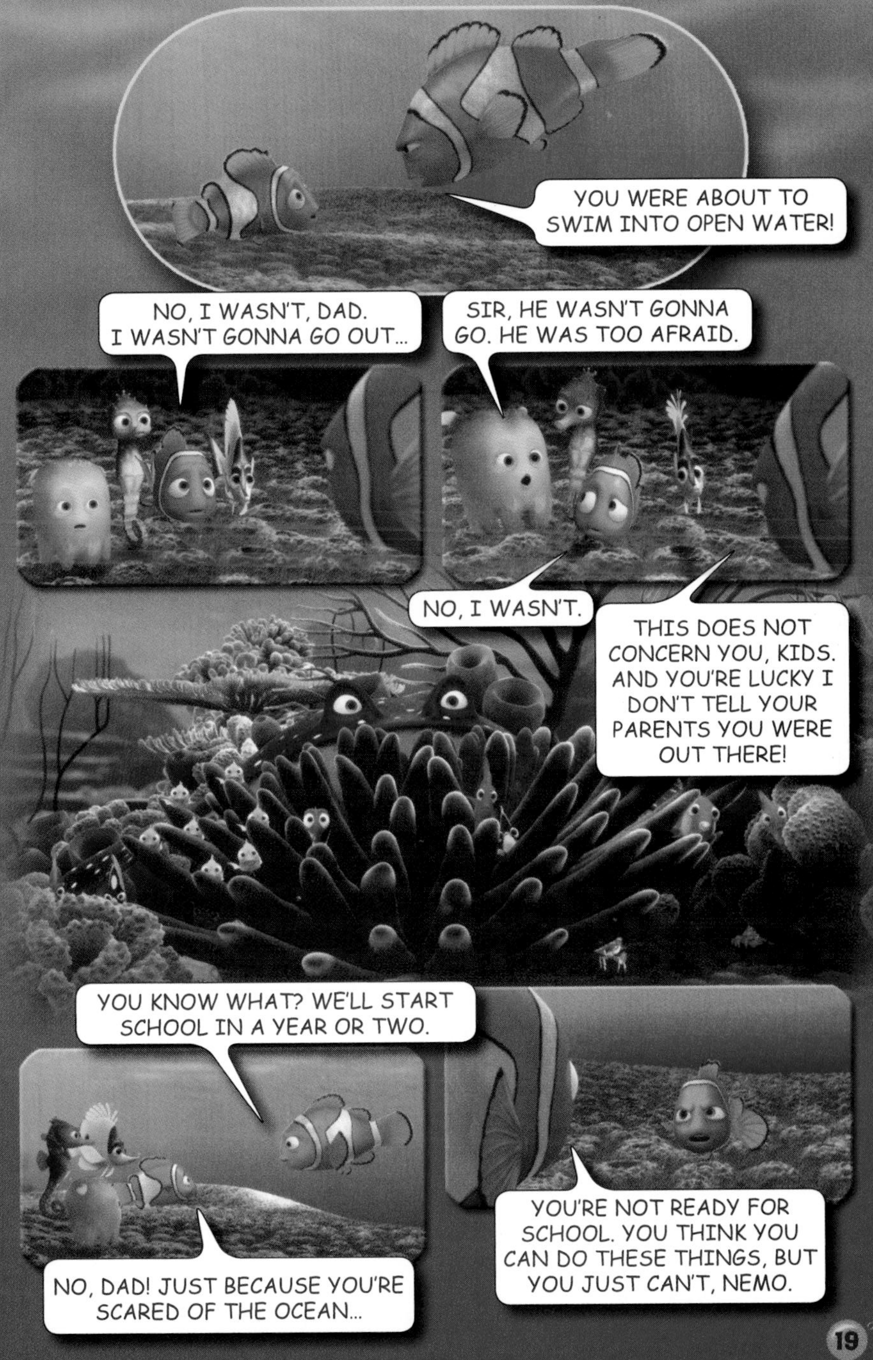
YOU WERE ABOUT TO SWIM INTO OPEN WATER!
NO, I WASN'T, DAD. I WASN'T GONNA GO OUT...
SIR, HE WASN'T GONNA GO. HE WAS TOO AFRAID.
NO, I WASN'T.
THIS DOES NOT CONCERN YOU, KIDS. AND YOU'RE LUCKY I DON'T TELL YOUR PARENTS YOU WERE OUT THERE!
YOU KNOW WHAT? WE'LL START SCHOOL IN A YEAR OR TWO.
NO, DAD! JUST BECAUSE YOU'RE SCARED OF THE OCEAN...
YOU'RE NOT READY FOR SCHOOL. YOU THINK YOU CAN DO THESE THINGS, BUT YOU JUST CAN'T, NEMO.

I HATE YOU.

EXCUSE ME, IS THERE ANYTHING I CAN DO?

YOU KNOW, I'M SORRY. I DIDN'T MEAN TO INTERRUPT THINGS. BUT YOU HAVE A LARGE CLASS, AND HE COULD GET LOST IF YOU'RE NOT LOOKING.

OH MY GOSH!!! NEMO'S SWIMMING OUT TO SEA!

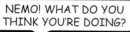

NEMO! WHAT DO YOU THINK YOU'RE DOING?

GET BACK HERE! I SAID GET BACK HERE, NOW! STOP!

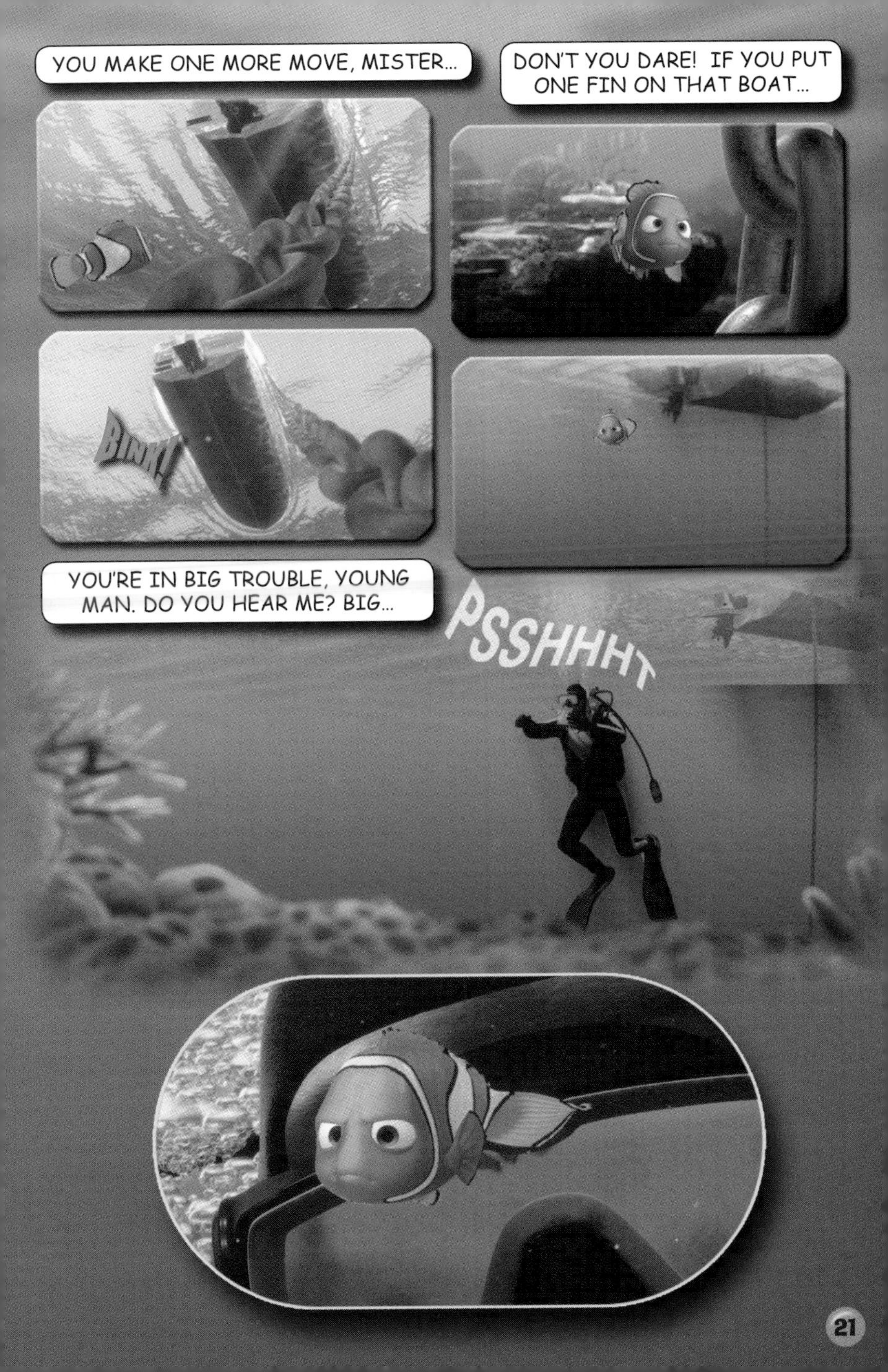
YOU MAKE ONE MORE MOVE, MISTER...
DON'T YOU DARE! IF YOU PUT ONE FIN ON THAT BOAT...
BINK!
YOU'RE IN BIG TROUBLE, YOUNG MAN. DO YOU HEAR ME? BIG...
PSSHHHT

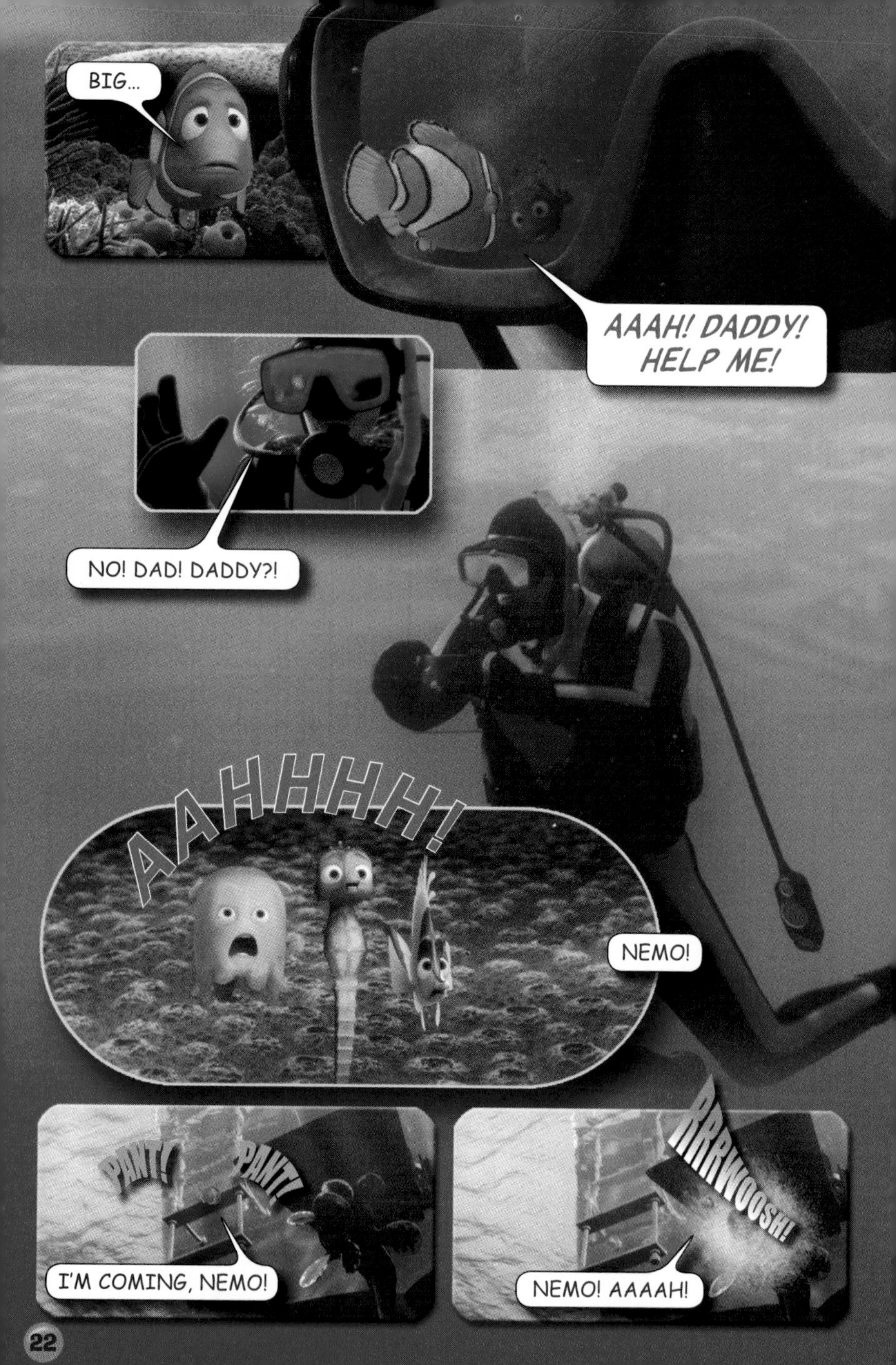
BIG...
AAAH! DADDY! HELP ME!
NO! DAD! DADDY?!
AAHHHH!
NEMO!
PANT!
PANT!
I'M COMING, NEMO!
RRRWOOSH!
NEMO! AAAAH!

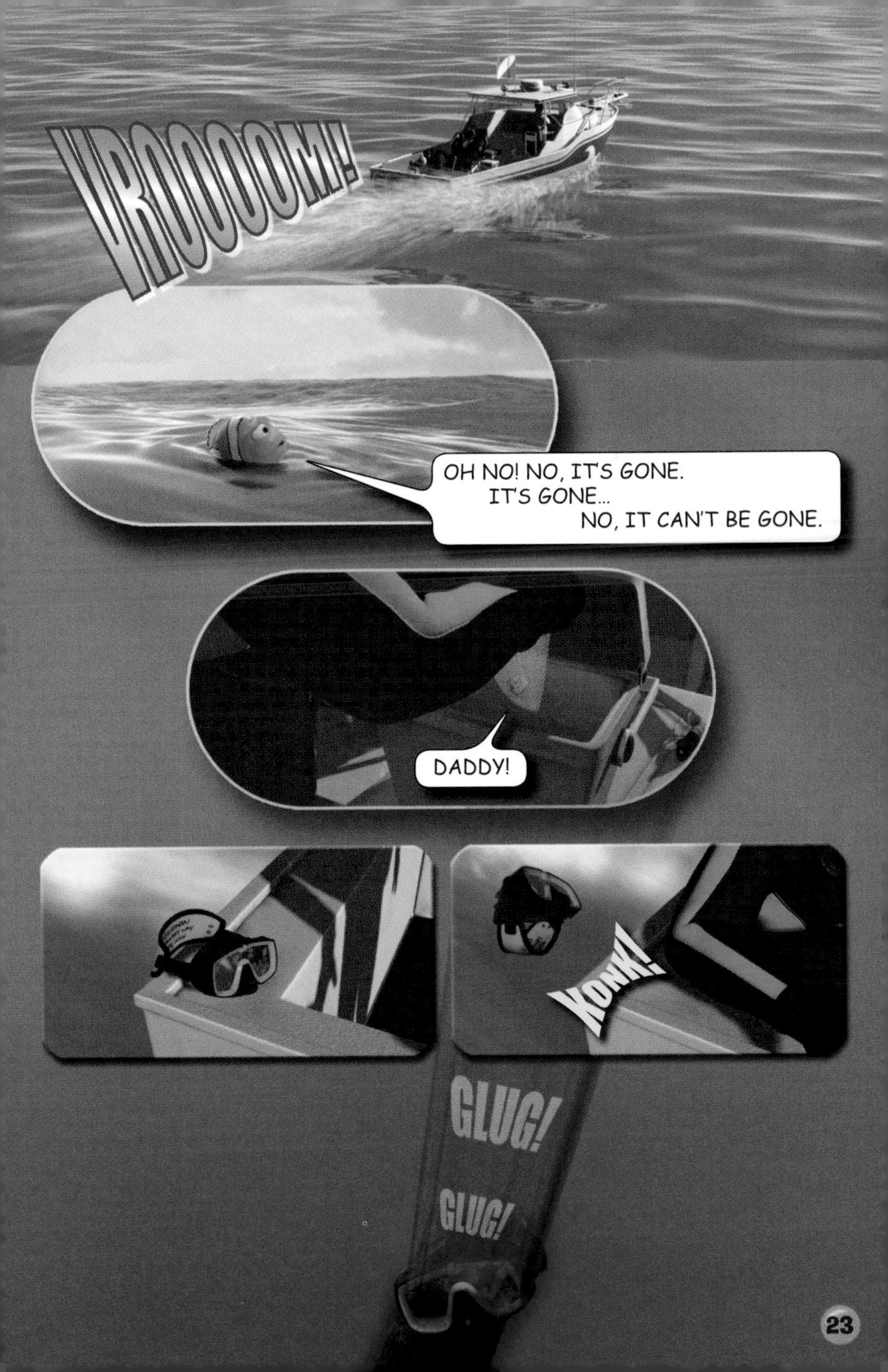
VROOOOM!
OH NO! NO, IT'S GONE. IT'S GONE... NO, IT CAN'T BE GONE.
DADDY!
KONK!
GLUG!
GLUG!

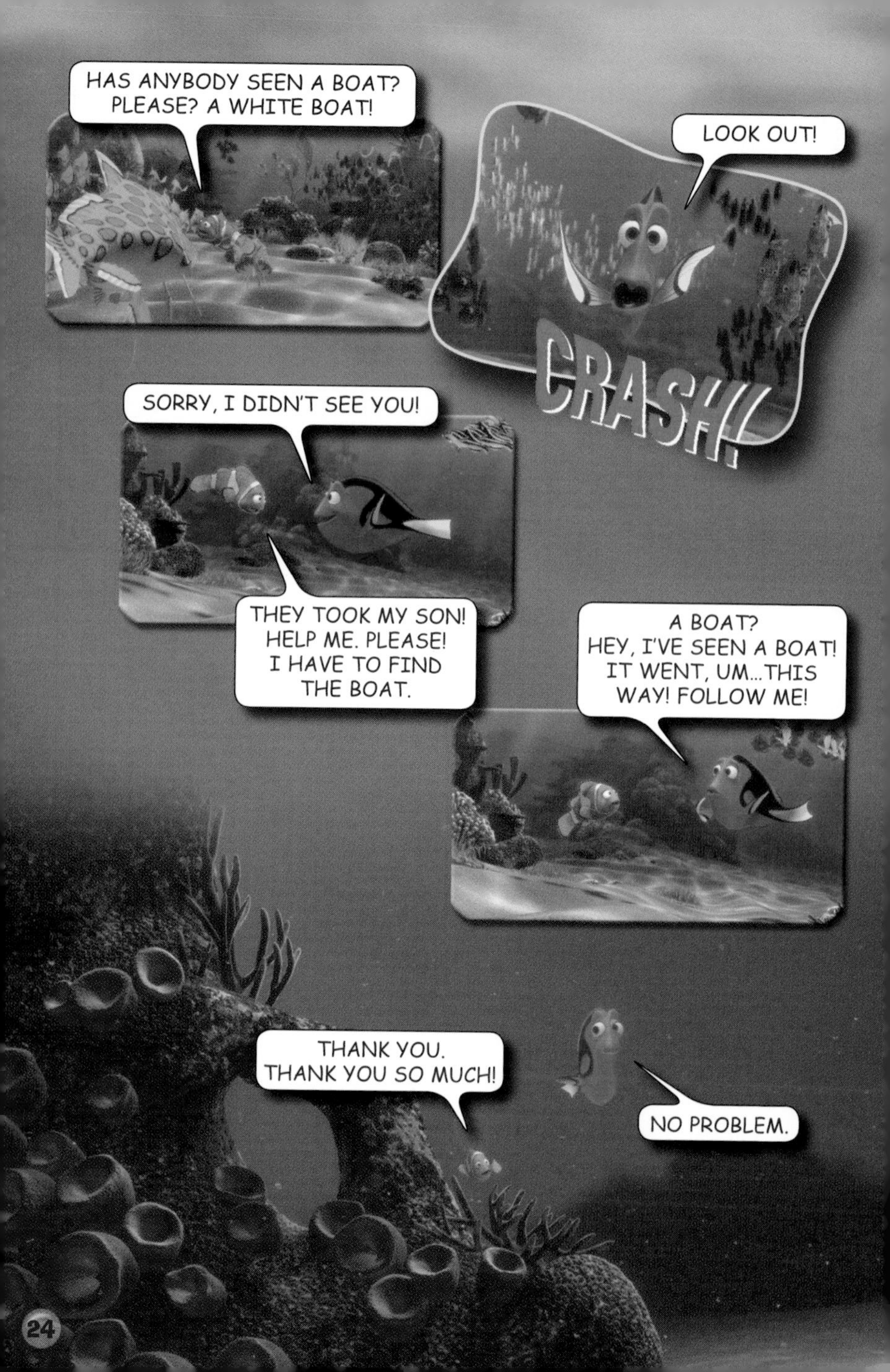
HAS ANYBODY SEEN A BOAT? PLEASE? A WHITE BOAT!
LOOK OUT!
CRASH!
SORRY, I DIDN'T SEE YOU!
THEY TOOK MY SON! HELP ME. PLEASE! I HAVE TO FIND THE BOAT.
A BOAT? HEY, I'VE SEEN A BOAT! IT WENT, UM...THIS WAY! FOLLOW ME!
THANK YOU. THANK YOU SO MUCH!
NO PROBLEM.

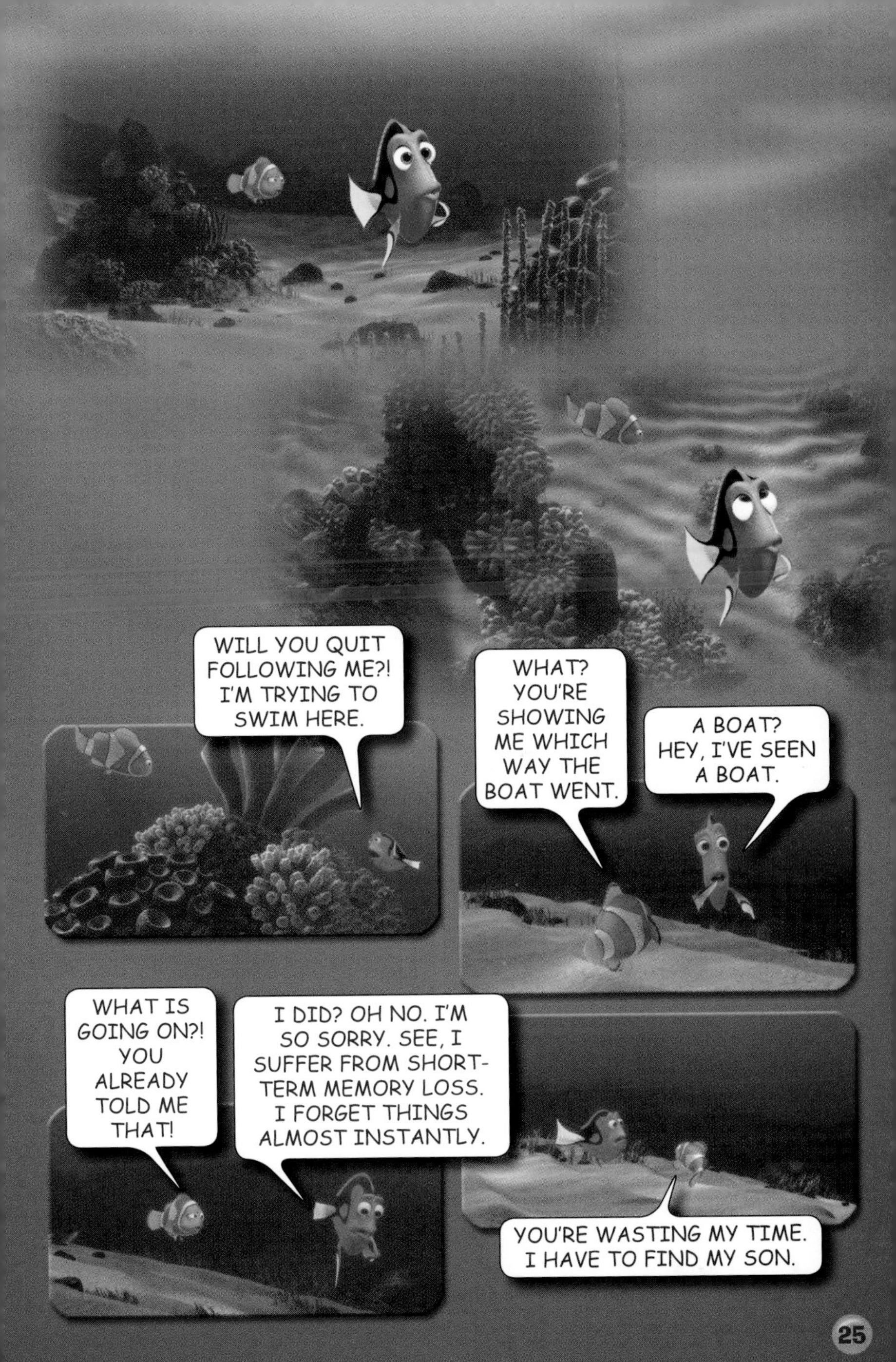
WILL YOU QUIT FOLLOWING ME?! I'M TRYING TO SWIM HERE.
WHAT? YOU'RE SHOWING ME WHICH WAY THE BOAT WENT.
A BOAT? HEY, I'VE SEEN A BOAT.
WHAT IS GOING ON?! YOU ALREADY TOLD ME THAT!
I DID? OH NO. I'M SO SORRY. SEE, I SUFFER FROM SHORT-TERM MEMORY LOSS. I FORGET THINGS ALMOST INSTANTLY.
YOU'RE WASTING MY TIME. I HAVE TO FIND MY SON.

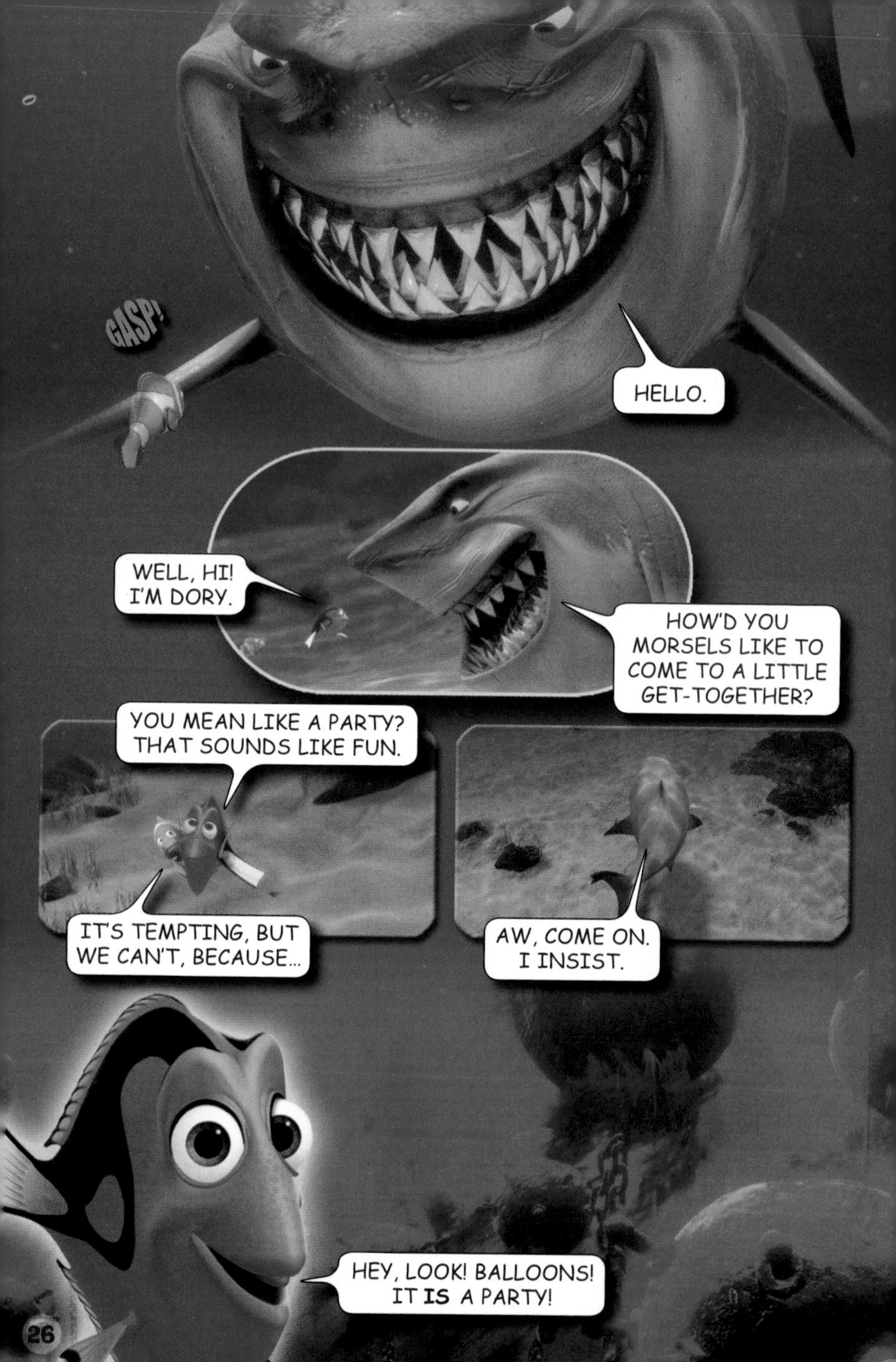
GASP!
HELLO.
WELL, HI! I'M DORY.
HOW'D YOU MORSELS LIKE TO COME TO A LITTLE GET-TOGETHER?
YOU MEAN LIKE A PARTY? THAT SOUNDS LIKE FUN.
IT'S TEMPTING, BUT WE CAN'T, BECAUSE...
AW, COME ON. I INSIST.
HEY, LOOK! BALLOONS! IT **IS** A PARTY!

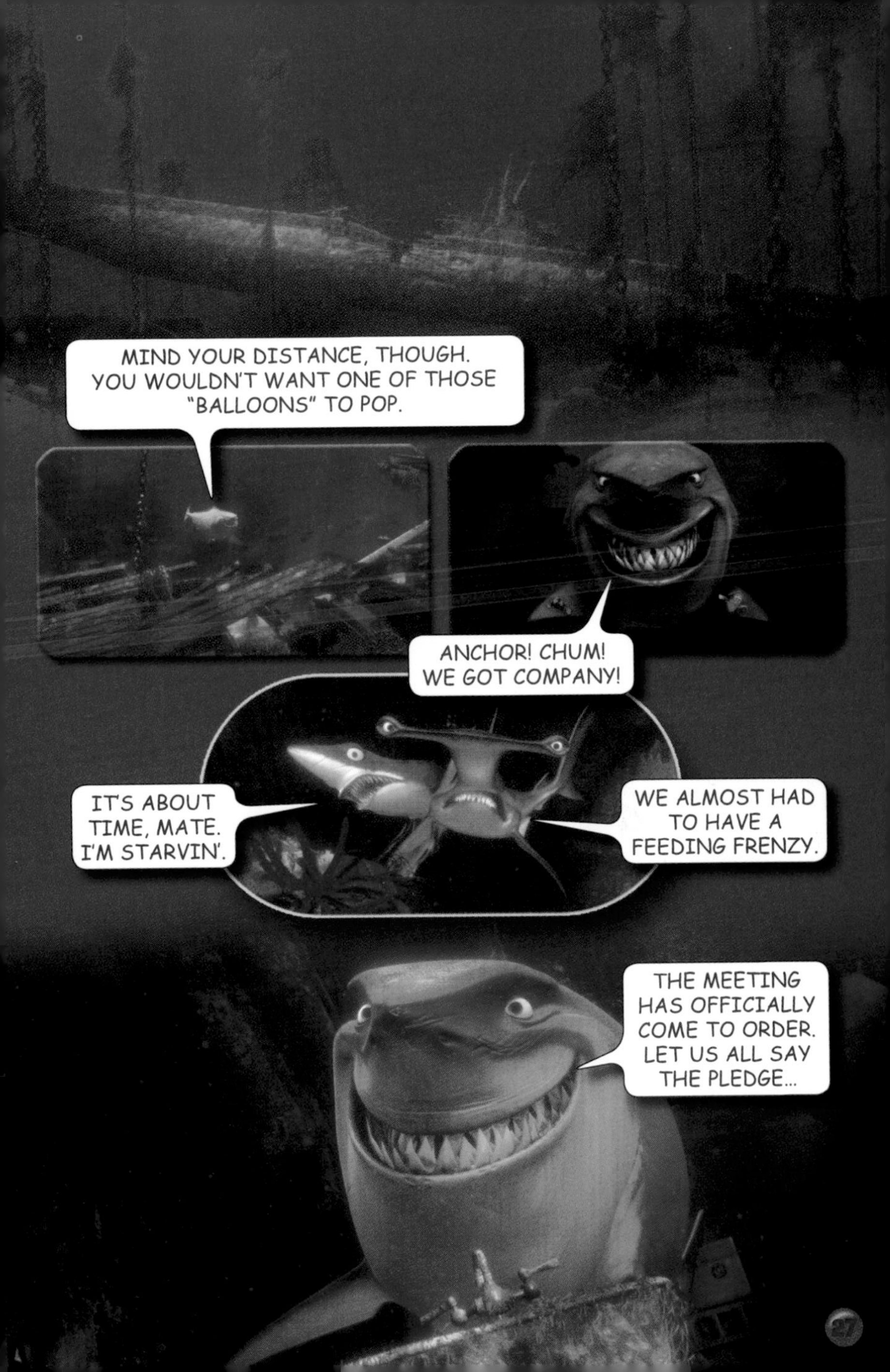
MIND YOUR DISTANCE, THOUGH. YOU WOULDN'T WANT ONE OF THOSE "BALLOONS" TO POP.
ANCHOR! CHUM! WE GOT COMPANY!
IT'S ABOUT TIME, MATE. I'M STARVIN'.
WE ALMOST HAD TO HAVE A FEEDING FRENZY.
THE MEETING HAS OFFICIALLY COME TO ORDER. LET US ALL SAY THE PLEDGE...

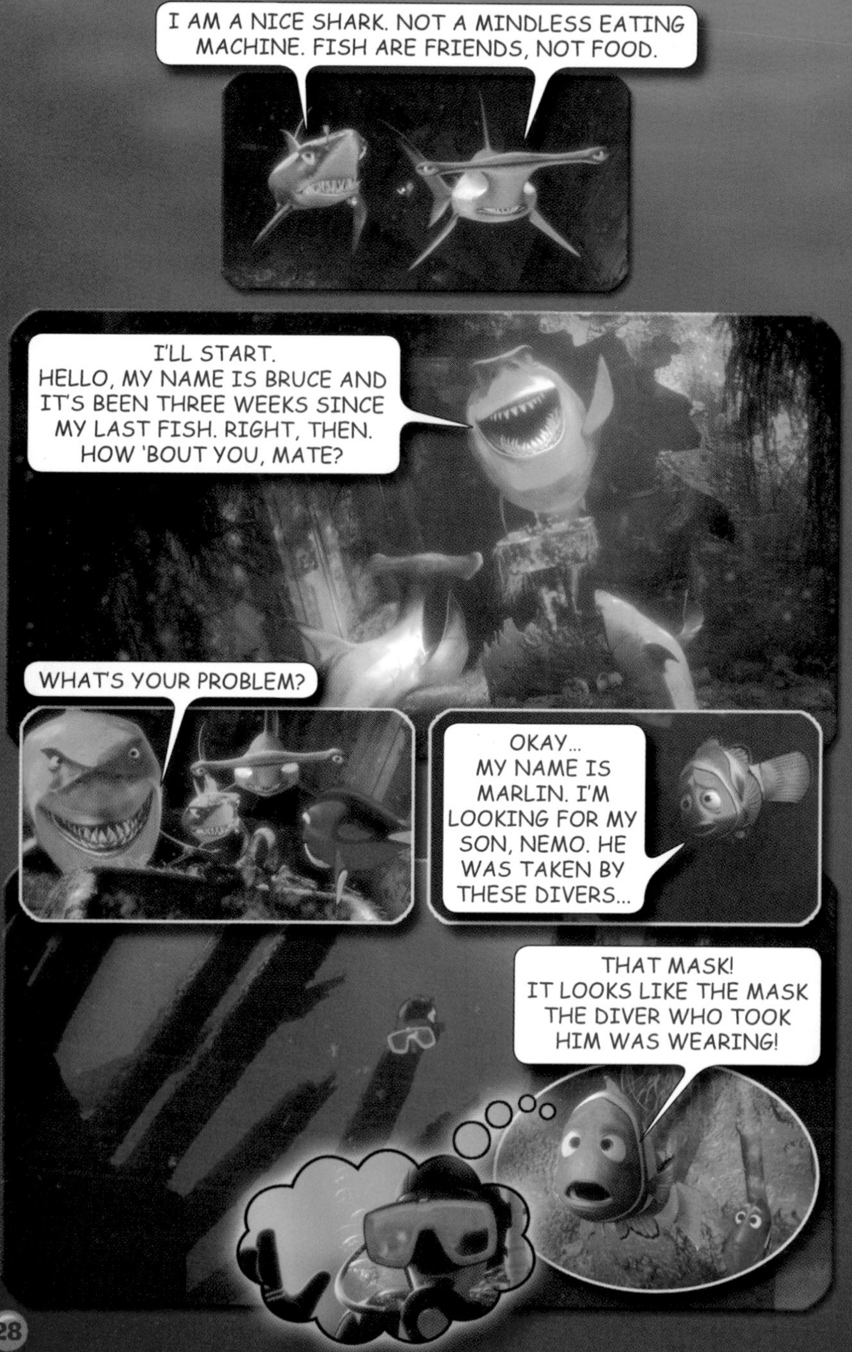
I AM A NICE SHARK. NOT A MINDLESS EATING MACHINE. FISH ARE FRIENDS, NOT FOOD.
I'LL START. HELLO, MY NAME IS BRUCE AND IT'S BEEN THREE WEEKS SINCE MY LAST FISH. RIGHT, THEN. HOW 'BOUT YOU, MATE?
WHAT'S YOUR PROBLEM?
OKAY... MY NAME IS MARLIN. I'M LOOKING FOR MY SON, NEMO. HE WAS TAKEN BY THESE DIVERS...
THAT MASK! IT LOOKS LIKE THE MASK THE DIVER WHO TOOK HIM WAS WEARING!

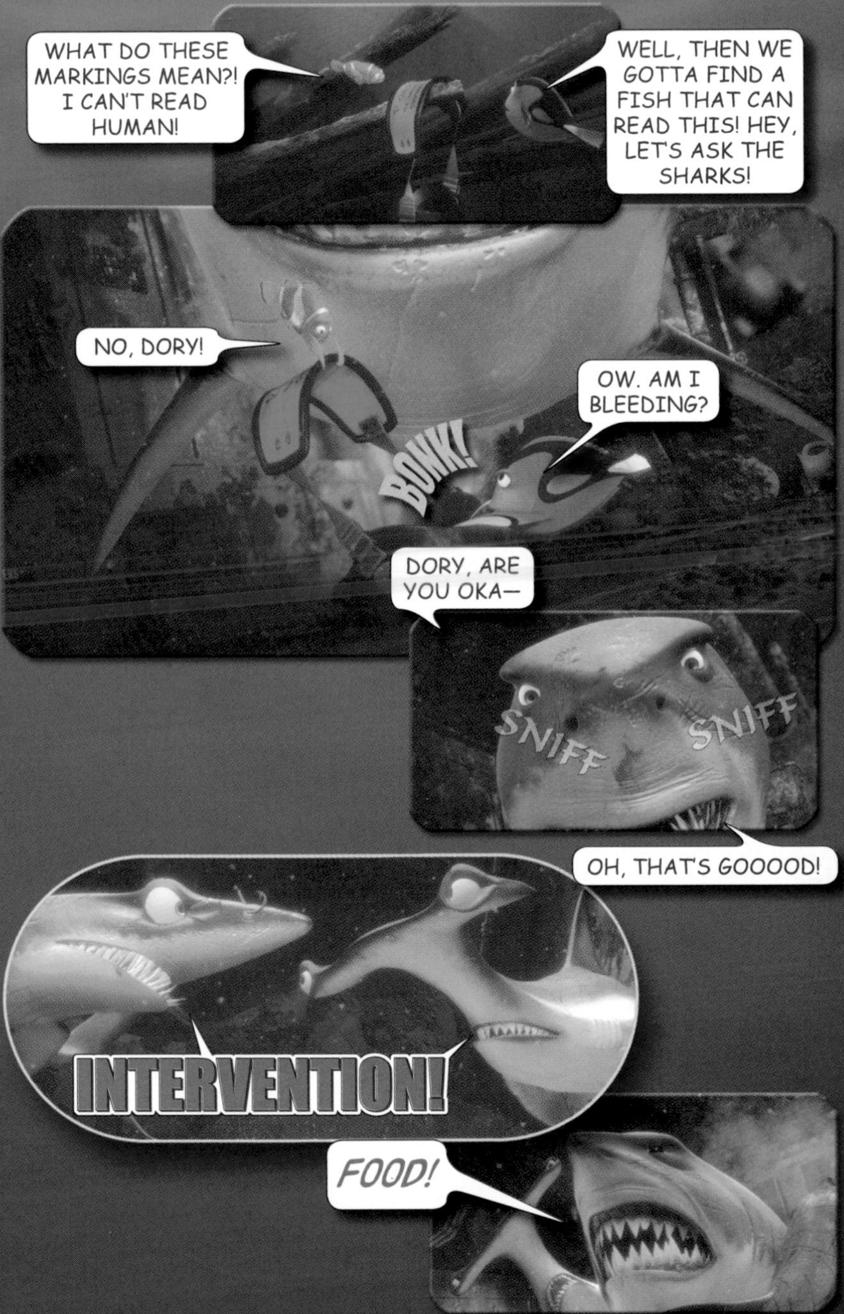
WHAT DO THESE MARKINGS MEAN?! I CAN'T READ HUMAN!
WELL, THEN WE GOTTA FIND A FISH THAT CAN READ THIS! HEY, LET'S ASK THE SHARKS!
NO, DORY!
BONK!
OW. AM I BLEEDING?
DORY, ARE YOU OKA—
SNIFF
SNIFF
OH, THAT'S GOOOOD!
INTERVENTION!
FOOD!

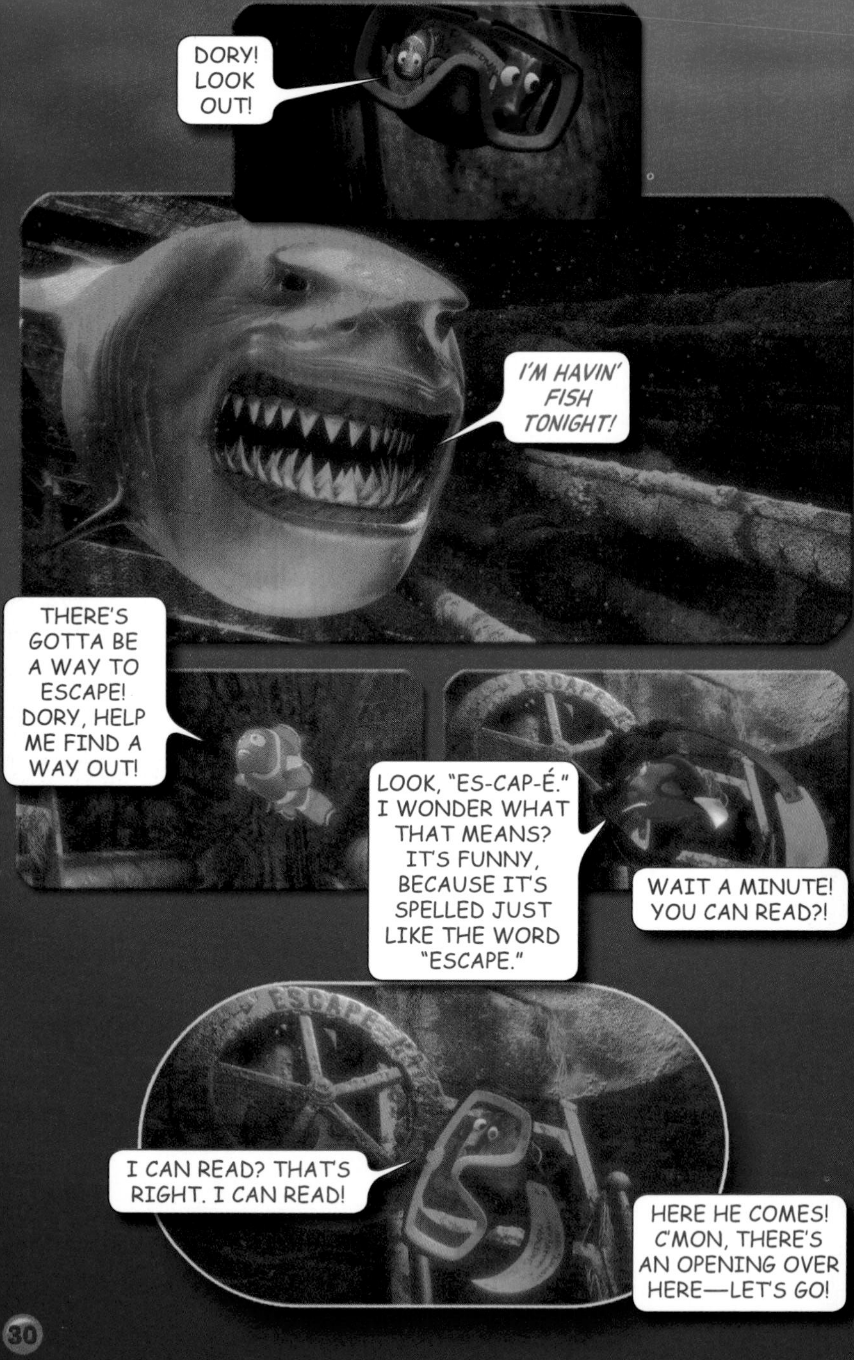
DORY! LOOK OUT!
I'M HAVIN' FISH TONIGHT!
THERE'S GOTTA BE A WAY TO ESCAPE! DORY, HELP ME FIND A WAY OUT!
ESCAPE
LOOK, "ES-CAP-É." I WONDER WHAT THAT MEANS? IT'S FUNNY, BECAUSE IT'S SPELLED JUST LIKE THE WORD "ESCAPE."
WAIT A MINUTE! YOU CAN READ?!
ESCAPE
I CAN READ? THAT'S RIGHT. I CAN READ!
HERE HE COMES! C'MON, THERE'S AN OPENING OVER HERE—LET'S GO!

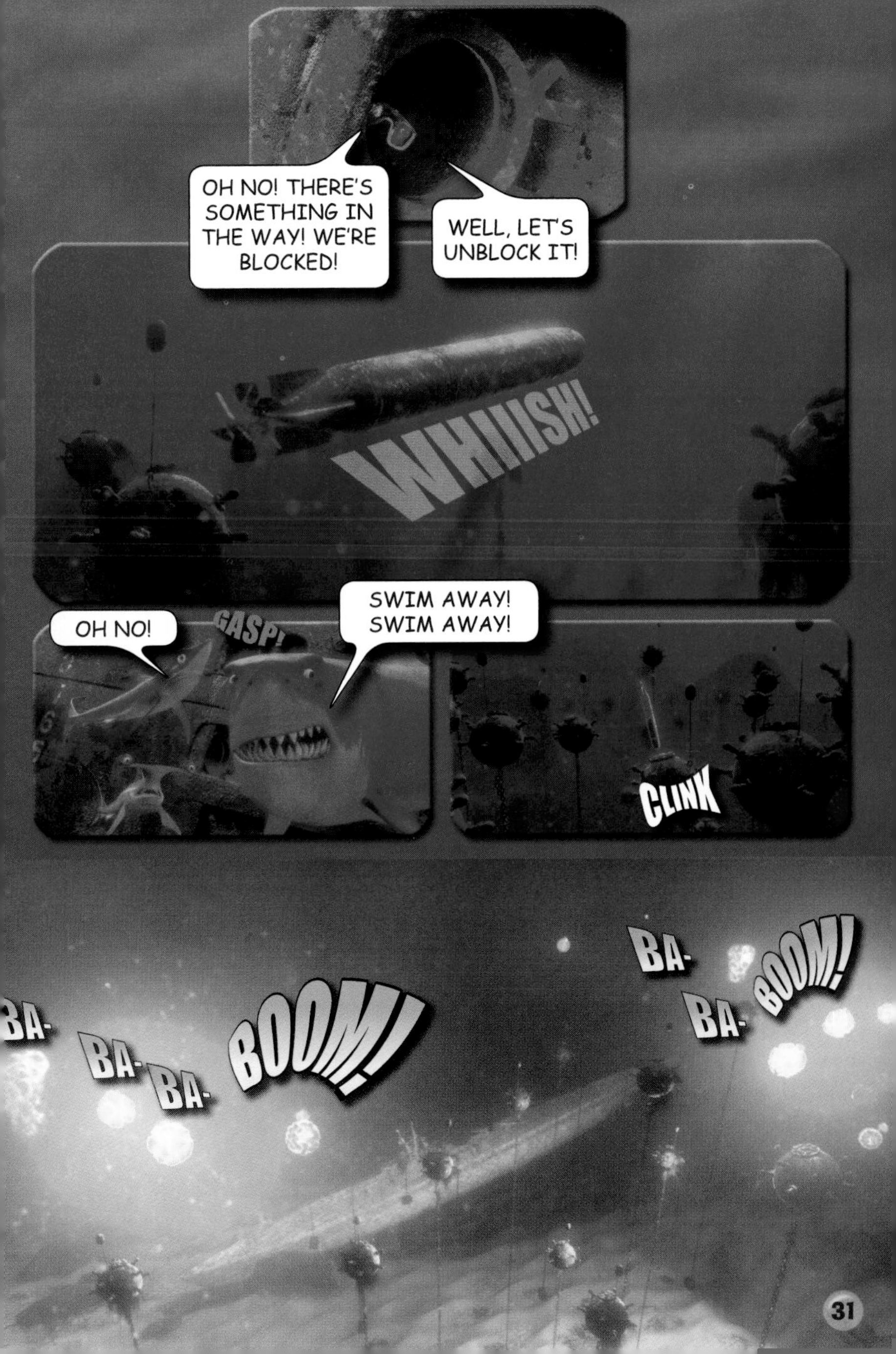
OH NO! THERE'S SOMETHING IN THE WAY! WE'RE BLOCKED!
WELL, LET'S UNBLOCK IT!
WHIIISH!
OH NO!
GASP!
SWIM AWAY! SWIM AWAY!
CLINK
BA- BA- BA- BOOM!
BA- BA- BOOM!

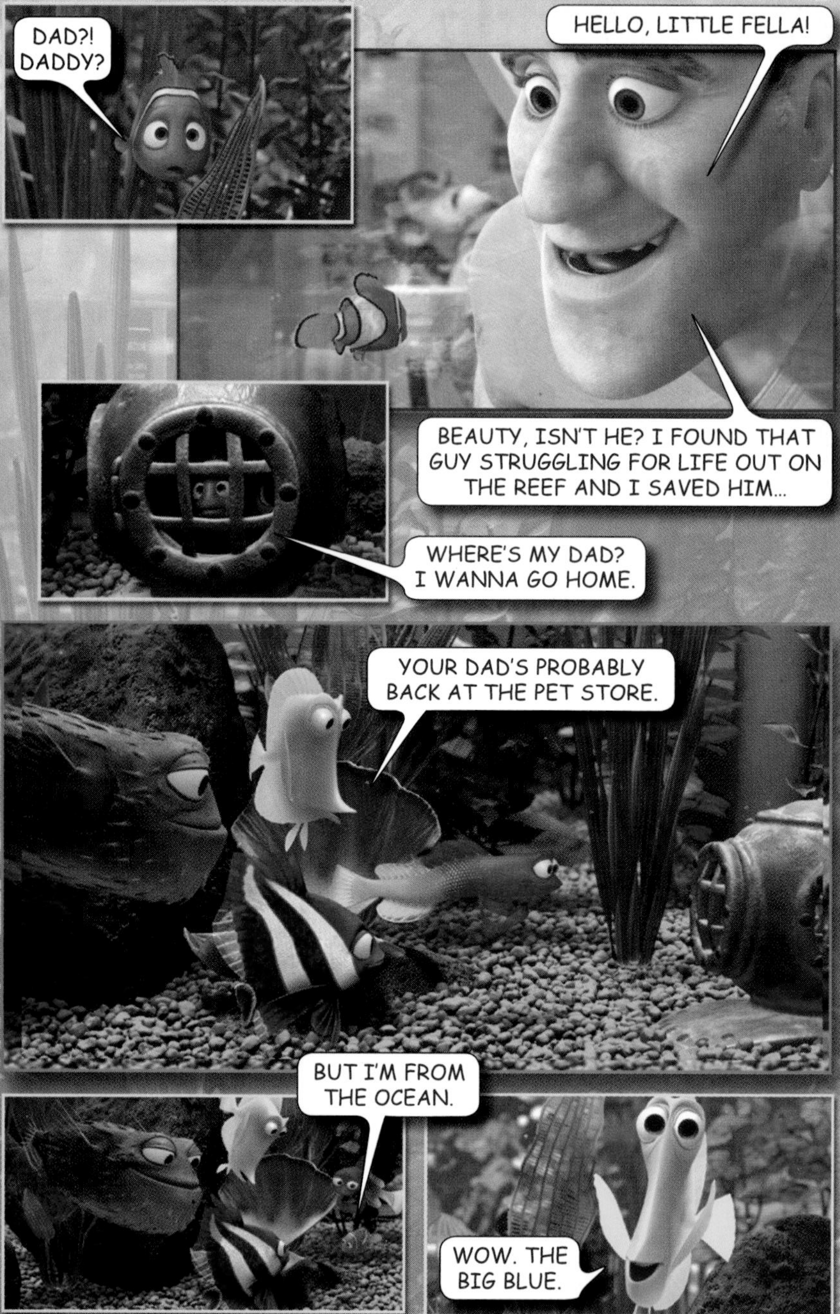
DAD?! DADDY?
HELLO, LITTLE FELLA!
BEAUTY, ISN'T HE? I FOUND THAT GUY STRUGGLING FOR LIFE OUT ON THE REEF AND I SAVED HIM...
WHERE'S MY DAD? I WANNA GO HOME.
YOUR DAD'S PROBABLY BACK AT THE PET STORE.
BUT I'M FROM THE OCEAN.
WOW. THE BIG BLUE.

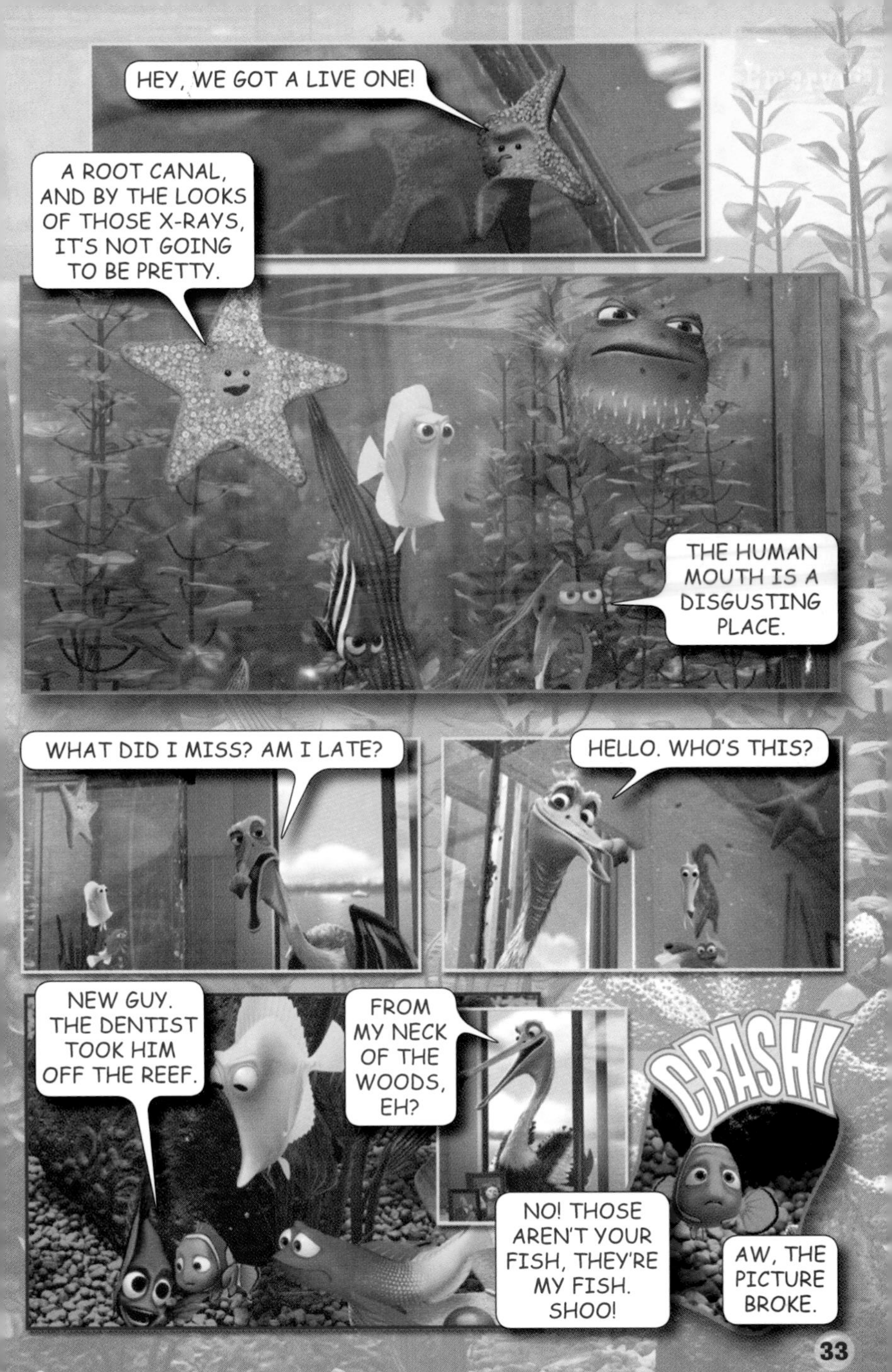
HEY, WE GOT A LIVE ONE!
A ROOT CANAL, AND BY THE LOOKS OF THOSE X-RAYS, IT'S NOT GOING TO BE PRETTY.
THE HUMAN MOUTH IS A DISGUSTING PLACE.
WHAT DID I MISS? AM I LATE?
HELLO. WHO'S THIS?
NEW GUY. THE DENTIST TOOK HIM OFF THE REEF.
FROM MY NECK OF THE WOODS, EH?
NO! THOSE AREN'T YOUR FISH, THEY'RE MY FISH. SHOO!
CRASH!
AW, THE PICTURE BROKE.

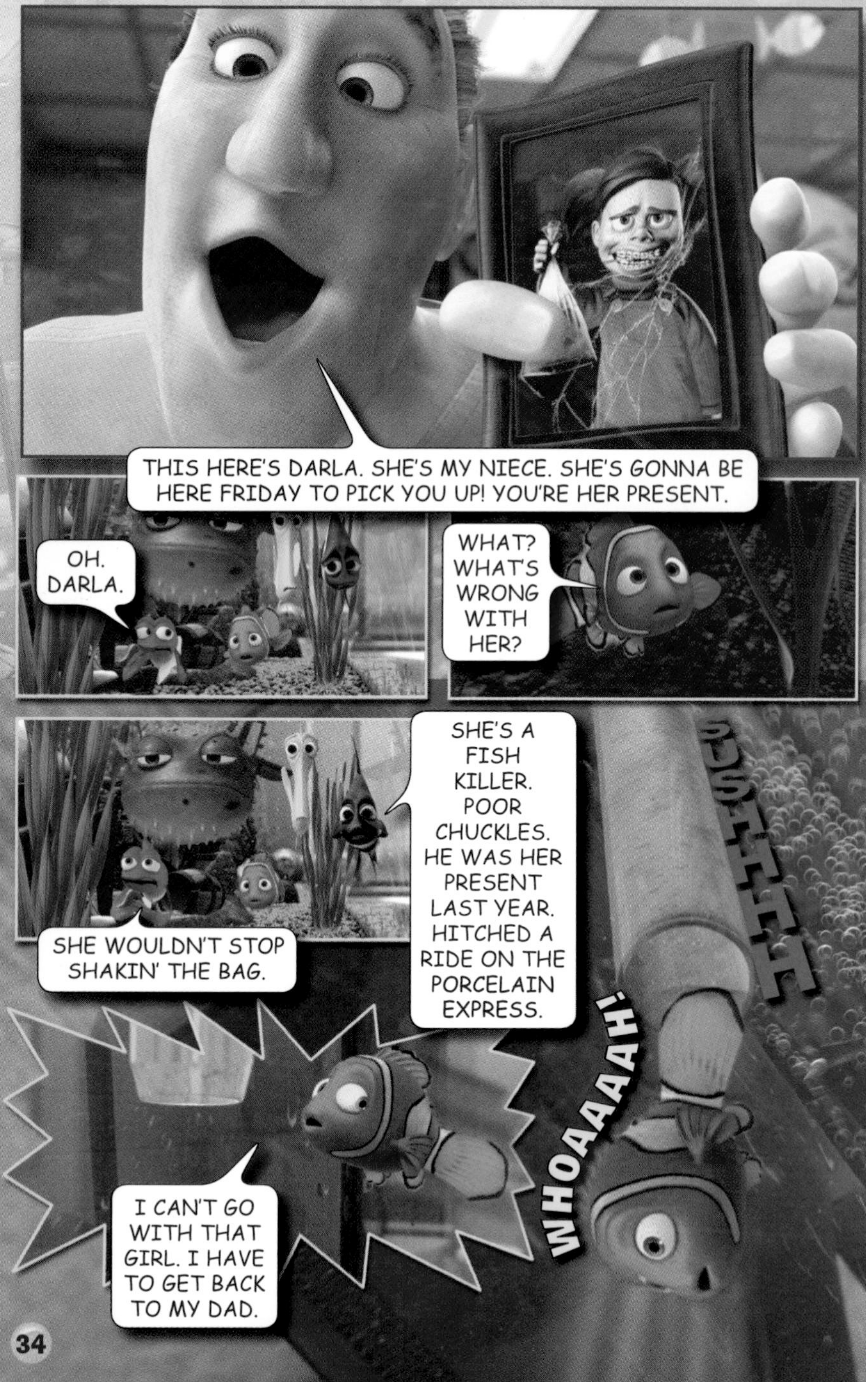
THIS HERE'S DARLA. SHE'S MY NIECE. SHE'S GONNA BE HERE FRIDAY TO PICK YOU UP! YOU'RE HER PRESENT.
OH. DARLA.
WHAT? WHAT'S WRONG WITH HER?
SHE'S A FISH KILLER. POOR CHUCKLES. HE WAS HER PRESENT LAST YEAR. HITCHED A RIDE ON THE PORCELAIN EXPRESS.
SHE WOULDN'T STOP SHAKIN' THE BAG.
I CAN'T GO WITH THAT GIRL. I HAVE TO GET BACK TO MY DAD.
SUSHHHH
WHOAAAAH!

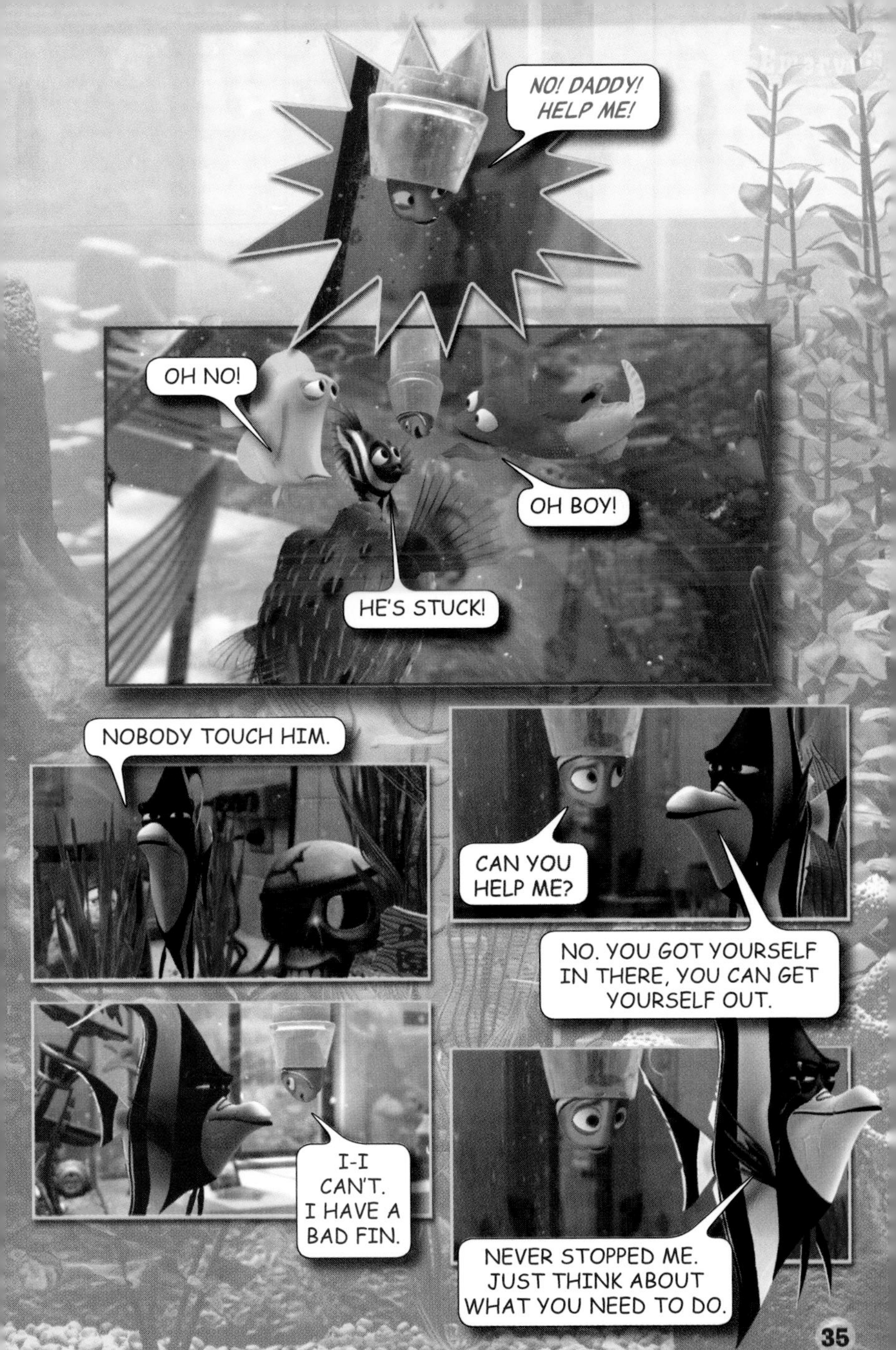
NO! DADDY! HELP ME!
OH NO!
OH BOY!
HE'S STUCK!
NOBODY TOUCH HIM.
CAN YOU HELP ME?
NO. YOU GOT YOURSELF IN THERE, YOU CAN GET YOURSELF OUT.
I-I CAN'T. I HAVE A BAD FIN.
NEVER STOPPED ME. JUST THINK ABOUT WHAT YOU NEED TO DO.

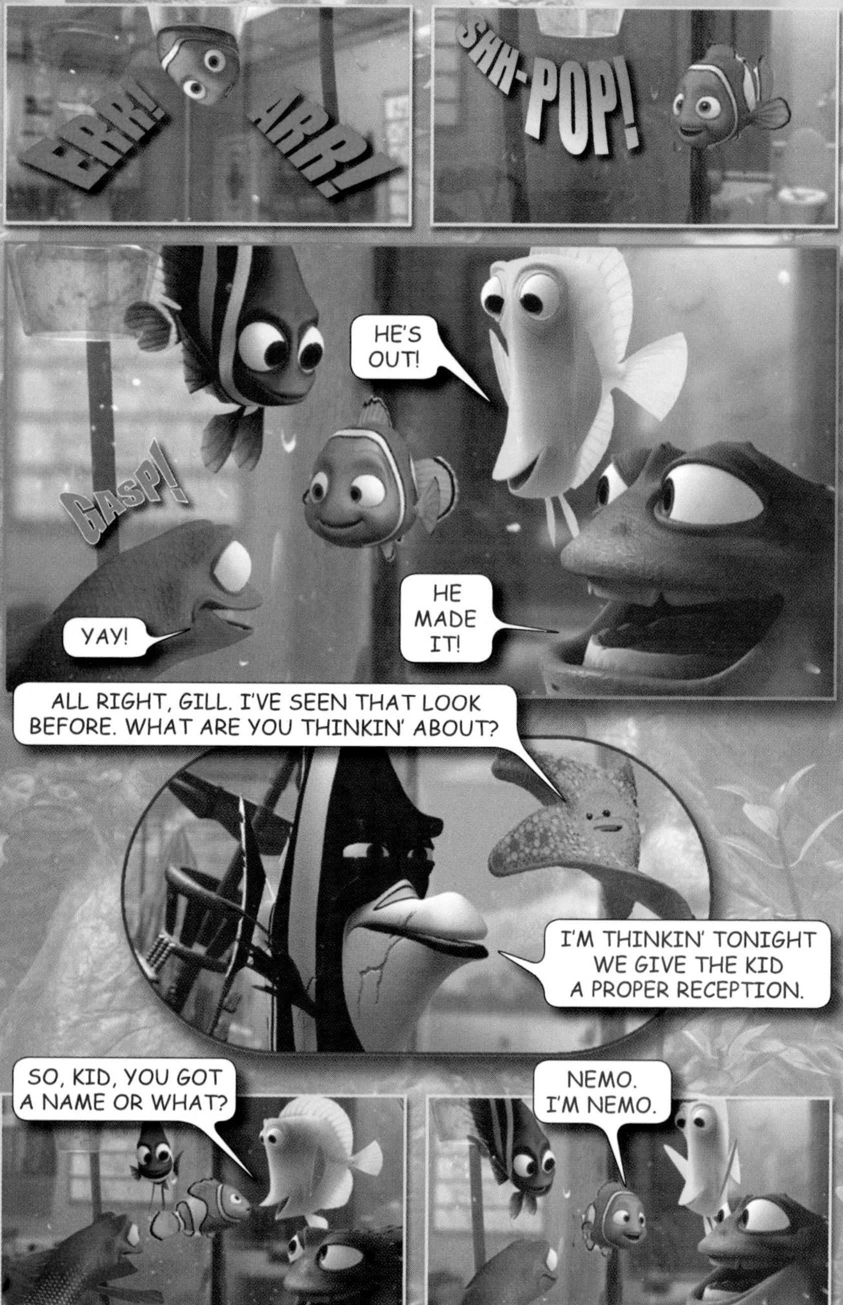
ERR!
ARR!
SHH-POP!
HE'S OUT!
GASP!
YAY!
HE MADE IT!
ALL RIGHT, GILL. I'VE SEEN THAT LOOK BEFORE. WHAT ARE YOU THINKIN' ABOUT?
I'M THINKIN' TONIGHT WE GIVE THE KID A PROPER RECEPTION.
SO, KID, YOU GOT A NAME OR WHAT?
NEMO. I'M NEMO.

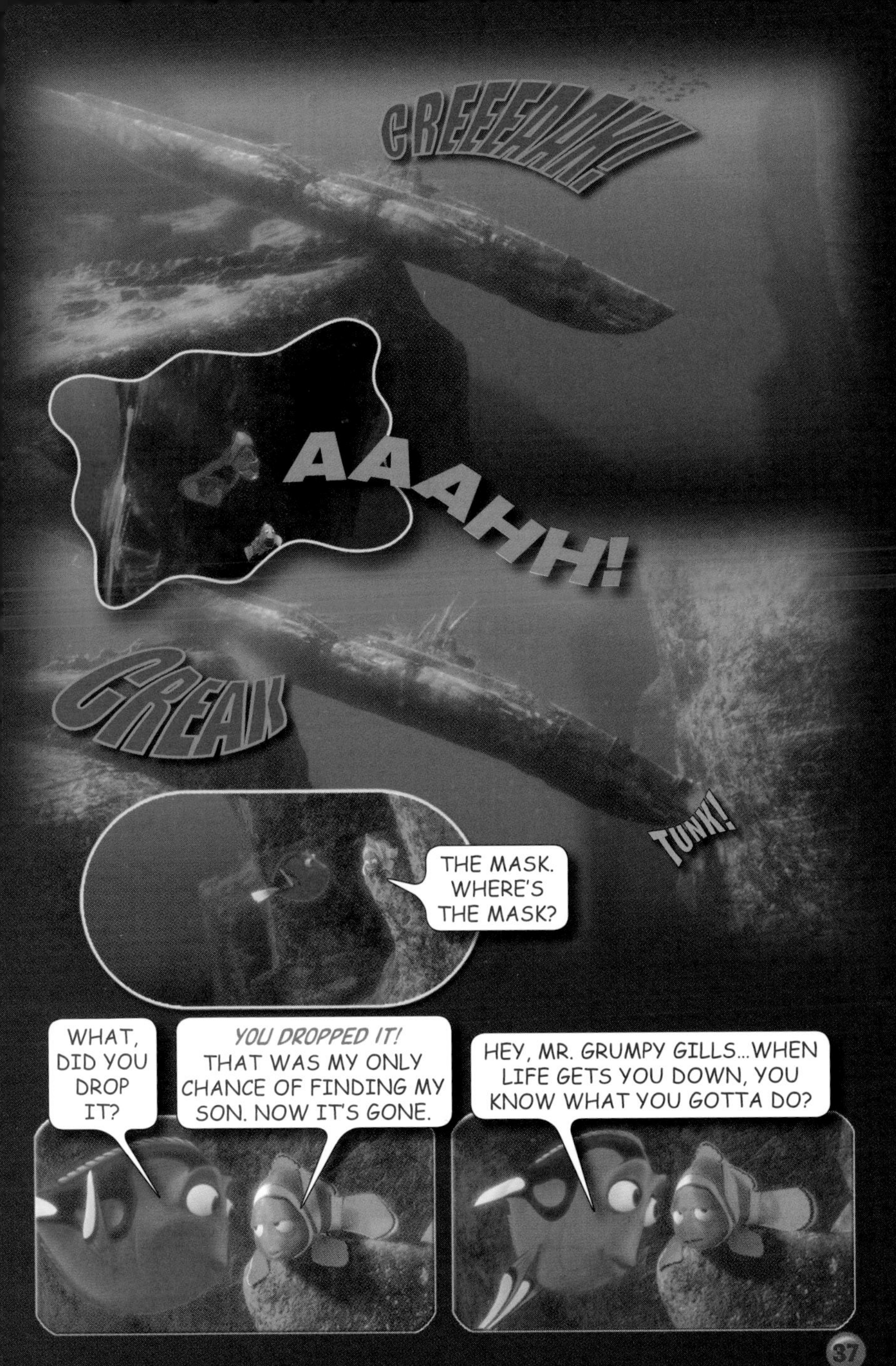
CREEEAAK!
AAAAHH!
CREAK
TUNK!
THE MASK. WHERE'S THE MASK?
WHAT, DID YOU DROP IT?
YOU DROPPED IT! THAT WAS MY ONLY CHANCE OF FINDING MY SON. NOW IT'S GONE.
HEY, MR. GRUMPY GILLS...WHEN LIFE GETS YOU DOWN, YOU KNOW WHAT YOU GOTTA DO?

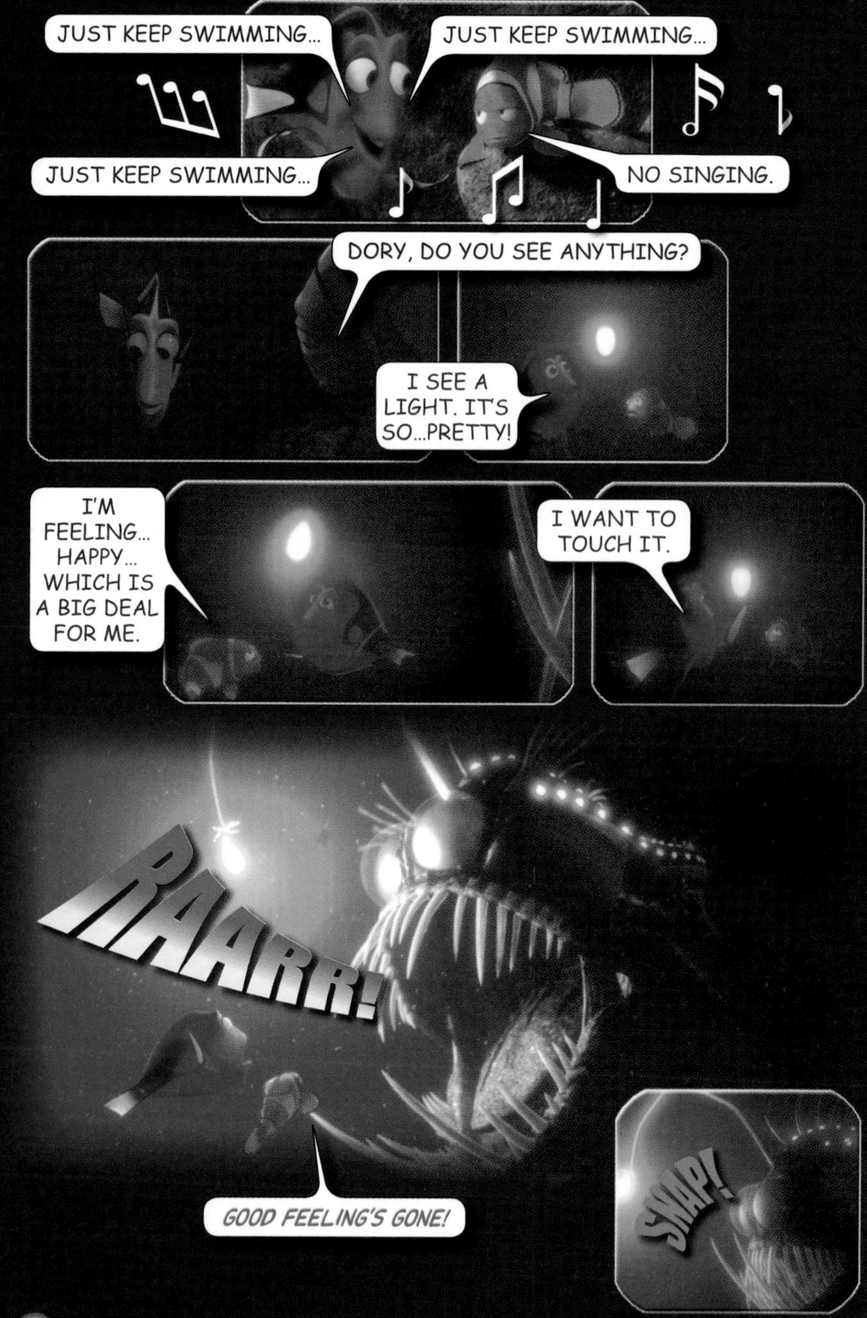
JUST KEEP SWIMMING...
JUST KEEP SWIMMING...
JUST KEEP SWIMMING...
NO SINGING.
DORY, DO YOU SEE ANYTHING?
I SEE A LIGHT. IT'S SO...PRETTY!
I'M FEELING... HAPPY... WHICH IS A BIG DEAL FOR ME.
I WANT TO TOUCH IT.
RAAARR!
GOOD FEELING'S GONE!
SNAP!

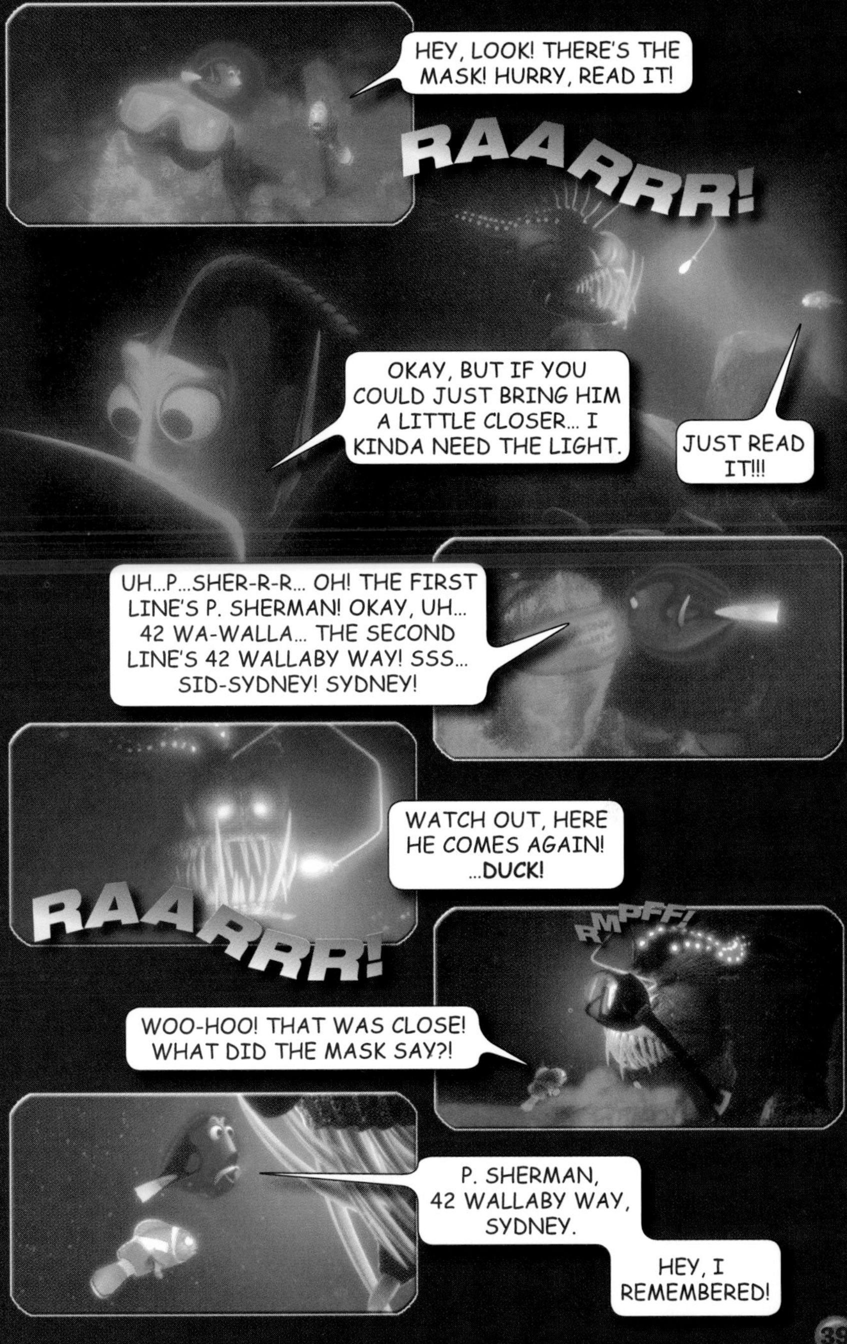
HEY, LOOK! THERE'S THE MASK! HURRY, READ IT!
RAAARRR!
OKAY, BUT IF YOU COULD JUST BRING HIM A LITTLE CLOSER... I KINDA NEED THE LIGHT.
JUST READ IT!!!
UH...P...SHER-R-R... OH! THE FIRST LINE'S P. SHERMAN! OKAY, UH... 42 WA-WALLA... THE SECOND LINE'S 42 WALLABY WAY! SSS... SID-SYDNEY! SYDNEY!
WATCH OUT, HERE HE COMES AGAIN! ...**DUCK!**
RAAARRR!
RMPFF!
WOO-HOO! THAT WAS CLOSE! WHAT DID THE MASK SAY?!
P. SHERMAN, 42 WALLABY WAY, SYDNEY.
HEY, I REMEMBERED!

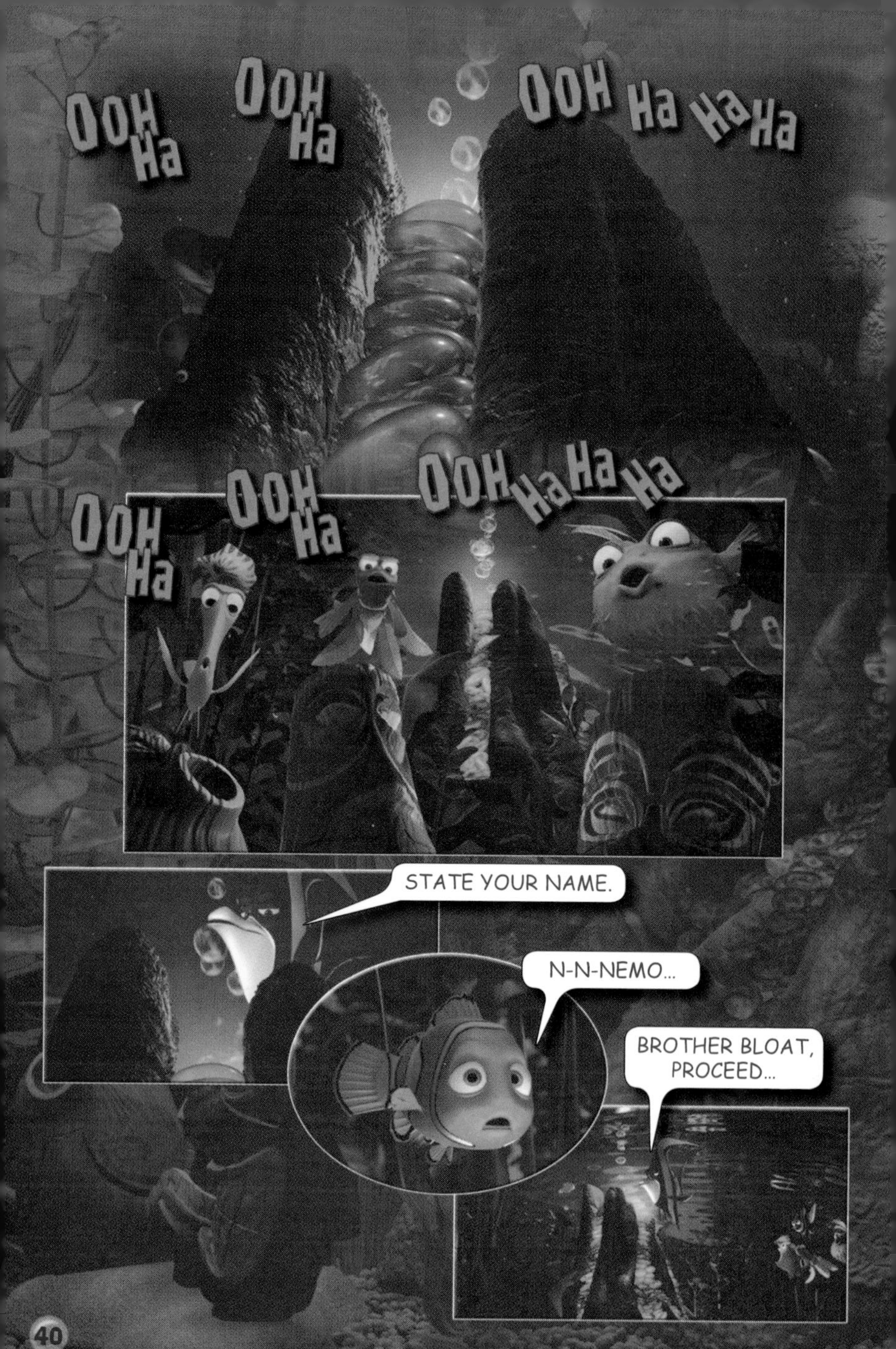
OOH HA
OOH HA
OOH HA HA HA
OOH HA
OOH HA
OOH HA HA HA
STATE YOUR NAME.
N-N-NEMO...
BROTHER BLOAT, PROCEED...

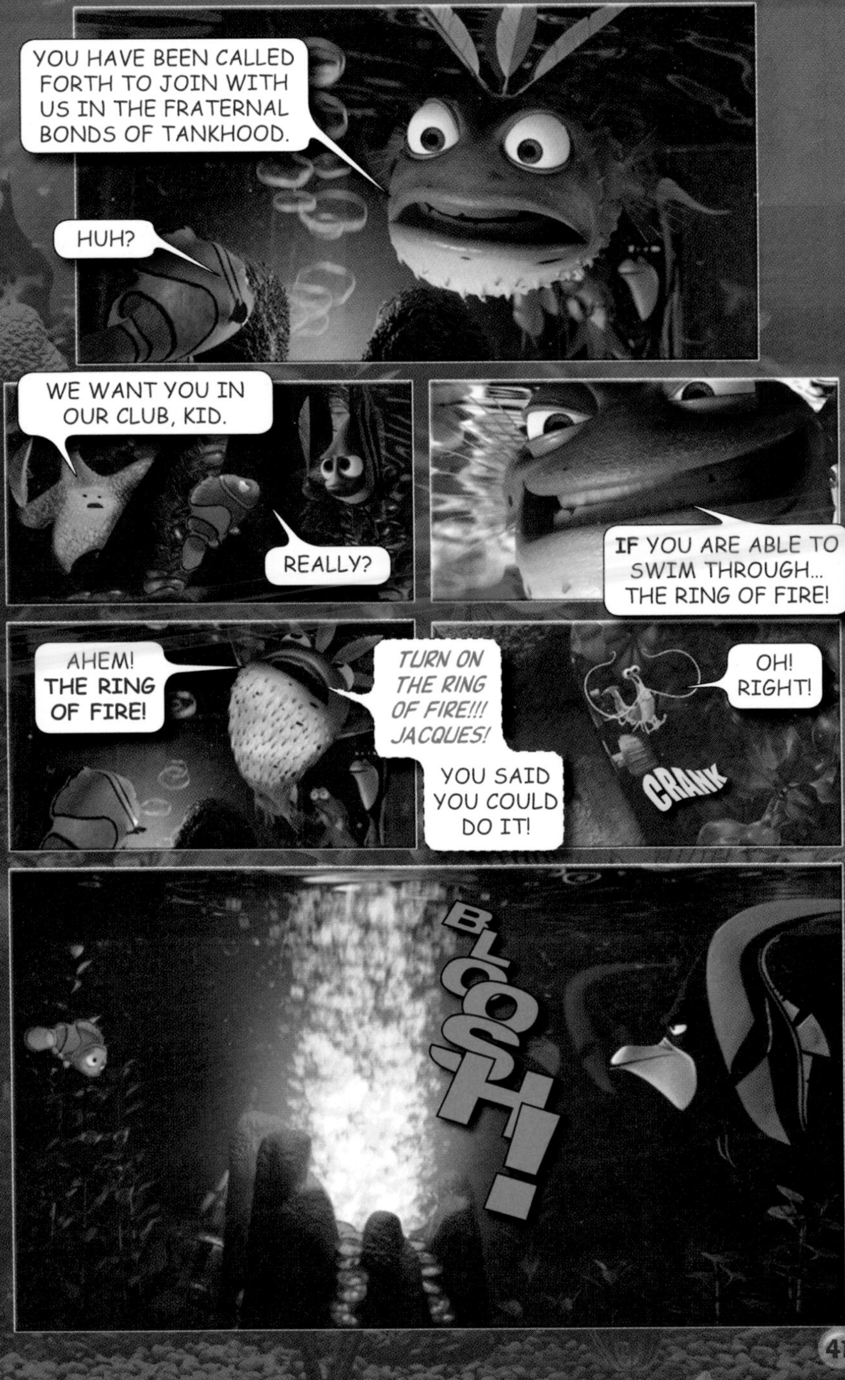

YOU HAVE BEEN CALLED FORTH TO JOIN WITH US IN THE FRATERNAL BONDS OF TANKHOOD.
HUH?
WE WANT YOU IN OUR CLUB, KID.
REALLY?
IF YOU ARE ABLE TO SWIM THROUGH... THE RING OF FIRE!
AHEM! THE RING OF FIRE!
TURN ON THE RING OF FIRE!!! JACQUES!
YOU SAID YOU COULD DO IT!
OH! RIGHT!
CRANK
BLOOSH!

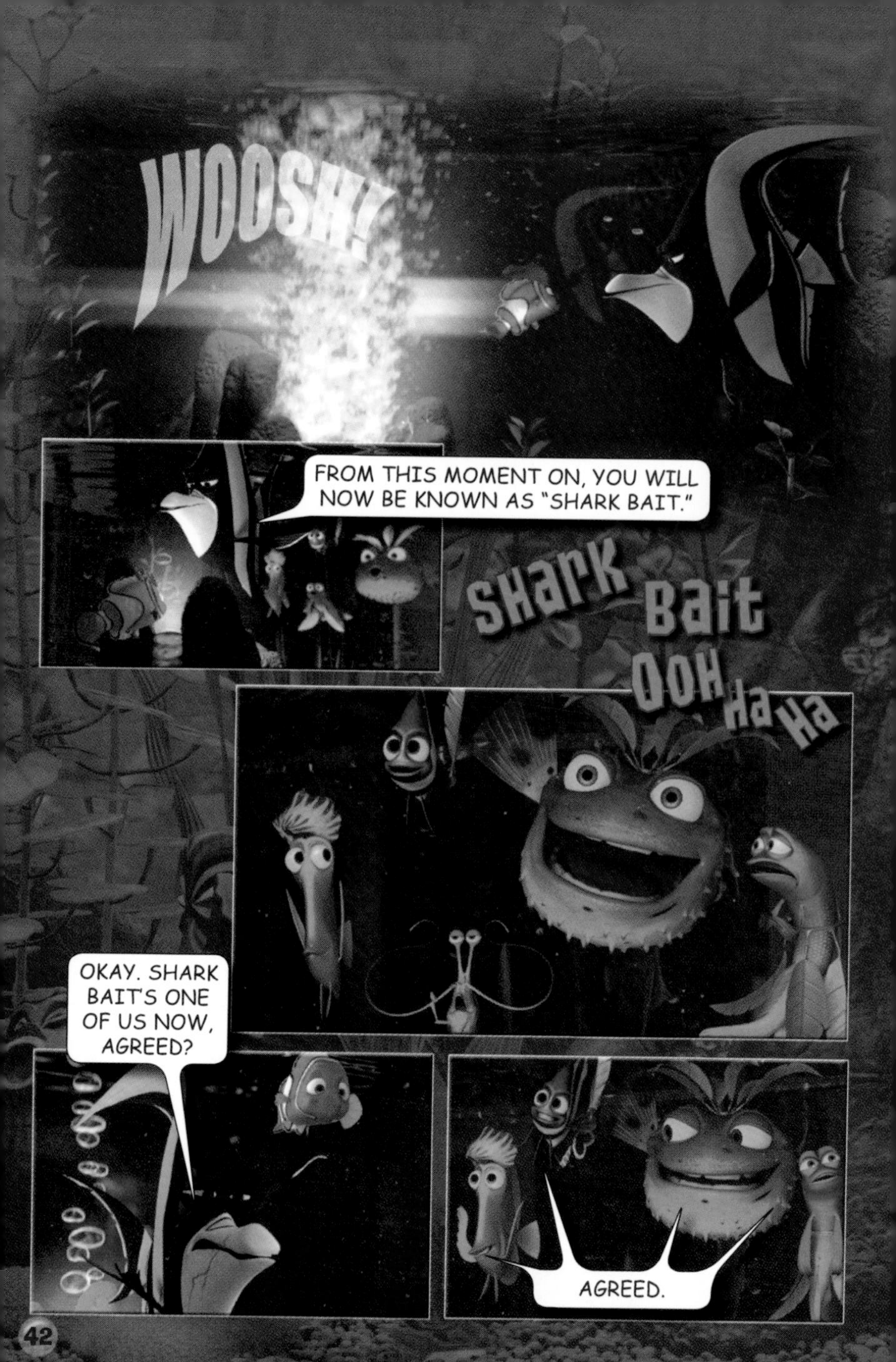
WOOSH!
FROM THIS MOMENT ON, YOU WILL NOW BE KNOWN AS "SHARK BAIT."
SHARK BAIT OOH HA HA
OKAY. SHARK BAIT'S ONE OF US NOW, AGREED?
AGREED.

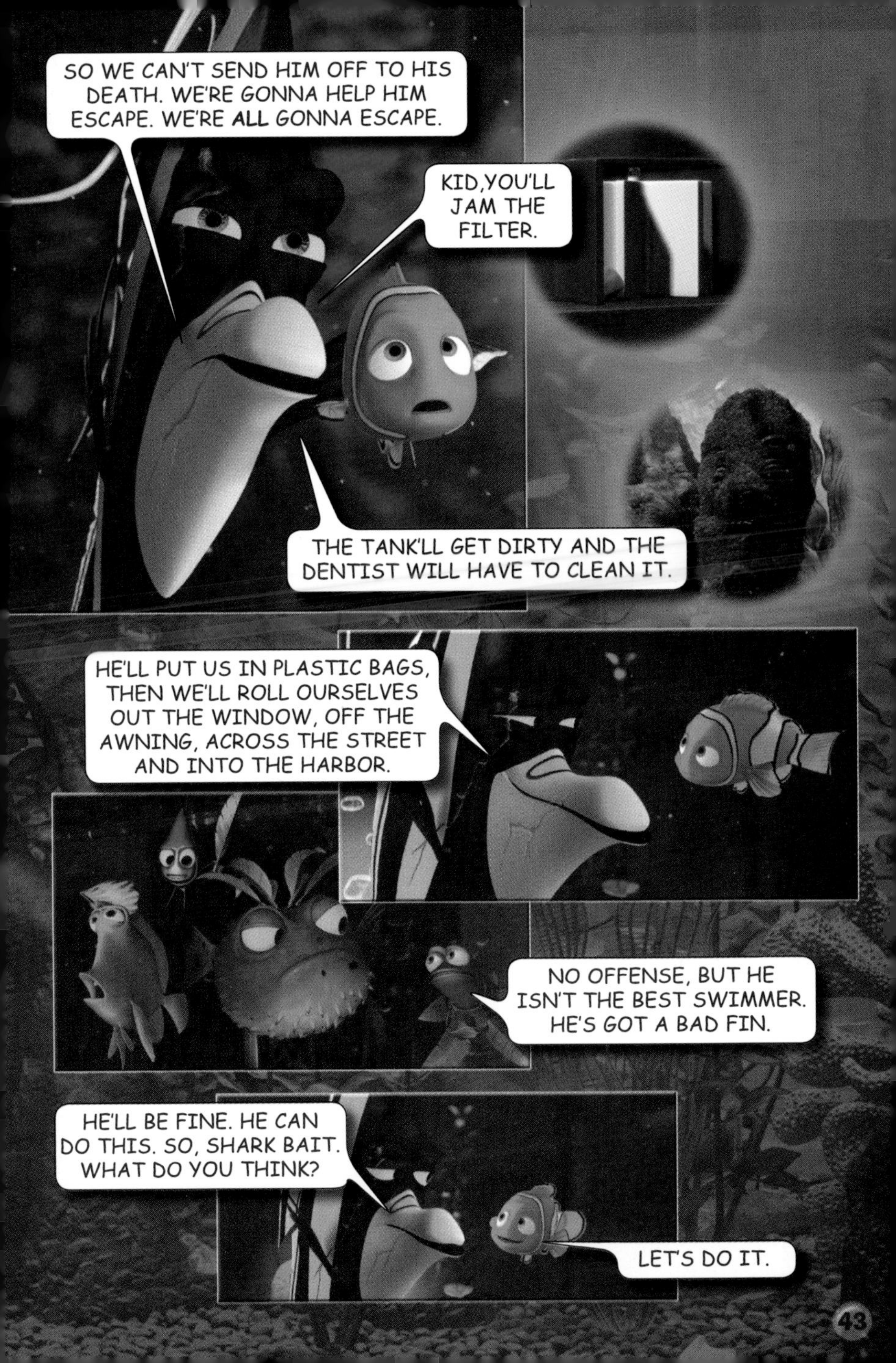
SO WE CAN'T SEND HIM OFF TO HIS DEATH. WE'RE GONNA HELP HIM ESCAPE. WE'RE **ALL** GONNA ESCAPE.
KID,YOU'LL JAM THE FILTER.
THE TANK'LL GET DIRTY AND THE DENTIST WILL HAVE TO CLEAN IT.
HE'LL PUT US IN PLASTIC BAGS, THEN WE'LL ROLL OURSELVES OUT THE WINDOW, OFF THE AWNING, ACROSS THE STREET AND INTO THE HARBOR.
NO OFFENSE, BUT HE ISN'T THE BEST SWIMMER. HE'S GOT A BAD FIN.
HE'LL BE FINE. HE CAN DO THIS. SO, SHARK BAIT. WHAT DO YOU THINK?
LET'S DO IT.

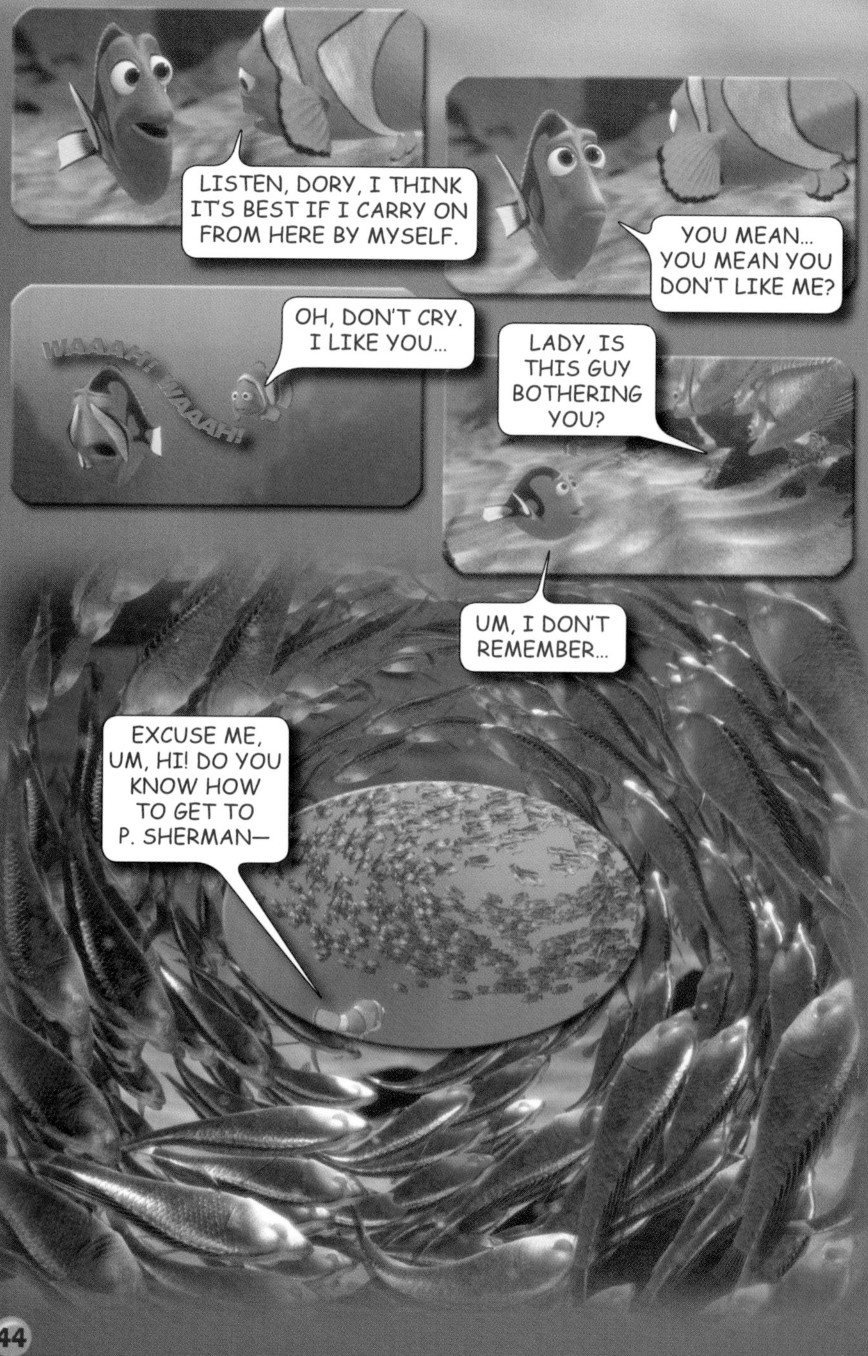
LISTEN, DORY, I THINK IT'S BEST IF I CARRY ON FROM HERE BY MYSELF.
YOU MEAN... YOU MEAN YOU DON'T LIKE ME?
WAAAH! WAAAH!
OH, DON'T CRY. I LIKE YOU...
LADY, IS THIS GUY BOTHERING YOU?
UM, I DON'T REMEMBER...
EXCUSE ME, UM, HI! DO YOU KNOW HOW TO GET TO P. SHERMAN—

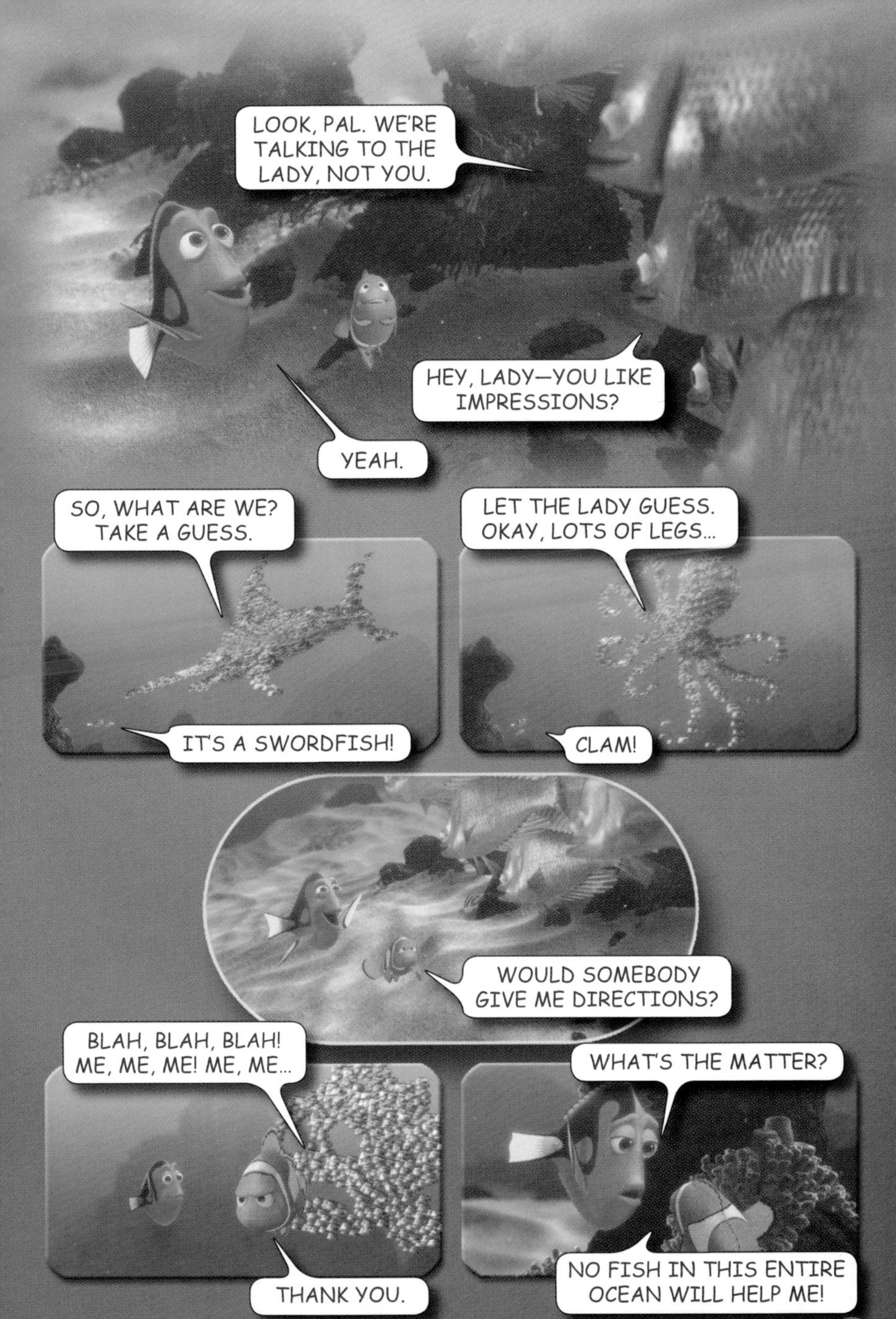
LOOK, PAL. WE'RE TALKING TO THE LADY, NOT YOU.
HEY, LADY—YOU LIKE IMPRESSIONS?
YEAH.
SO, WHAT ARE WE? TAKE A GUESS.
IT'S A SWORDFISH!
LET THE LADY GUESS. OKAY, LOTS OF LEGS...
CLAM!
WOULD SOMEBODY GIVE ME DIRECTIONS?
BLAH, BLAH, BLAH! ME, ME, ME! ME, ME...
THANK YOU.
WHAT'S THE MATTER?
NO FISH IN THIS ENTIRE OCEAN WILL HELP ME!

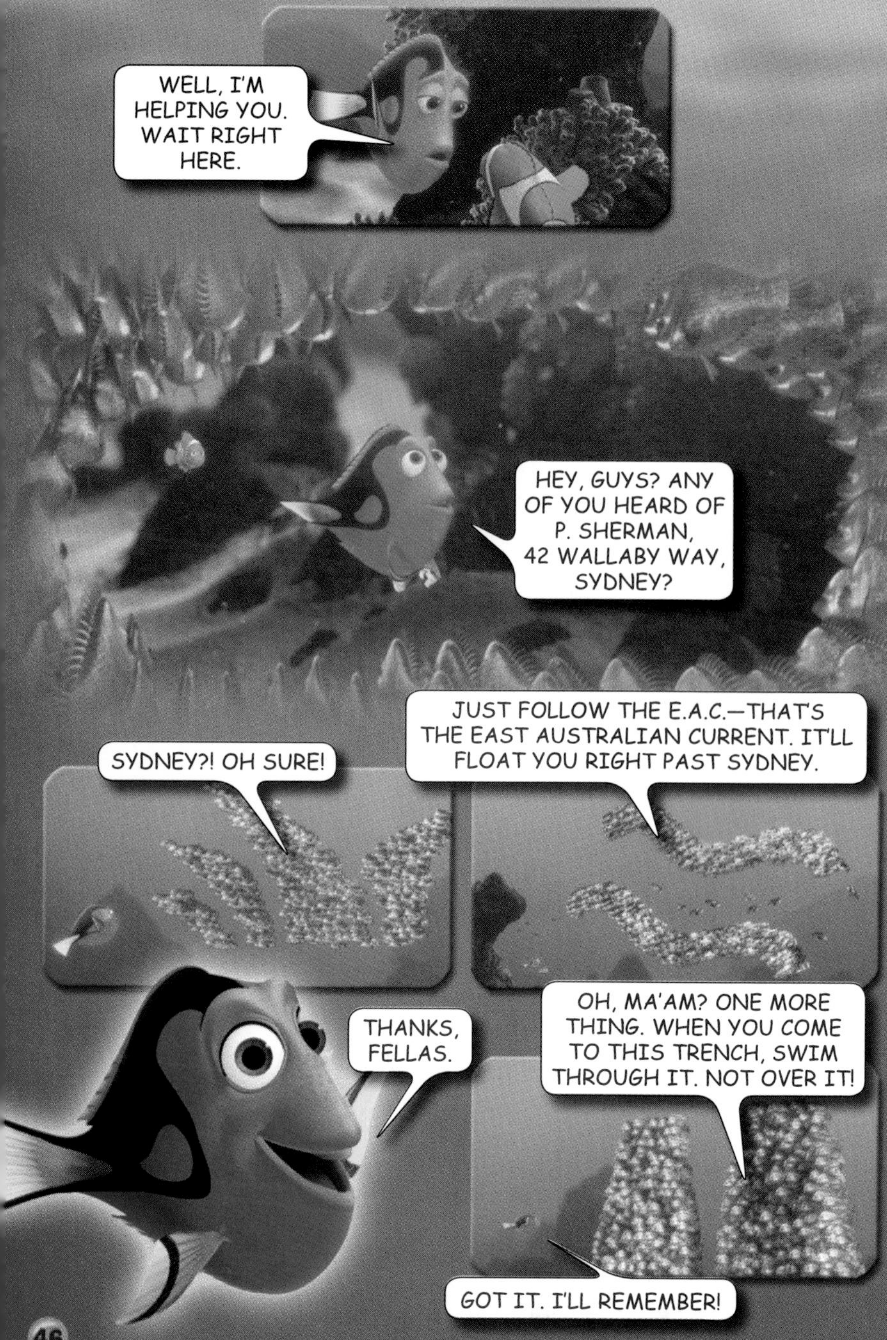

WELL, I'M HELPING YOU. WAIT RIGHT HERE.
HEY, GUYS? ANY OF YOU HEARD OF P. SHERMAN, 42 WALLABY WAY, SYDNEY?
SYDNEY?! OH SURE!
JUST FOLLOW THE E.A.C.—THAT'S THE EAST AUSTRALIAN CURRENT. IT'LL FLOAT YOU RIGHT PAST SYDNEY.
THANKS, FELLAS.
OH, MA'AM? ONE MORE THING. WHEN YOU COME TO THIS TRENCH, SWIM THROUGH IT. NOT OVER IT!
GOT IT. I'LL REMEMBER!

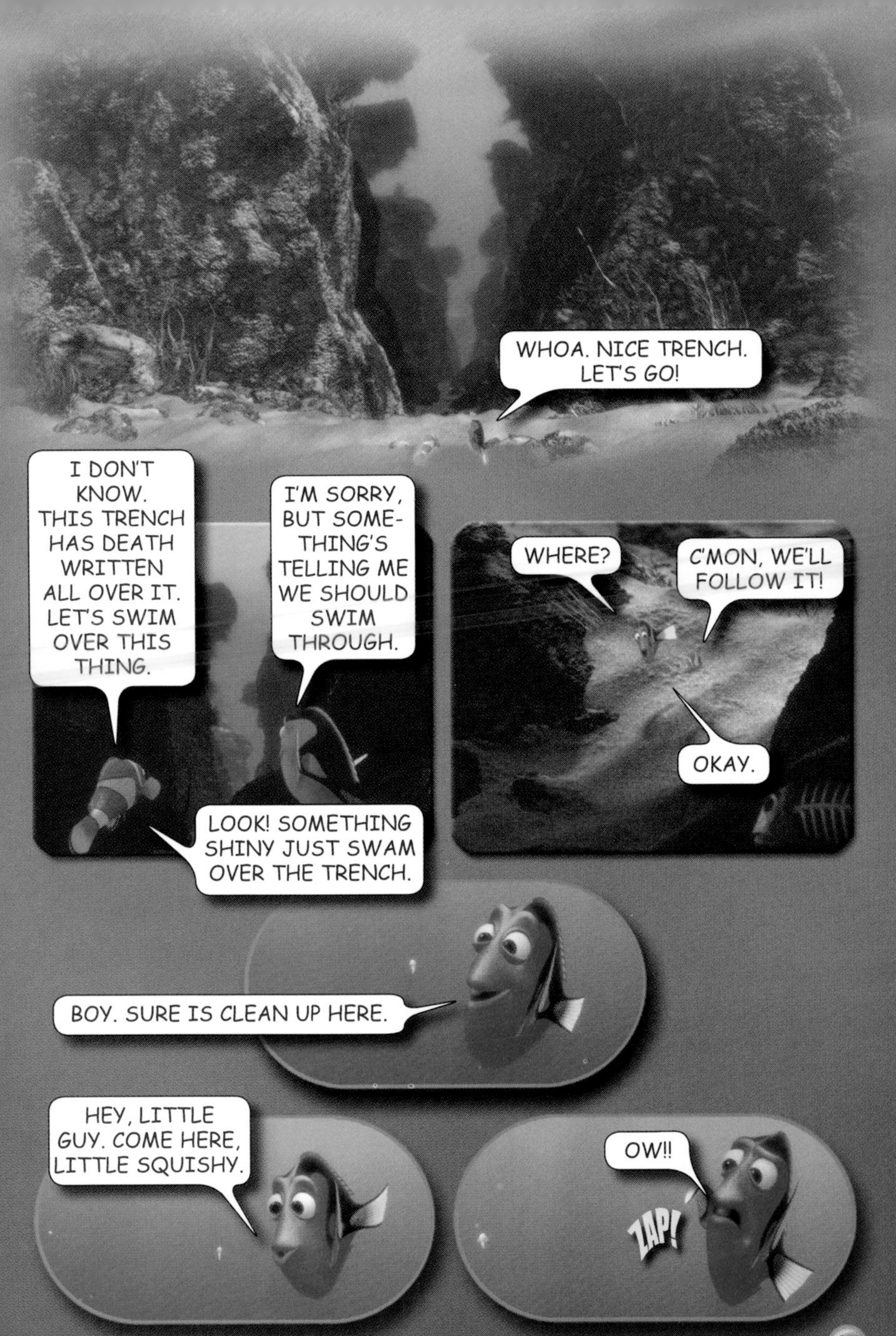
WHOA. NICE TRENCH. LET'S GO!
I DON'T KNOW. THIS TRENCH HAS DEATH WRITTEN ALL OVER IT. LET'S SWIM OVER THIS THING.
I'M SORRY, BUT SOME-THING'S TELLING ME WE SHOULD SWIM THROUGH.
LOOK! SOMETHING SHINY JUST SWAM OVER THE TRENCH.
WHERE?
C'MON, WE'LL FOLLOW IT!
OKAY.
BOY. SURE IS CLEAN UP HERE.
HEY, LITTLE GUY. COME HERE, LITTLE SQUISHY.
OW!!
ZAP!

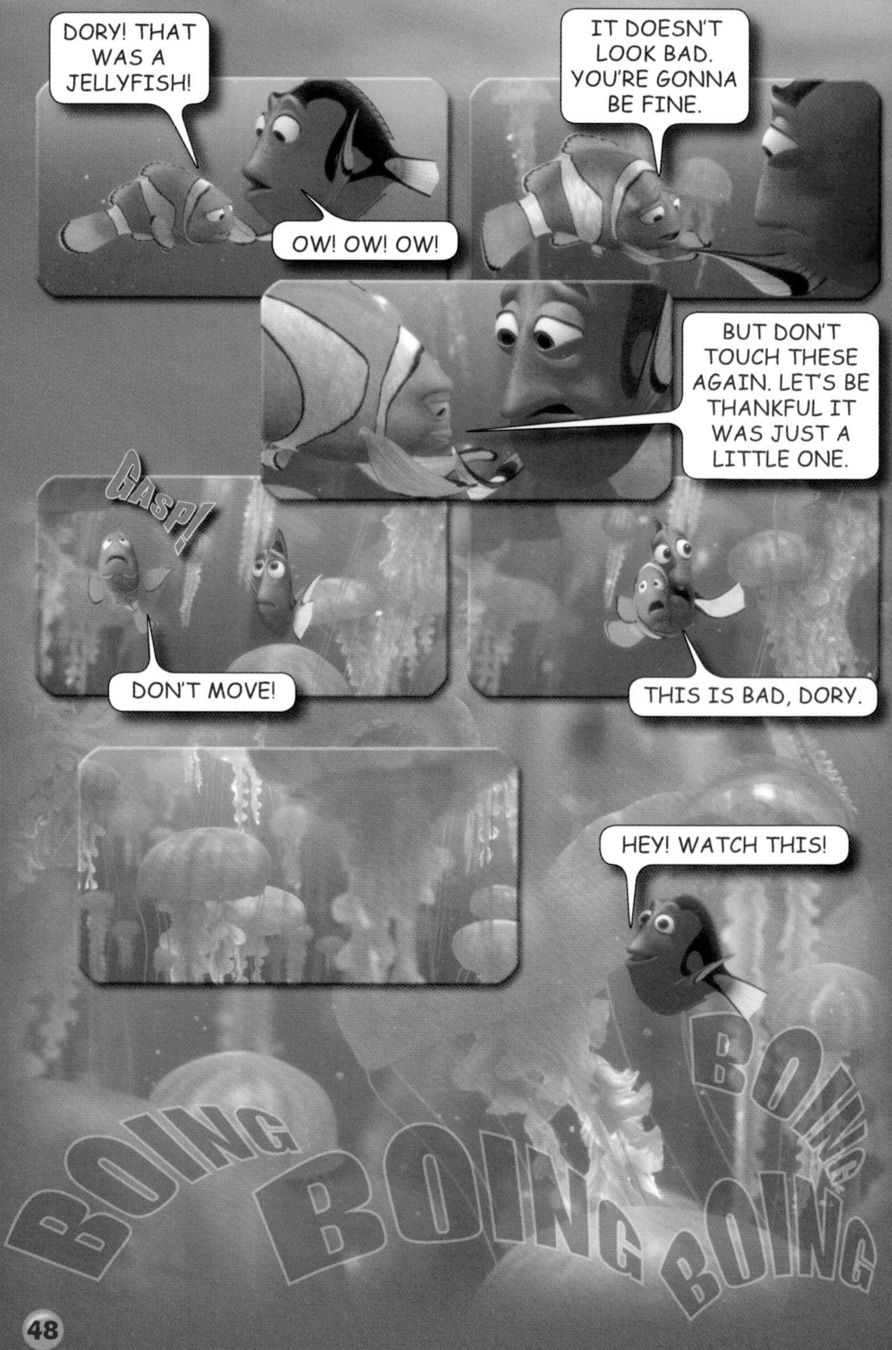
DORY! THAT WAS A JELLYFISH!
OW! OW! OW!
IT DOESN'T LOOK BAD. YOU'RE GONNA BE FINE.
BUT DON'T TOUCH THESE AGAIN. LET'S BE THANKFUL IT WAS JUST A LITTLE ONE.
GASP!
DON'T MOVE!
THIS IS BAD, DORY.
HEY! WATCH THIS!
BOING
BOING
BOING
BOING

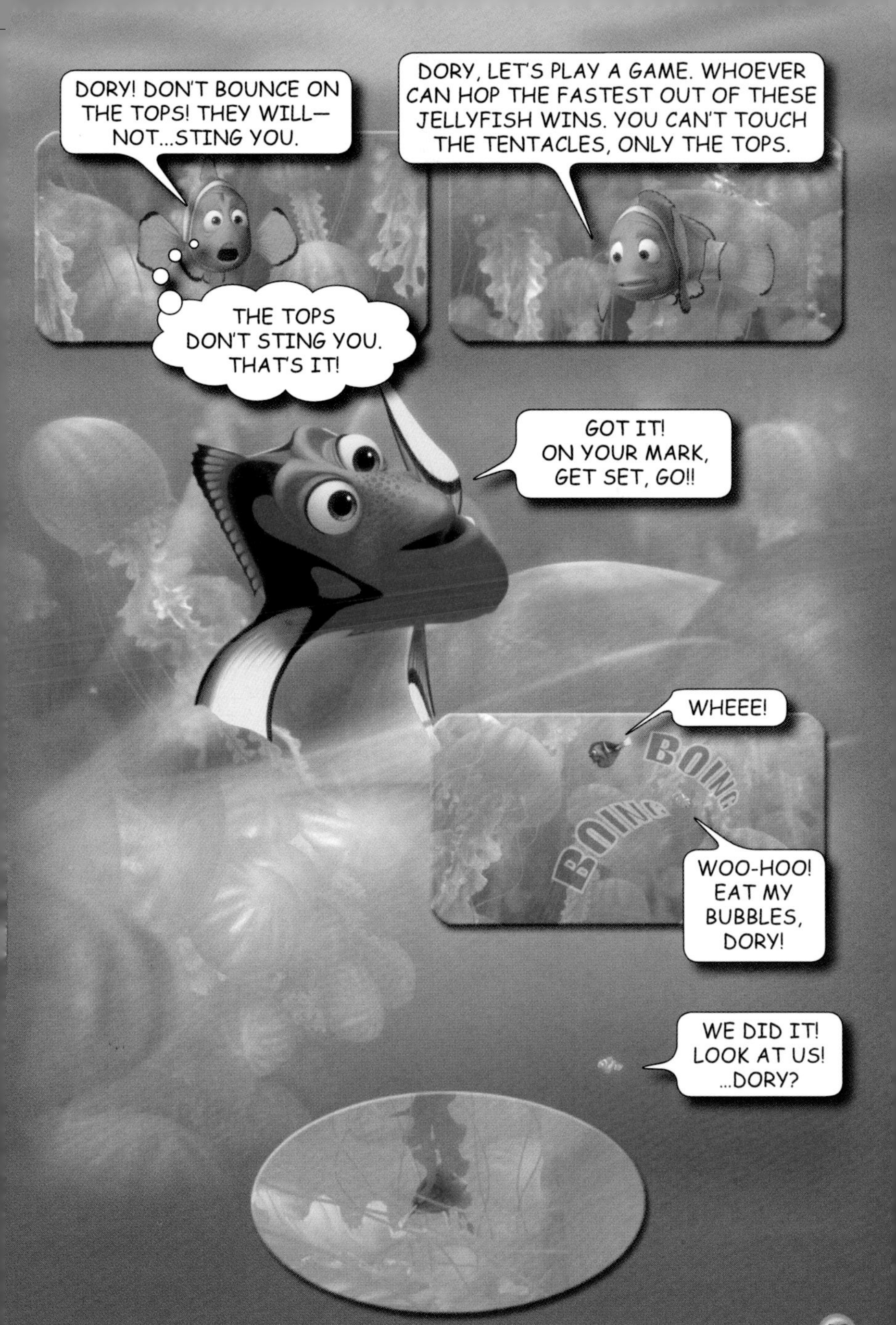
DORY! DON'T BOUNCE ON THE TOPS! THEY WILL— NOT...STING YOU.
THE TOPS DON'T STING YOU. THAT'S IT!
DORY, LET'S PLAY A GAME. WHOEVER CAN HOP THE FASTEST OUT OF THESE JELLYFISH WINS. YOU CAN'T TOUCH THE TENTACLES, ONLY THE TOPS.
GOT IT! ON YOUR MARK, GET SET, GO!!
WHEEE!
BOING
BOING
BOING
WOO-HOO! EAT MY BUBBLES, DORY!
WE DID IT! LOOK AT US! ...DORY?

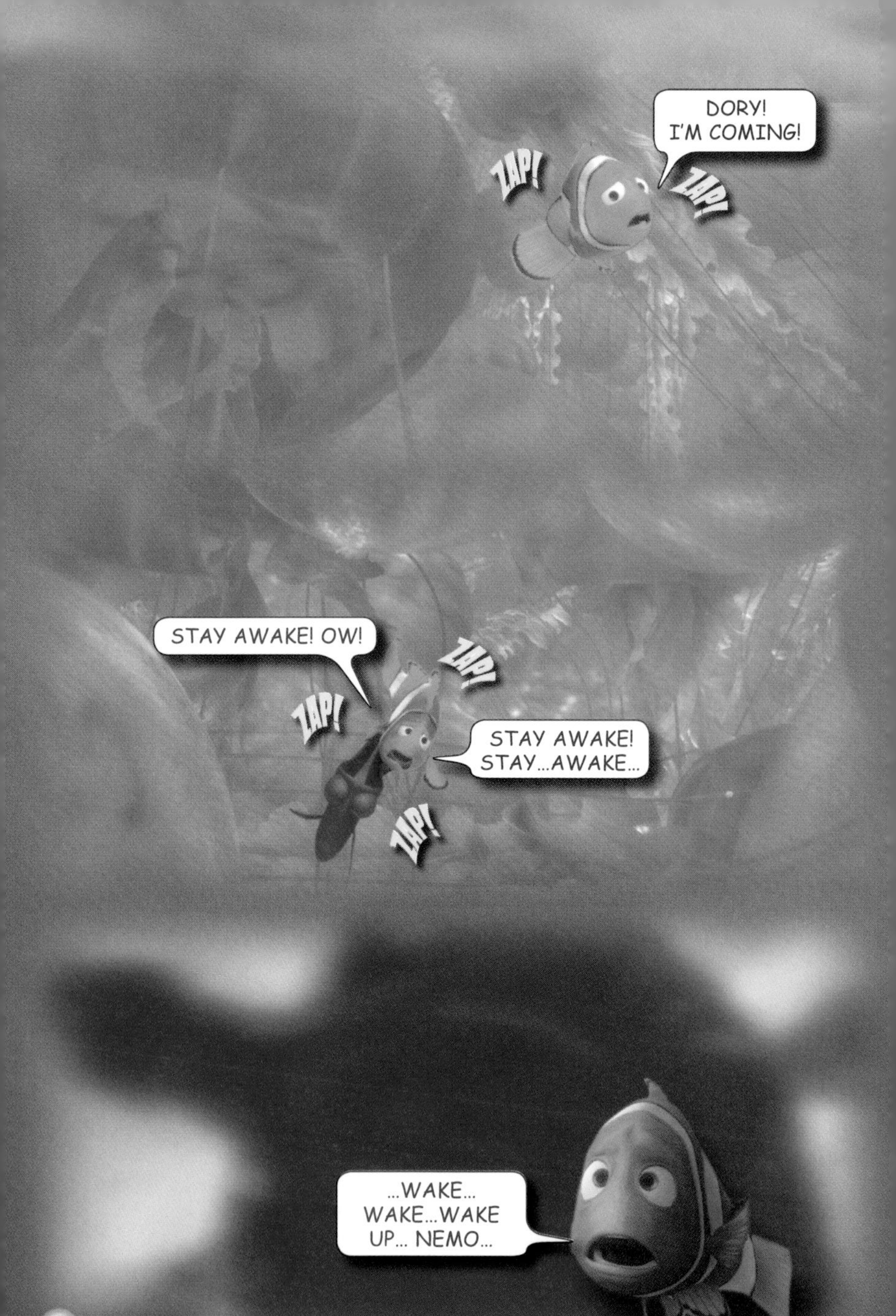
ZAP!
DORY! I'M COMING!
ZAP!
STAY AWAKE! OW!
ZAP!
ZAP!
STAY AWAKE! STAY...AWAKE...
ZAP!
...WAKE... WAKE...WAKE UP... NEMO...

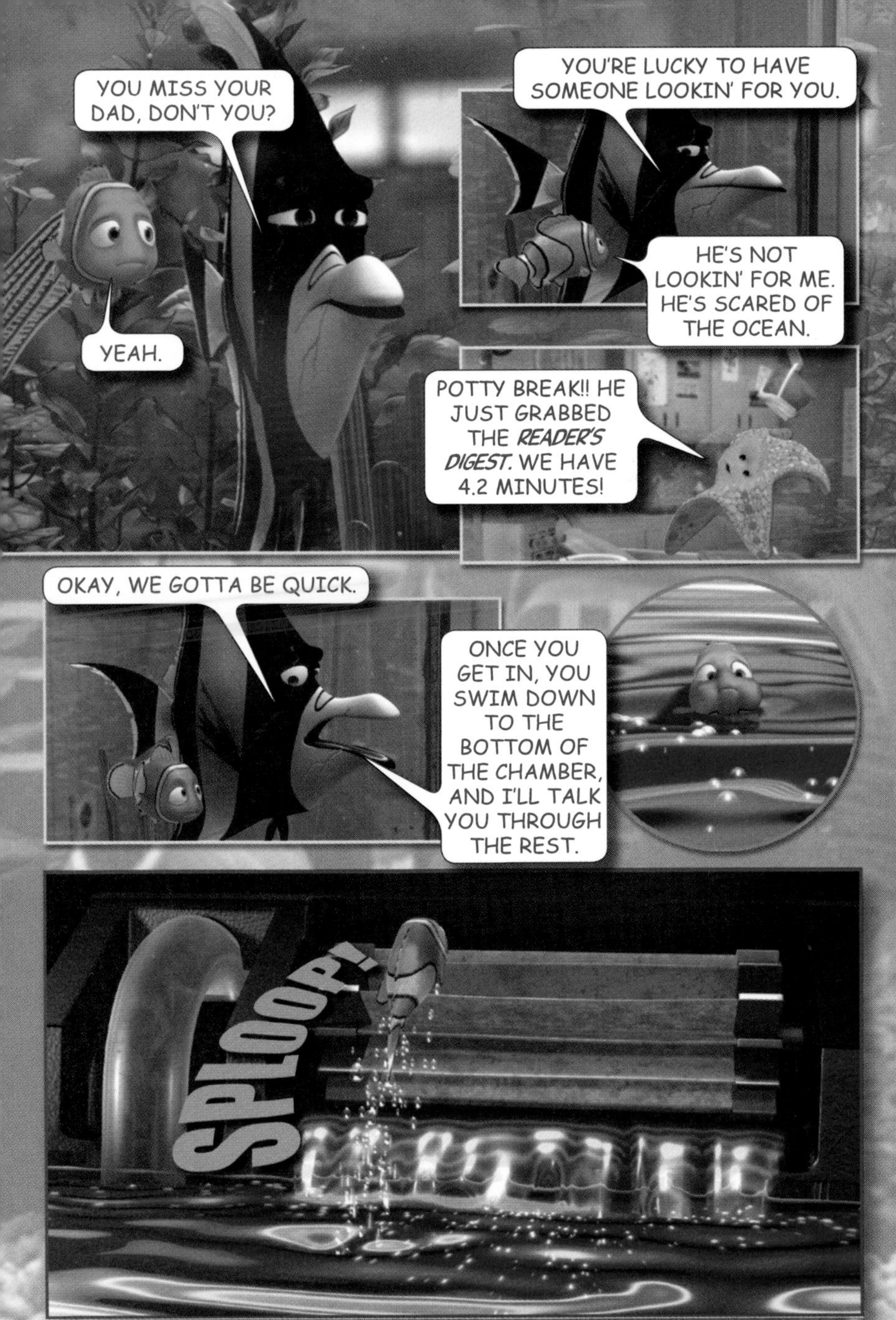

YOU MISS YOUR DAD, DON'T YOU?
YEAH.
YOU'RE LUCKY TO HAVE SOMEONE LOOKIN' FOR YOU.
HE'S NOT LOOKIN' FOR ME. HE'S SCARED OF THE OCEAN.
POTTY BREAK!! HE JUST GRABBED THE *READER'S DIGEST.* WE HAVE 4.2 MINUTES!
OKAY, WE GOTTA BE QUICK.
ONCE YOU GET IN, YOU SWIM DOWN TO THE BOTTOM OF THE CHAMBER, AND I'LL TALK YOU THROUGH THE REST.
SPLOOP!

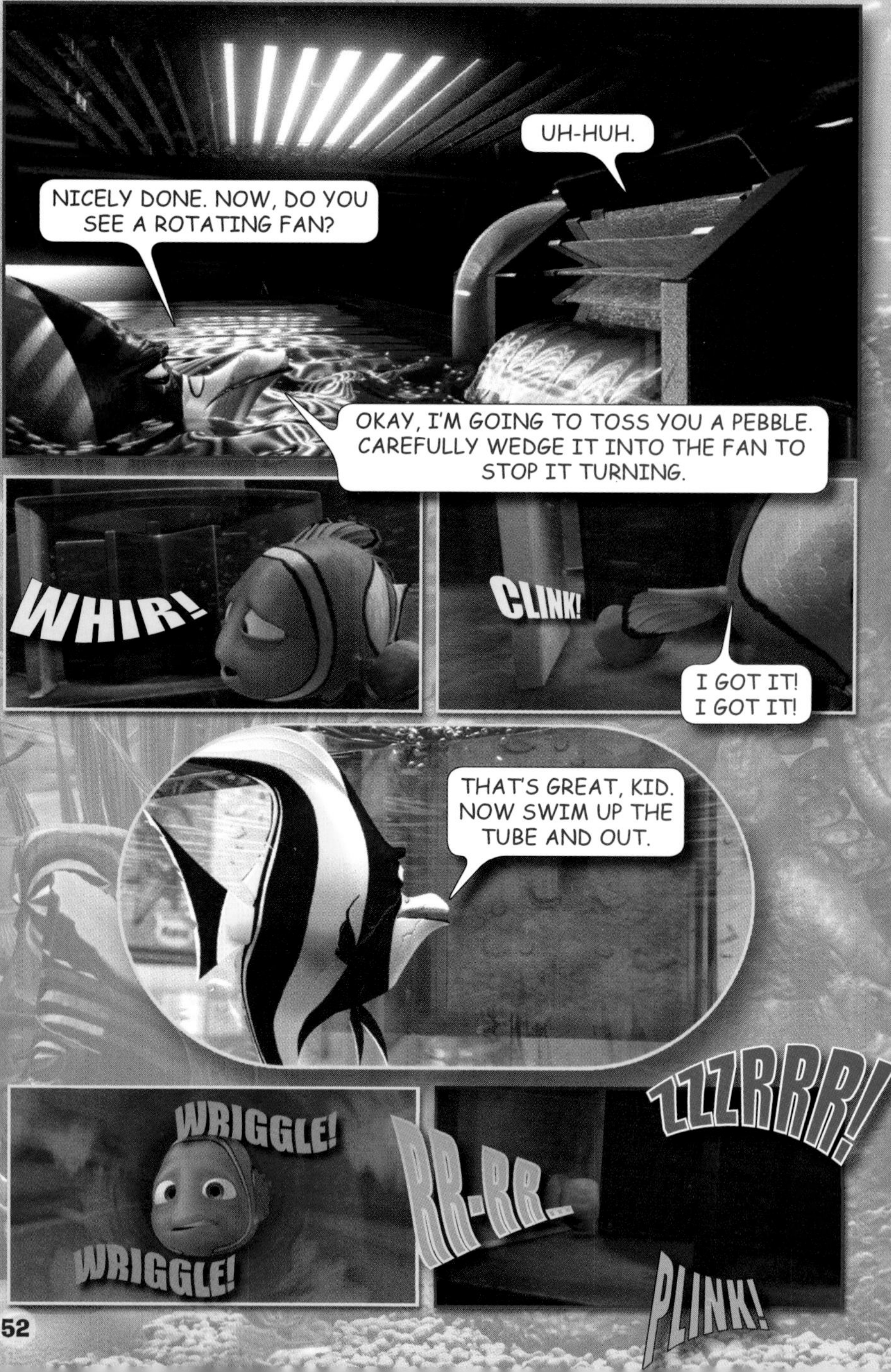

NICELY DONE. NOW, DO YOU SEE A ROTATING FAN?
UH-HUH.
OKAY, I'M GOING TO TOSS YOU A PEBBLE. CAREFULLY WEDGE IT INTO THE FAN TO STOP IT TURNING.
WHIR!
CLINK!
I GOT IT! I GOT IT!
THAT'S GREAT, KID. NOW SWIM UP THE TUBE AND OUT.
WRIGGLE!
WRIGGLE!
RR-RR...
ZZZRRR!
PLINK!

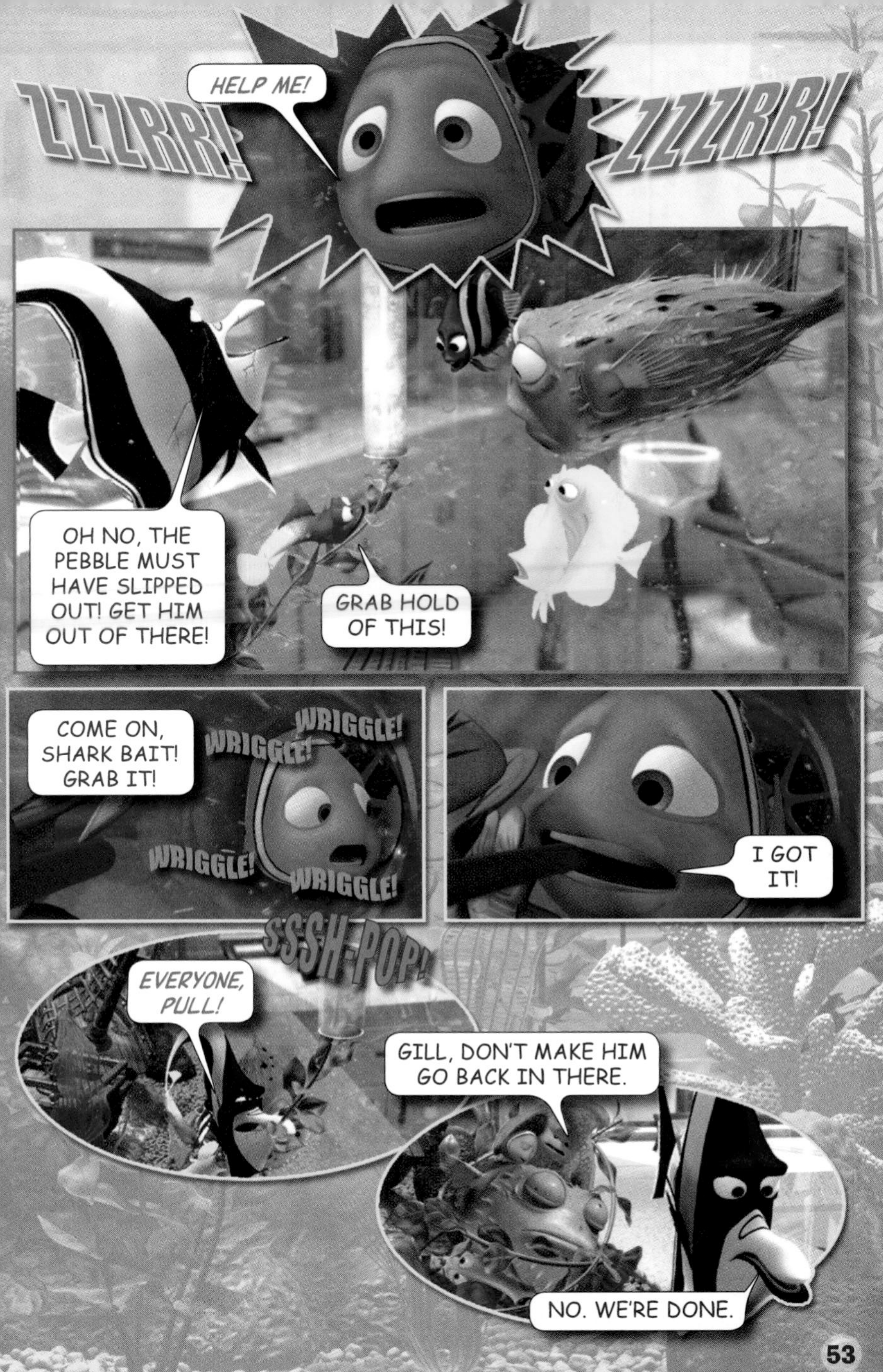
ZZZRR!
HELP ME!
ZZZRR!
OH NO, THE PEBBLE MUST HAVE SLIPPED OUT! GET HIM OUT OF THERE!
GRAB HOLD OF THIS!
COME ON, SHARK BAIT! GRAB IT!
WRIGGLE!
WRIGGLE!
WRIGGLE!
WRIGGLE!
I GOT IT!
SSSH-POP!
EVERYONE, PULL!
GILL, DON'T MAKE HIM GO BACK IN THERE.
NO. WE'RE DONE.

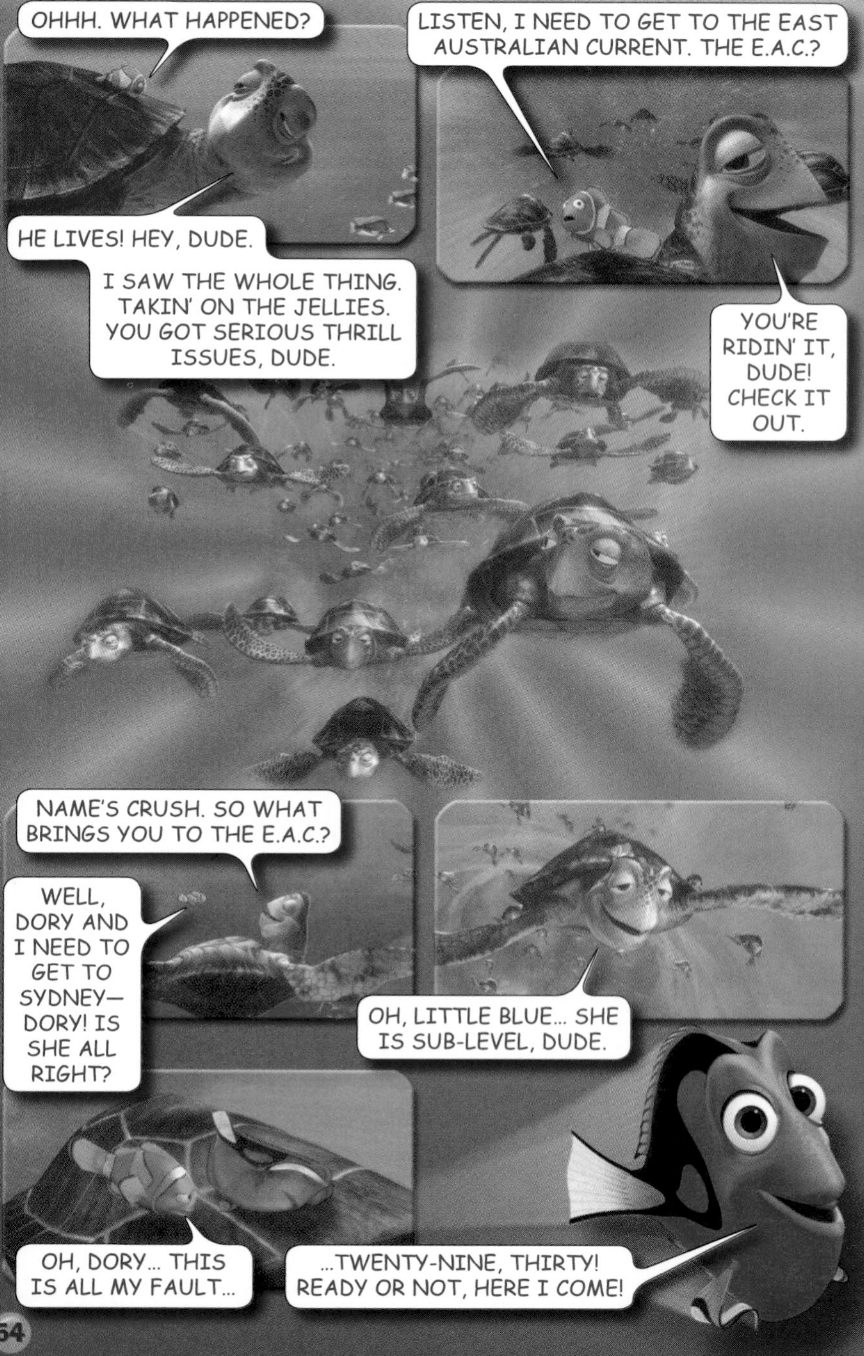
OHHH. WHAT HAPPENED?
HE LIVES! HEY, DUDE.
I SAW THE WHOLE THING. TAKIN' ON THE JELLIES. YOU GOT SERIOUS THRILL ISSUES, DUDE.
LISTEN, I NEED TO GET TO THE EAST AUSTRALIAN CURRENT. THE E.A.C.?
YOU'RE RIDIN' IT, DUDE! CHECK IT OUT.
NAME'S CRUSH. SO WHAT BRINGS YOU TO THE E.A.C.?
WELL, DORY AND I NEED TO GET TO SYDNEY— DORY! IS SHE ALL RIGHT?
OH, LITTLE BLUE... SHE IS SUB-LEVEL, DUDE.
OH, DORY... THIS IS ALL MY FAULT...
...TWENTY-NINE, THIRTY! READY OR NOT, HERE I COME!

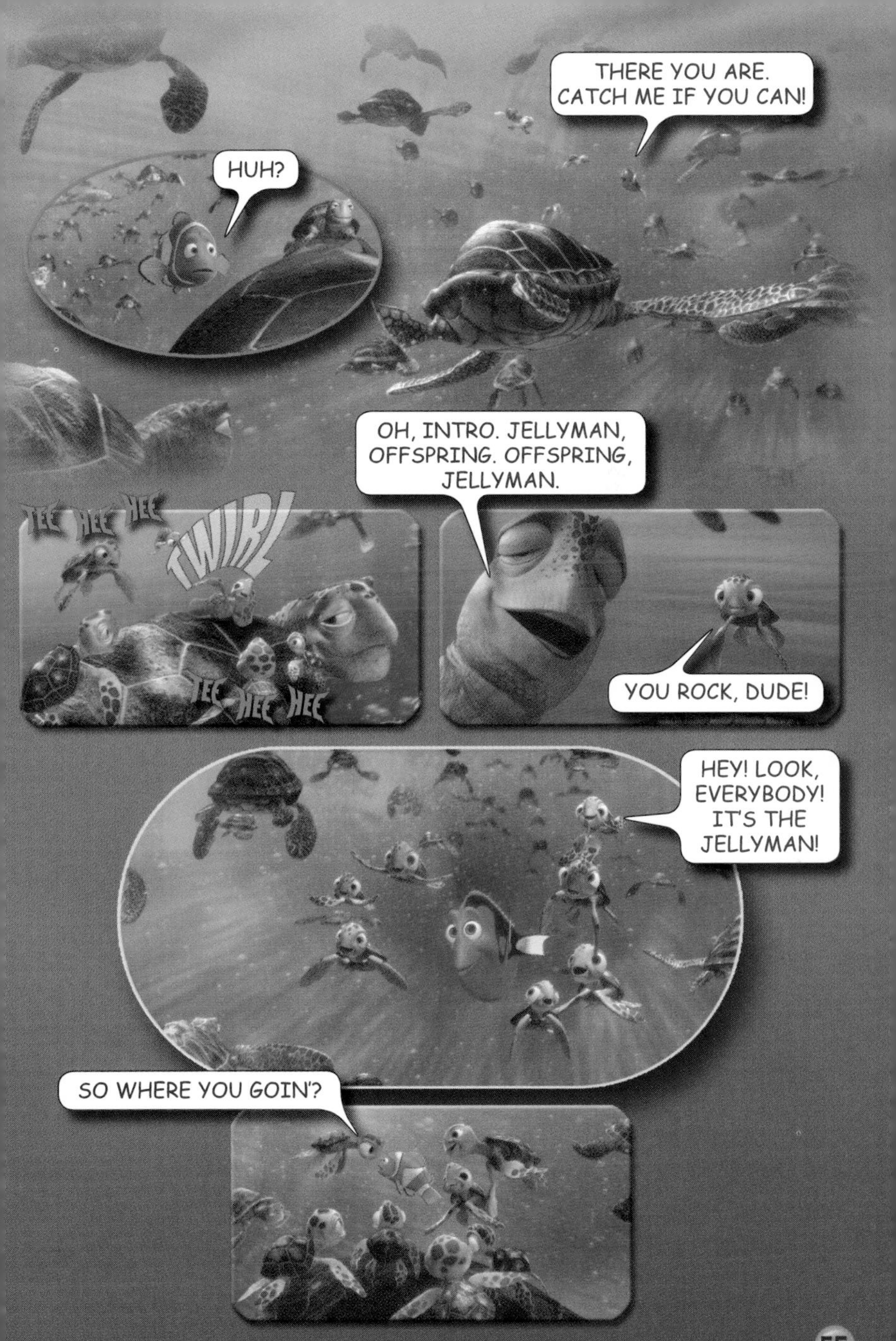
THERE YOU ARE. CATCH ME IF YOU CAN!
HUH?
TEE HEE HEE
TWIRL
TEE HEE HEE
OH, INTRO. JELLYMAN, OFFSPRING. OFFSPRING, JELLYMAN.
YOU ROCK, DUDE!
HEY! LOOK, EVERYBODY! IT'S THE JELLYMAN!
SO WHERE YOU GOIN'?

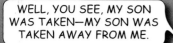

WELL, YOU SEE, MY SON WAS TAKEN—MY SON WAS TAKEN AWAY FROM ME.

NO WAY.

WHAT HAPPENED?

WELL, OKAY. I LIVE ON THIS REEF, A LONG, LONG WAY FROM HERE...

OH BOY, THIS IS GONNA BE GOOD, I CAN TELL.

...AND MY SON, NEMO, SWAM OUT IN THE OPEN WATER TO THIS BOAT, AND WHEN HE WAS OUT THERE, THESE DIVERS APPEARED.

AND I TRIED TO STOP THEM. BUT THE BOAT WAS TOO FAST. SO WE SWAM OUT INTO THE OCEAN TO FOLLOW IT...

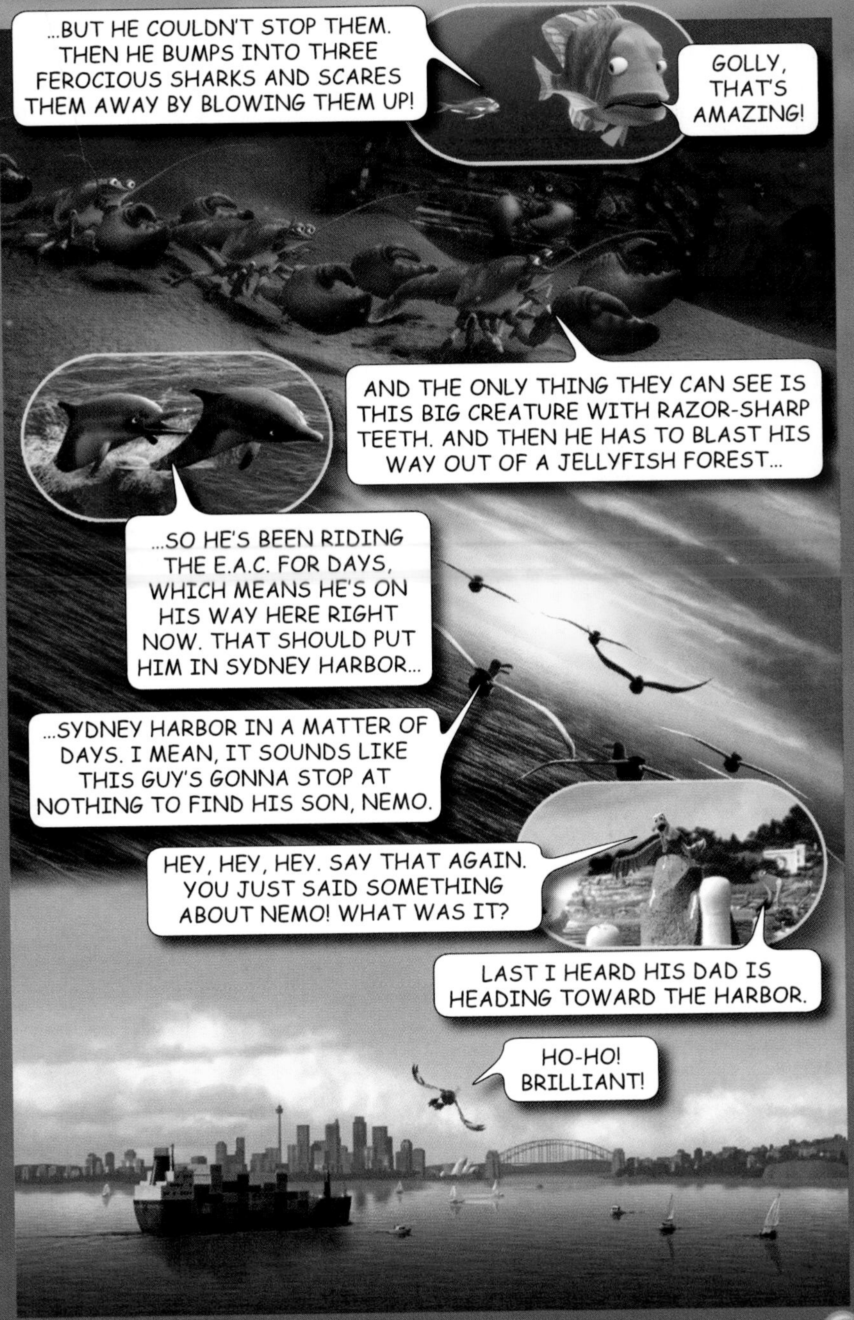
...BUT HE COULDN'T STOP THEM. THEN HE BUMPS INTO THREE FEROCIOUS SHARKS AND SCARES THEM AWAY BY BLOWING THEM UP!
GOLLY, THAT'S AMAZING!
AND THE ONLY THING THEY CAN SEE IS THIS BIG CREATURE WITH RAZOR-SHARP TEETH. AND THEN HE HAS TO BLAST HIS WAY OUT OF A JELLYFISH FOREST...
...SO HE'S BEEN RIDING THE E.A.C. FOR DAYS, WHICH MEANS HE'S ON HIS WAY HERE RIGHT NOW. THAT SHOULD PUT HIM IN SYDNEY HARBOR...
...SYDNEY HARBOR IN A MATTER OF DAYS. I MEAN, IT SOUNDS LIKE THIS GUY'S GONNA STOP AT NOTHING TO FIND HIS SON, NEMO.
HEY, HEY, HEY. SAY THAT AGAIN. YOU JUST SAID SOMETHING ABOUT NEMO! WHAT WAS IT?
LAST I HEARD HIS DAD IS HEADING TOWARD THE HARBOR.
HO-HO! BRILLIANT!

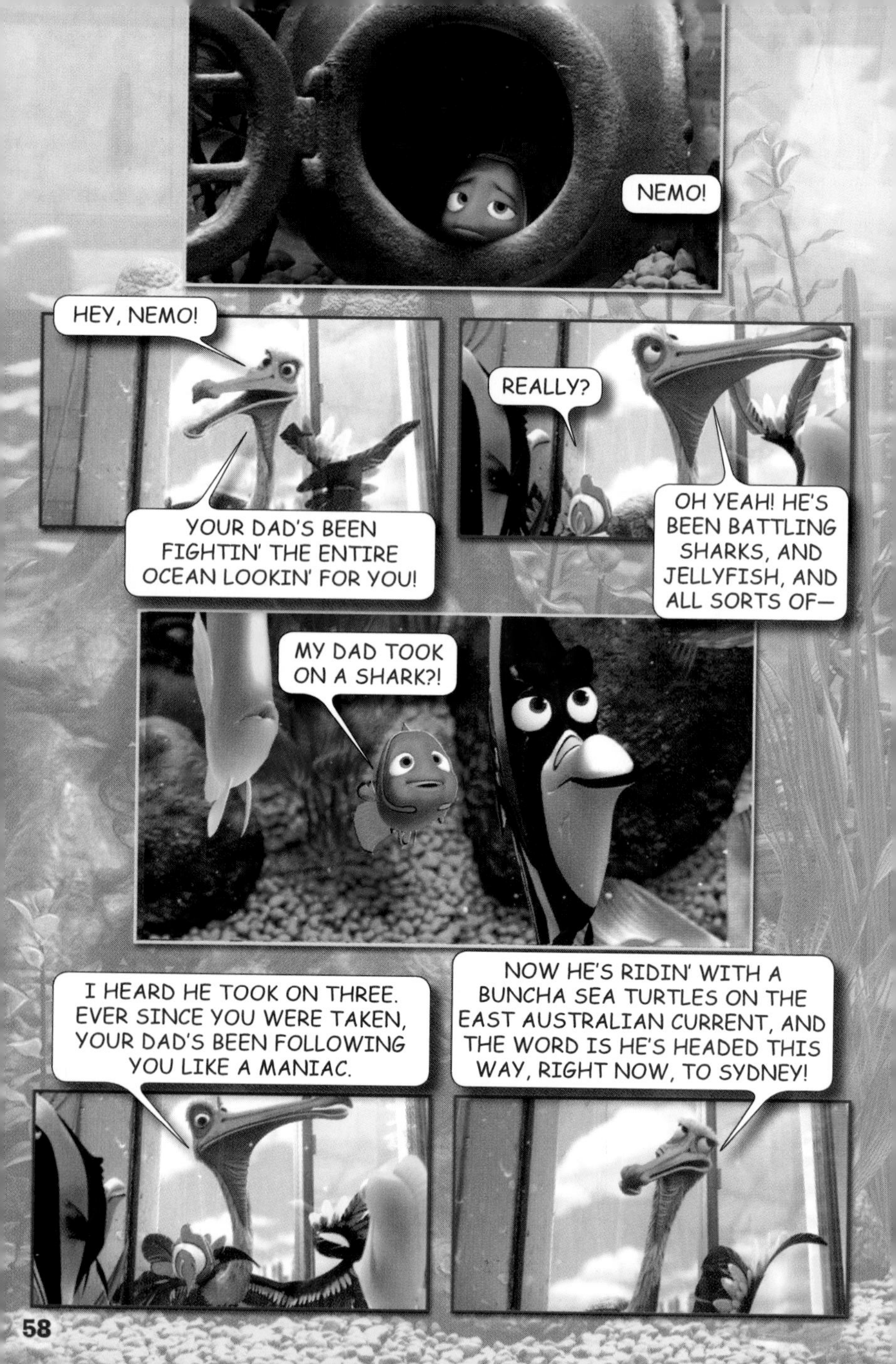
NEMO!
HEY, NEMO!
YOUR DAD'S BEEN FIGHTIN' THE ENTIRE OCEAN LOOKIN' FOR YOU!
REALLY?
OH YEAH! HE'S BEEN BATTLING SHARKS, AND JELLYFISH, AND ALL SORTS OF—
MY DAD TOOK ON A SHARK?!
I HEARD HE TOOK ON THREE. EVER SINCE YOU WERE TAKEN, YOUR DAD'S BEEN FOLLOWING YOU LIKE A MANIAC.
NOW HE'S RIDIN' WITH A BUNCHA SEA TURTLES ON THE EAST AUSTRALIAN CURRENT, AND THE WORD IS HE'S HEADED THIS WAY, RIGHT NOW, TO SYDNEY!

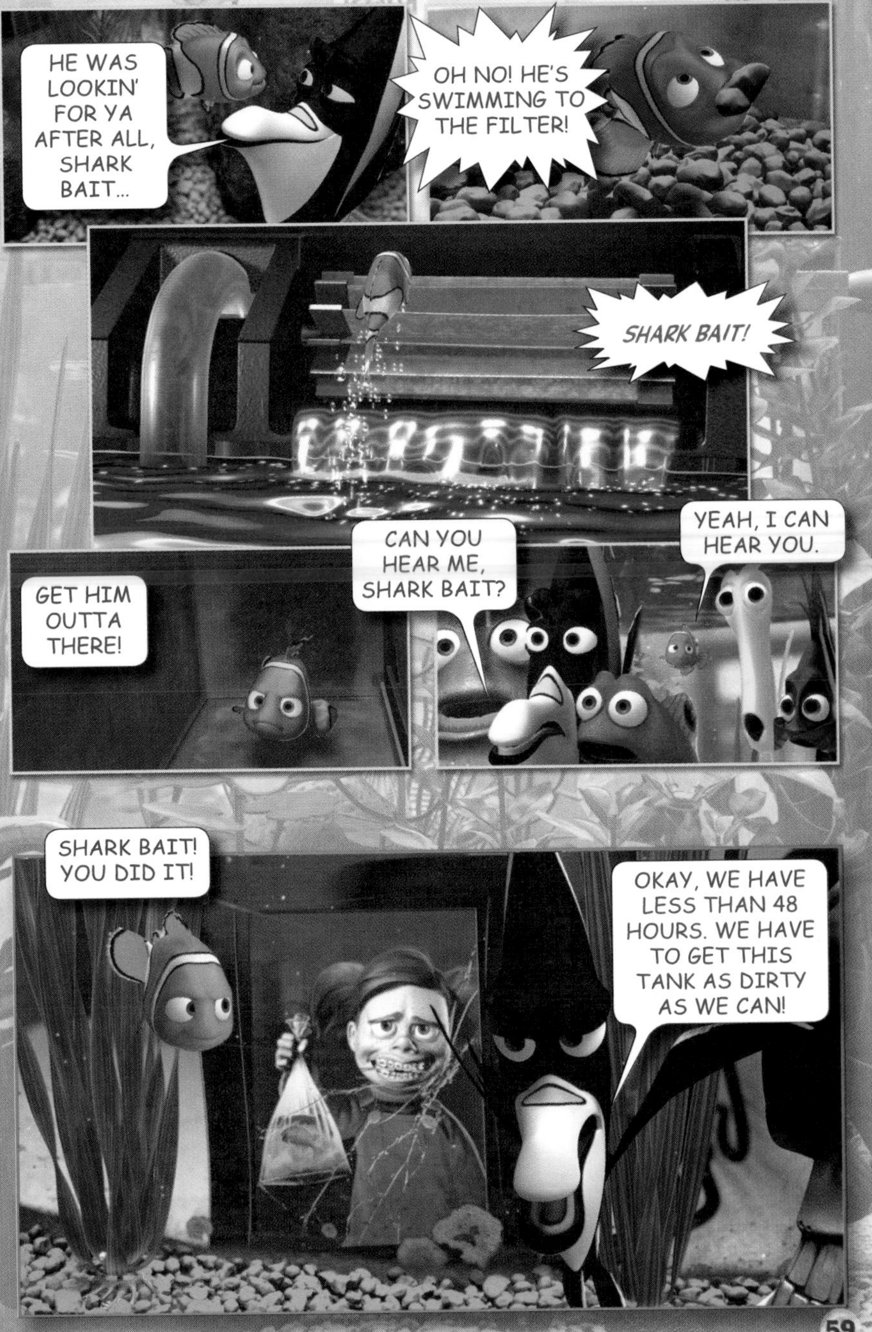
HE WAS LOOKIN' FOR YA AFTER ALL, SHARK BAIT...
OH NO! HE'S SWIMMING TO THE FILTER!
SHARK BAIT!
GET HIM OUTTA THERE!
CAN YOU HEAR ME, SHARK BAIT?
YEAH, I CAN HEAR YOU.
SHARK BAIT! YOU DID IT!
OKAY, WE HAVE LESS THAN 48 HOURS. WE HAVE TO GET THIS TANK AS DIRTY AS WE CAN!

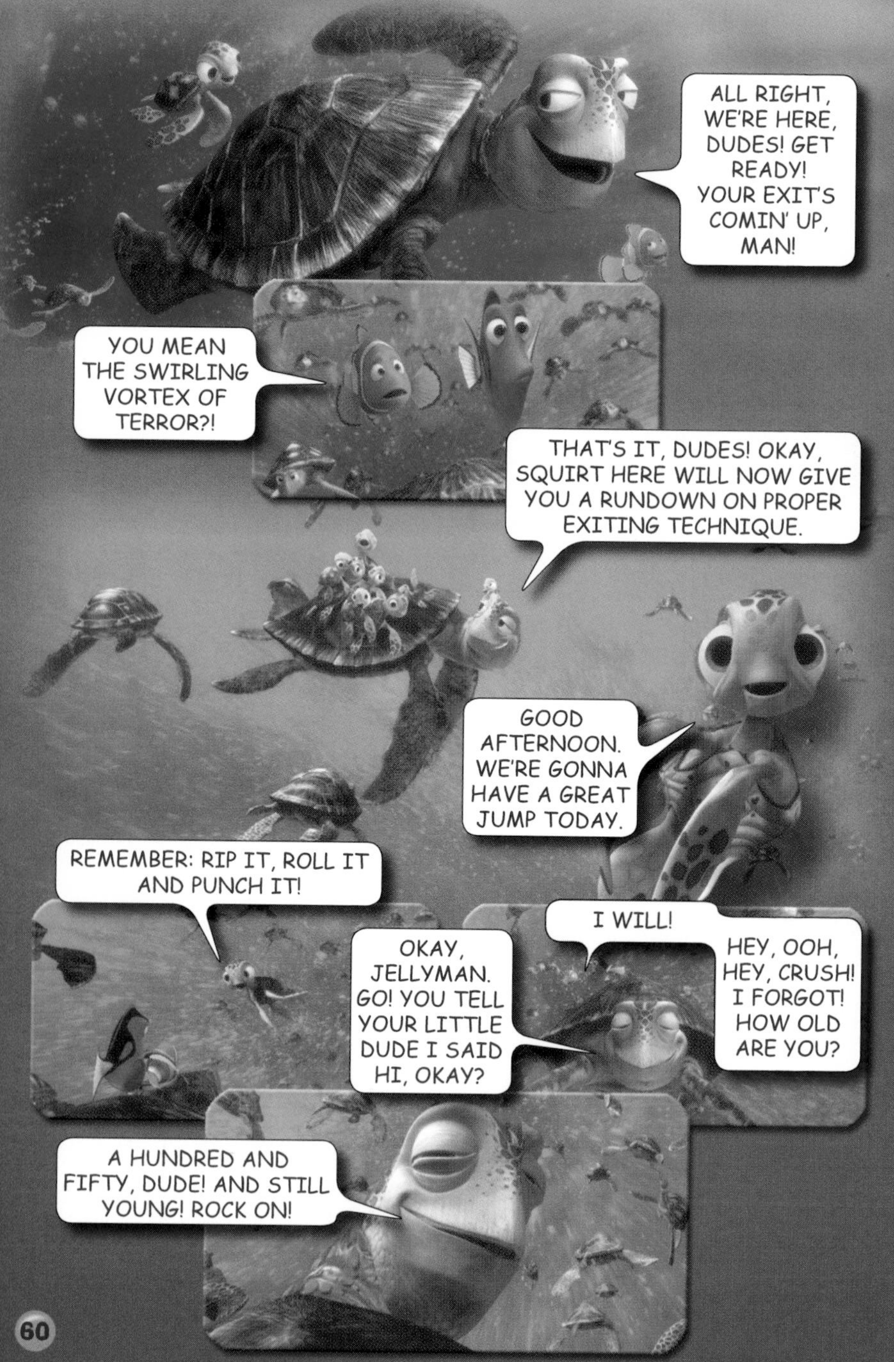
ALL RIGHT, WE'RE HERE, DUDES! GET READY! YOUR EXIT'S COMIN' UP, MAN!
YOU MEAN THE SWIRLING VORTEX OF TERROR?!
THAT'S IT, DUDES! OKAY, SQUIRT HERE WILL NOW GIVE YOU A RUNDOWN ON PROPER EXITING TECHNIQUE.
GOOD AFTERNOON. WE'RE GONNA HAVE A GREAT JUMP TODAY.
REMEMBER: RIP IT, ROLL IT AND PUNCH IT!
OKAY, JELLYMAN. GO! YOU TELL YOUR LITTLE DUDE I SAID HI, OKAY?
I WILL!
HEY, OOH, HEY, CRUSH! I FORGOT! HOW OLD ARE YOU?
A HUNDRED AND FIFTY, DUDE! AND STILL YOUNG! ROCK ON!

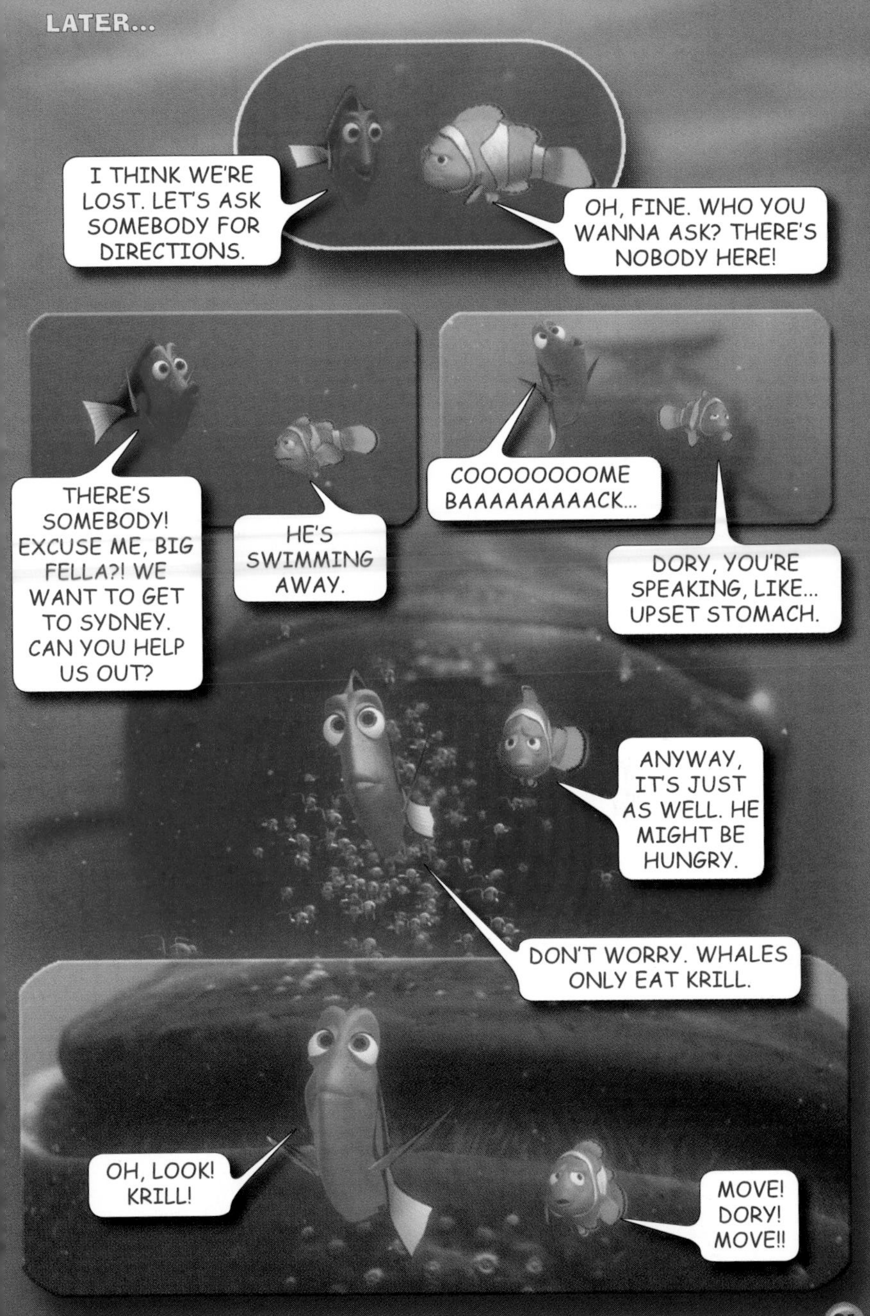
LATER...
I THINK WE'RE LOST. LET'S ASK SOMEBODY FOR DIRECTIONS.
OH, FINE. WHO YOU WANNA ASK? THERE'S NOBODY HERE!
THERE'S SOMEBODY! EXCUSE ME, BIG FELLA?! WE WANT TO GET TO SYDNEY. CAN YOU HELP US OUT?
HE'S SWIMMING AWAY.
COOOOOOOOME BAAAAAAAAACK...
DORY, YOU'RE SPEAKING, LIKE... UPSET STOMACH.
ANYWAY, IT'S JUST AS WELL. HE MIGHT BE HUNGRY.
DON'T WORRY. WHALES ONLY EAT KRILL.
OH, LOOK! KRILL!
MOVE! DORY! MOVE!!

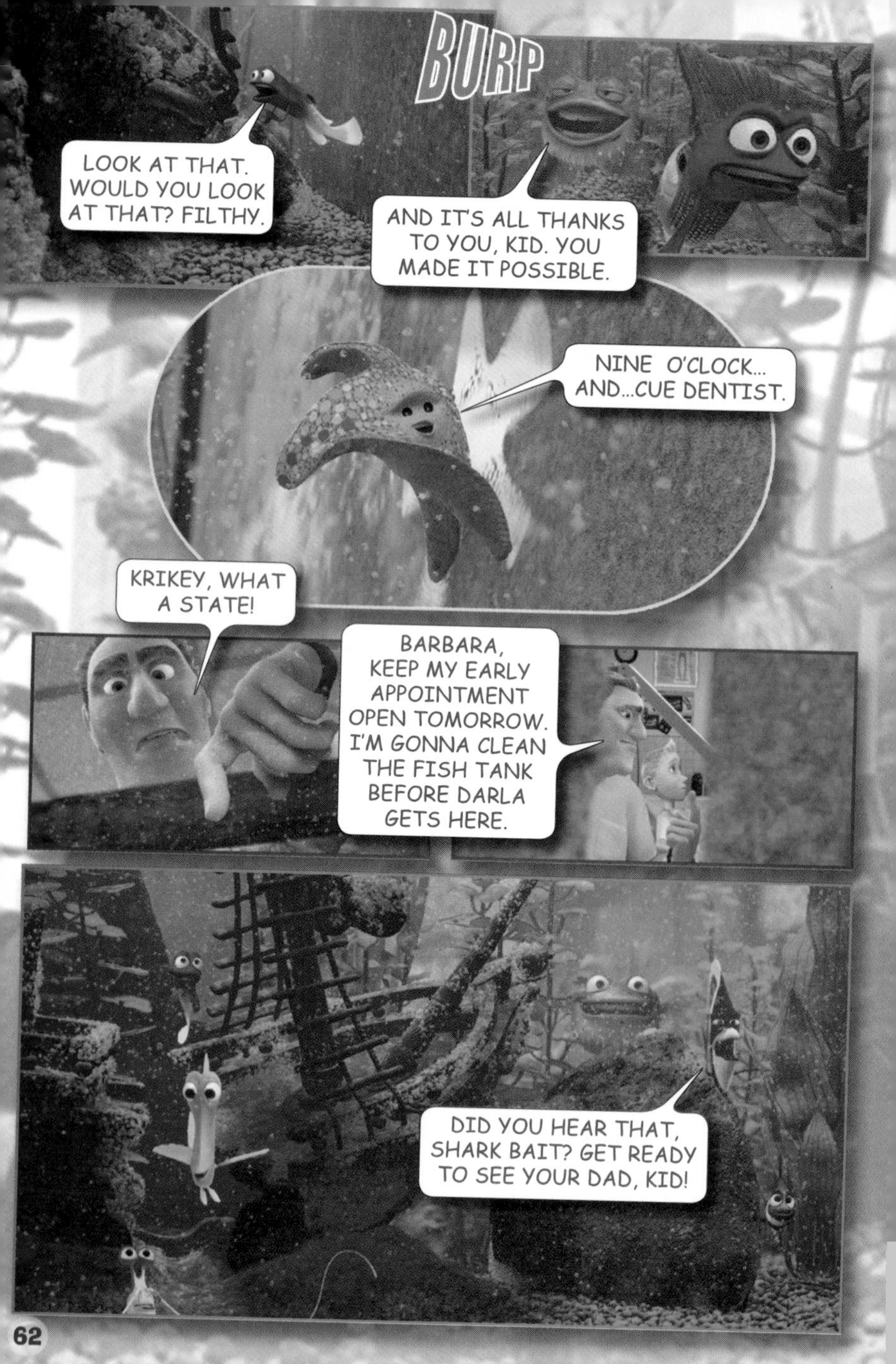
LOOK AT THAT. WOULD YOU LOOK AT THAT? FILTHY.
BURP
AND IT'S ALL THANKS TO YOU, KID. YOU MADE IT POSSIBLE.
NINE O'CLOCK... AND...CUE DENTIST.
KRIKEY, WHAT A STATE!
BARBARA, KEEP MY EARLY APPOINTMENT OPEN TOMORROW. I'M GONNA CLEAN THE FISH TANK BEFORE DARLA GETS HERE.
DID YOU HEAR THAT, SHARK BAIT? GET READY TO SEE YOUR DAD, KID!

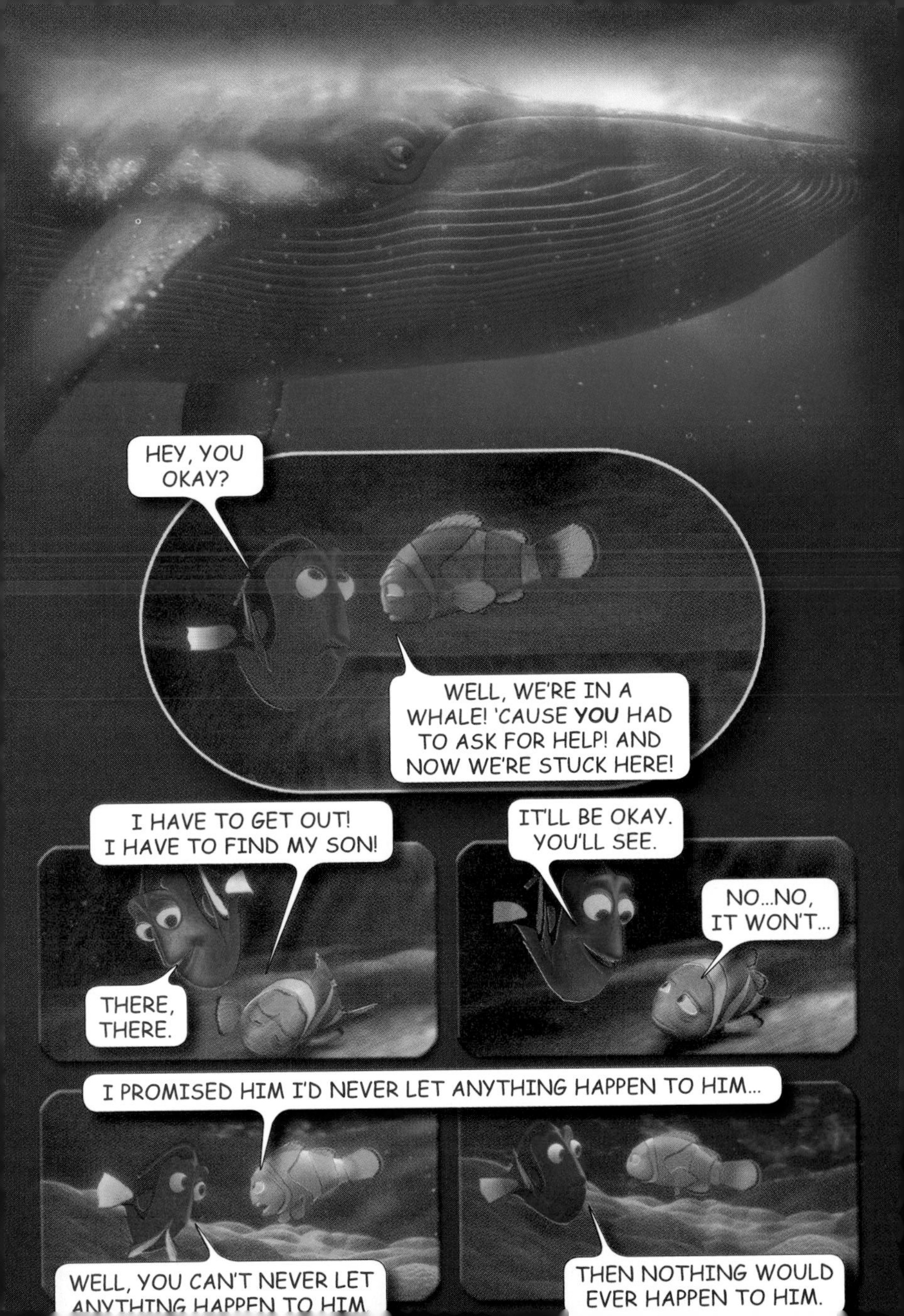
HEY, YOU OKAY?
WELL, WE'RE IN A WHALE! 'CAUSE **YOU** HAD TO ASK FOR HELP! AND NOW WE'RE STUCK HERE!
I HAVE TO GET OUT! I HAVE TO FIND MY SON!
THERE, THERE.
IT'LL BE OKAY. YOU'LL SEE.
NO...NO, IT WON'T...
I PROMISED HIM I'D NEVER LET ANYTHING HAPPEN TO HIM...
WELL, YOU CAN'T NEVER LET ANYTHING HAPPEN TO HIM.
THEN NOTHING WOULD EVER HAPPEN TO HIM.

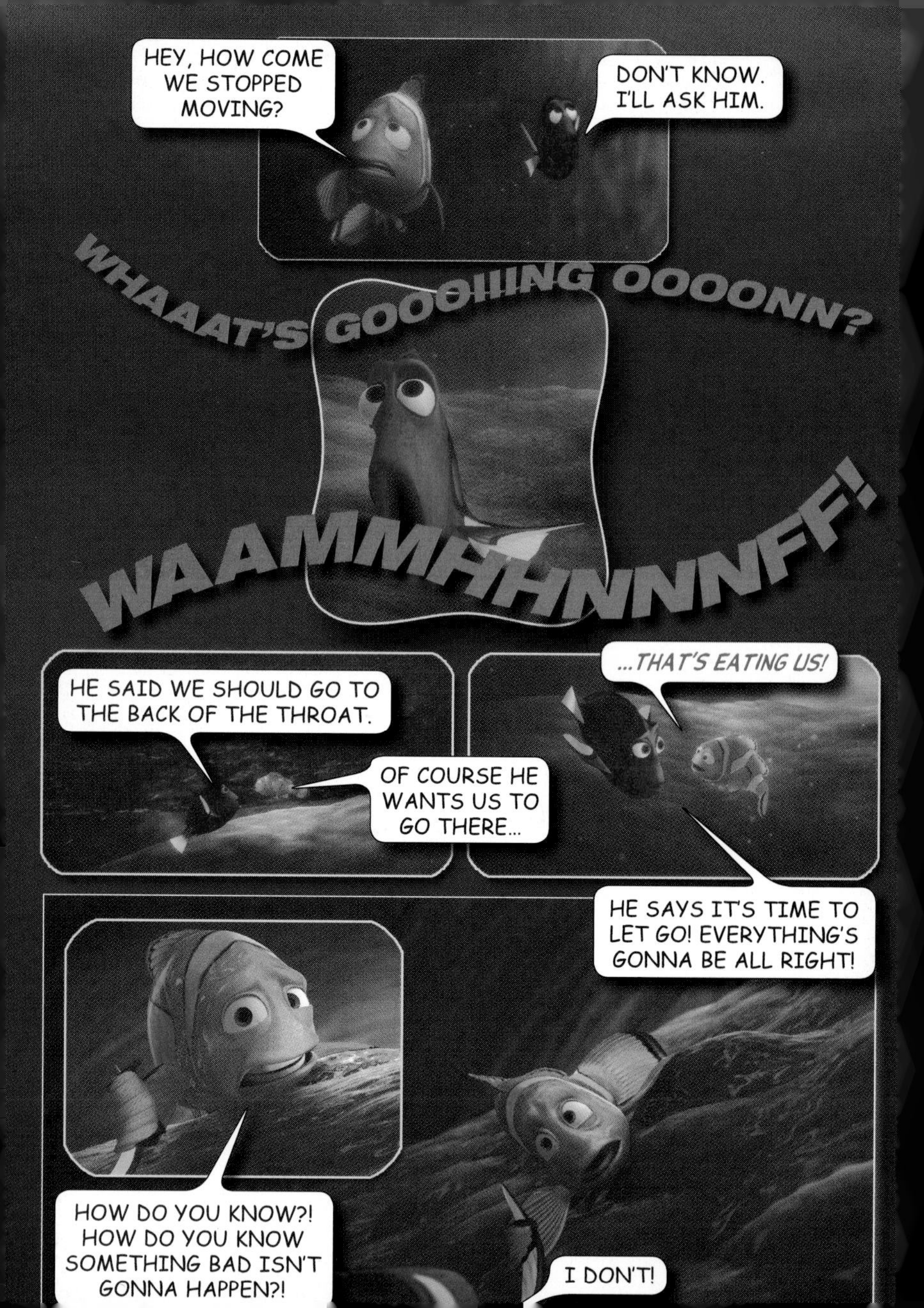
HEY, HOW COME WE STOPPED MOVING?
DON'T KNOW. I'LL ASK HIM.
WHAAAT'S GOOOIIIING OOOOONN?
WAAMMHHNNNFF!
HE SAID WE SHOULD GO TO THE BACK OF THE THROAT.
OF COURSE HE WANTS US TO GO THERE...
...THAT'S EATING US!
HE SAYS IT'S TIME TO LET GO! EVERYTHING'S GONNA BE ALL RIGHT!
HOW DO YOU KNOW?! HOW DO YOU KNOW SOMETHING BAD ISN'T GONNA HAPPEN?!
I DON'T!

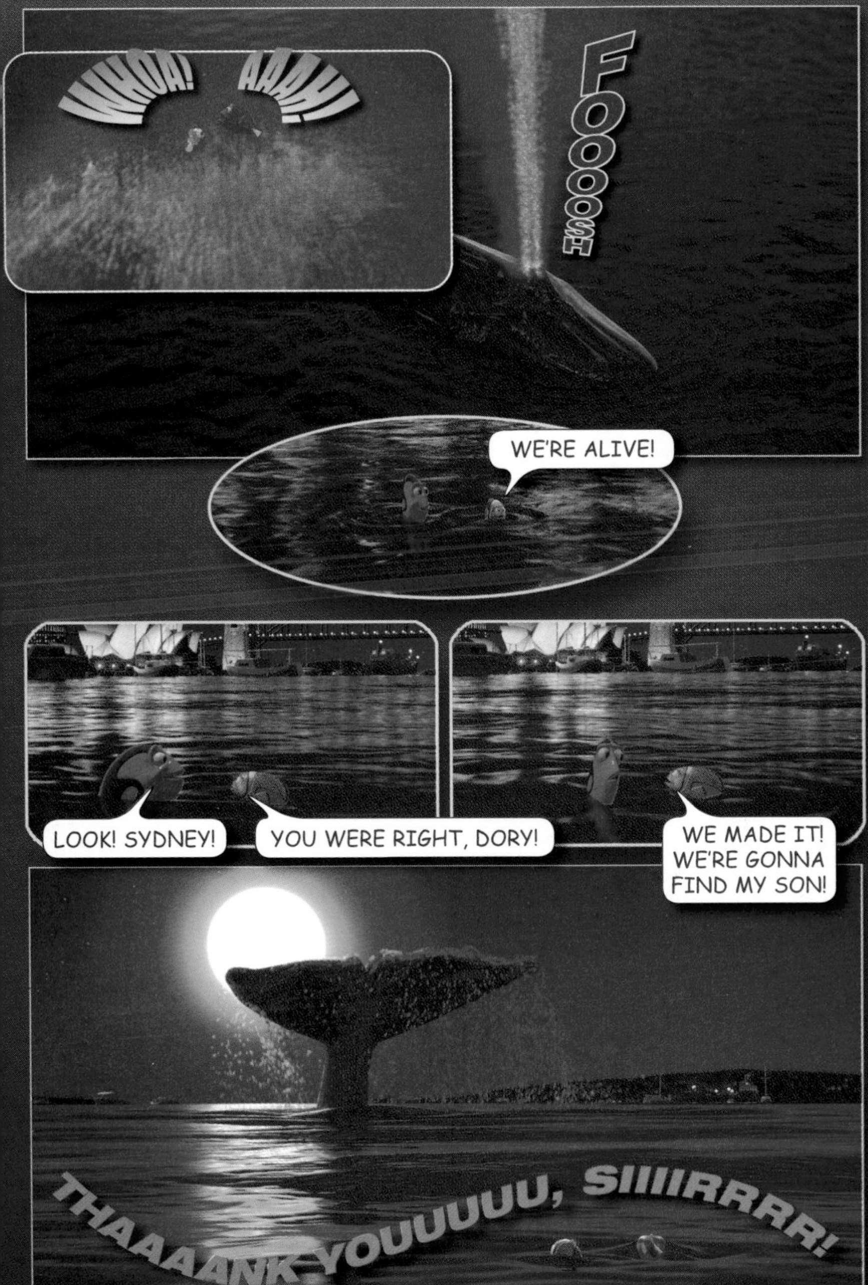
WHOA!
AAAAH!
FOOOOSH
WE'RE ALIVE!
LOOK! SYDNEY!
YOU WERE RIGHT, DORY!
WE MADE IT! WE'RE GONNA FIND MY SON!
THAAAANK YOUUUUU, SIIIIRRRR!

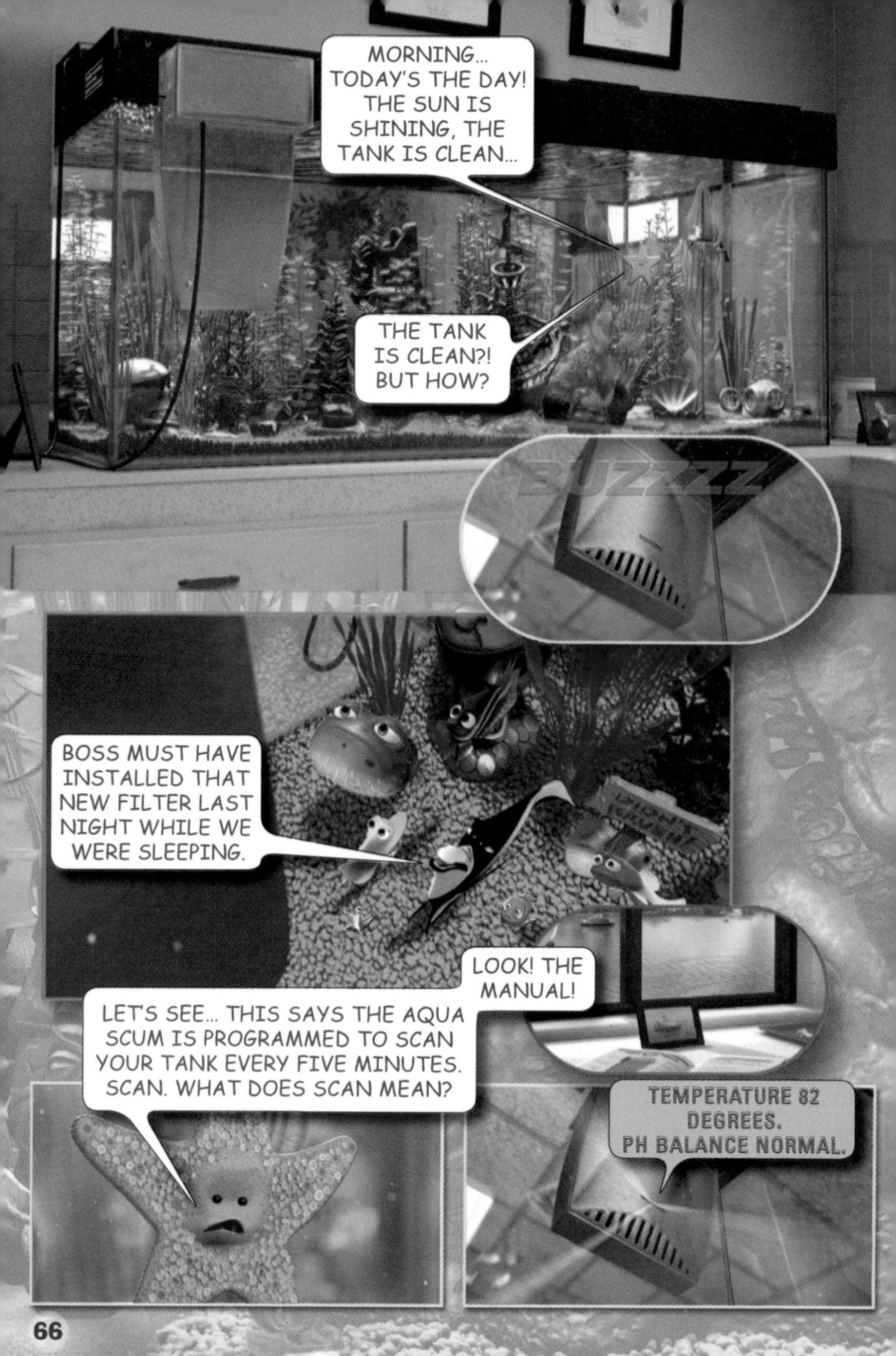
MORNING... TODAY'S THE DAY! THE SUN IS SHINING, THE TANK IS CLEAN...
THE TANK IS CLEAN?! BUT HOW?
BUZZZ
BOSS MUST HAVE INSTALLED THAT NEW FILTER LAST NIGHT WHILE WE WERE SLEEPING.
LOOK! THE MANUAL!
LET'S SEE... THIS SAYS THE AQUA SCUM IS PROGRAMMED TO SCAN YOUR TANK EVERY FIVE MINUTES. SCAN. WHAT DOES SCAN MEAN?
TEMPERATURE 82 DEGREES. PH BALANCE NORMAL.

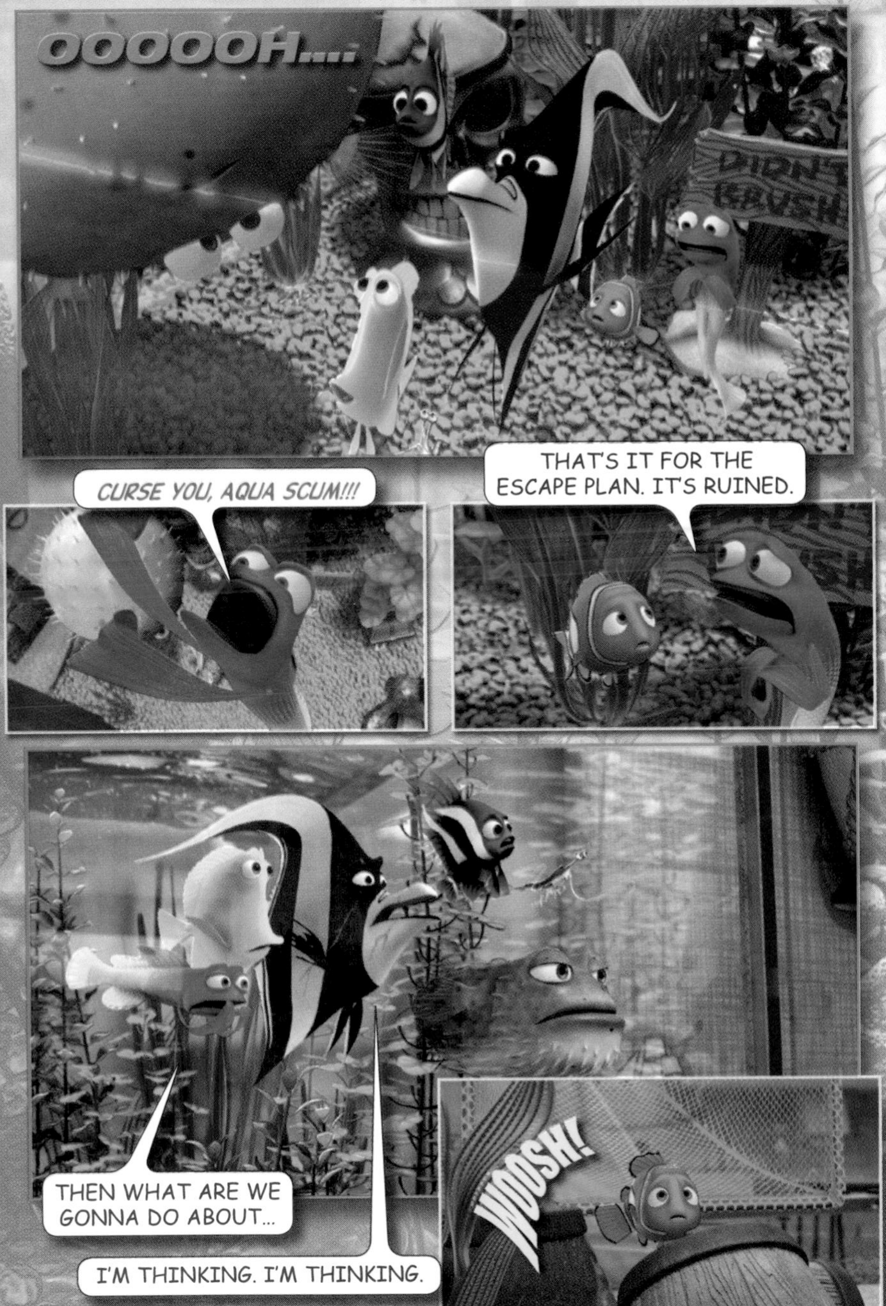
OOOOOH....
CURSE YOU, AQUA SCUM!!!
THAT'S IT FOR THE ESCAPE PLAN. IT'S RUINED.
THEN WHAT ARE WE GONNA DO ABOUT...
I'M THINKING. I'M THINKING.
WOOSH!

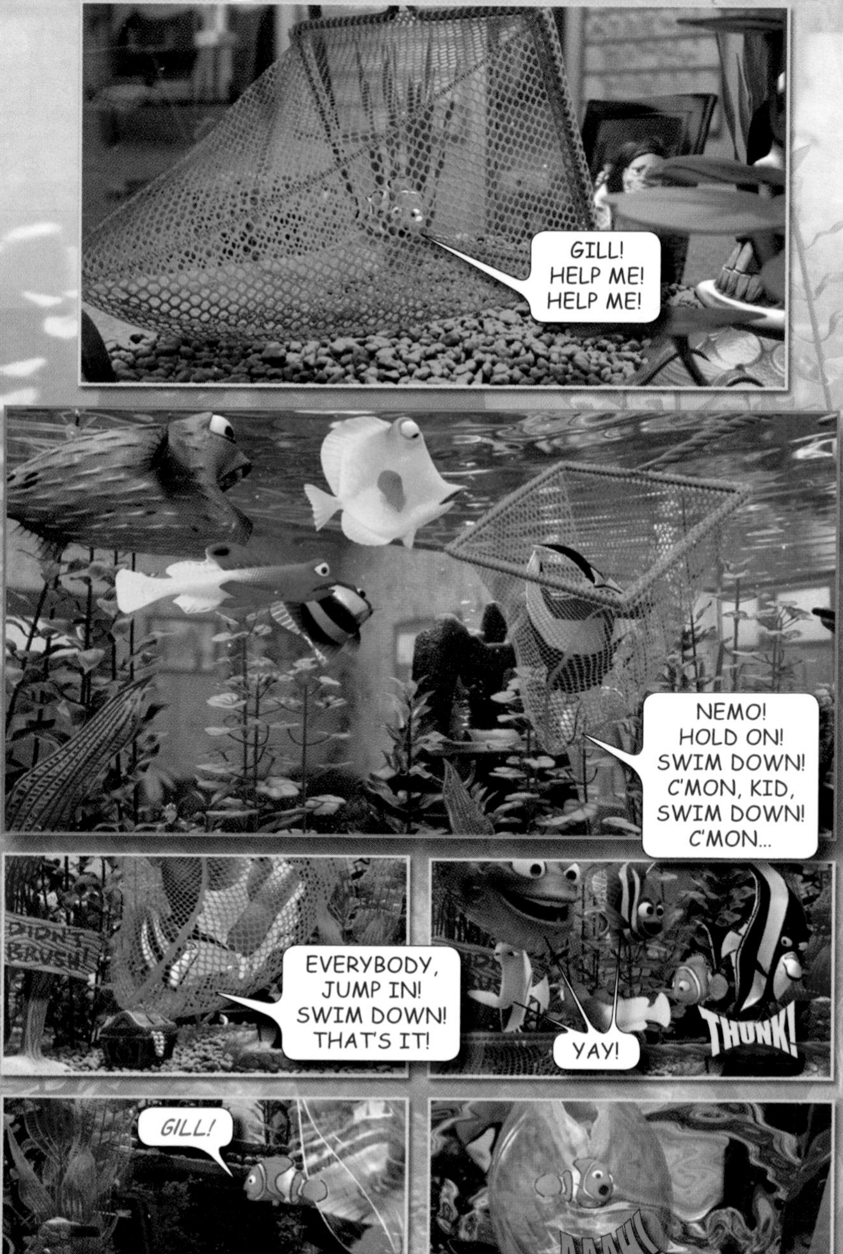
GILL! HELP ME! HELP ME!
NEMO! HOLD ON! SWIM DOWN! C'MON, KID, SWIM DOWN! C'MON...
EVERYBODY, JUMP IN! SWIM DOWN! THAT'S IT!
YAY!
THUNK!
GILL!
AAAH!

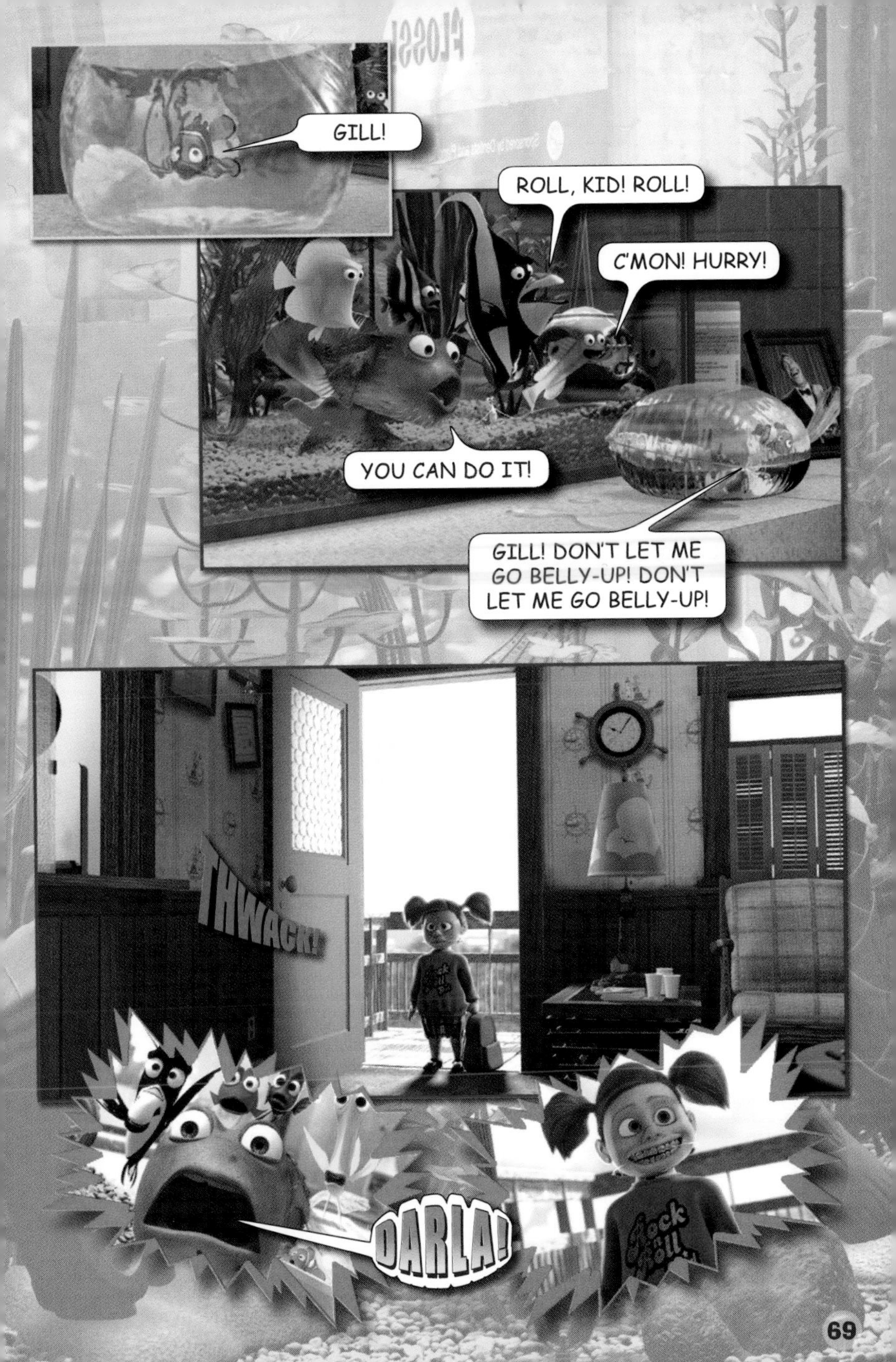
GILL!
ROLL, KID! ROLL!
C'MON! HURRY!
YOU CAN DO IT!
GILL! DON'T LET ME GO BELLY-UP! DON'T LET ME GO BELLY-UP!
THWACK!
DARLA!

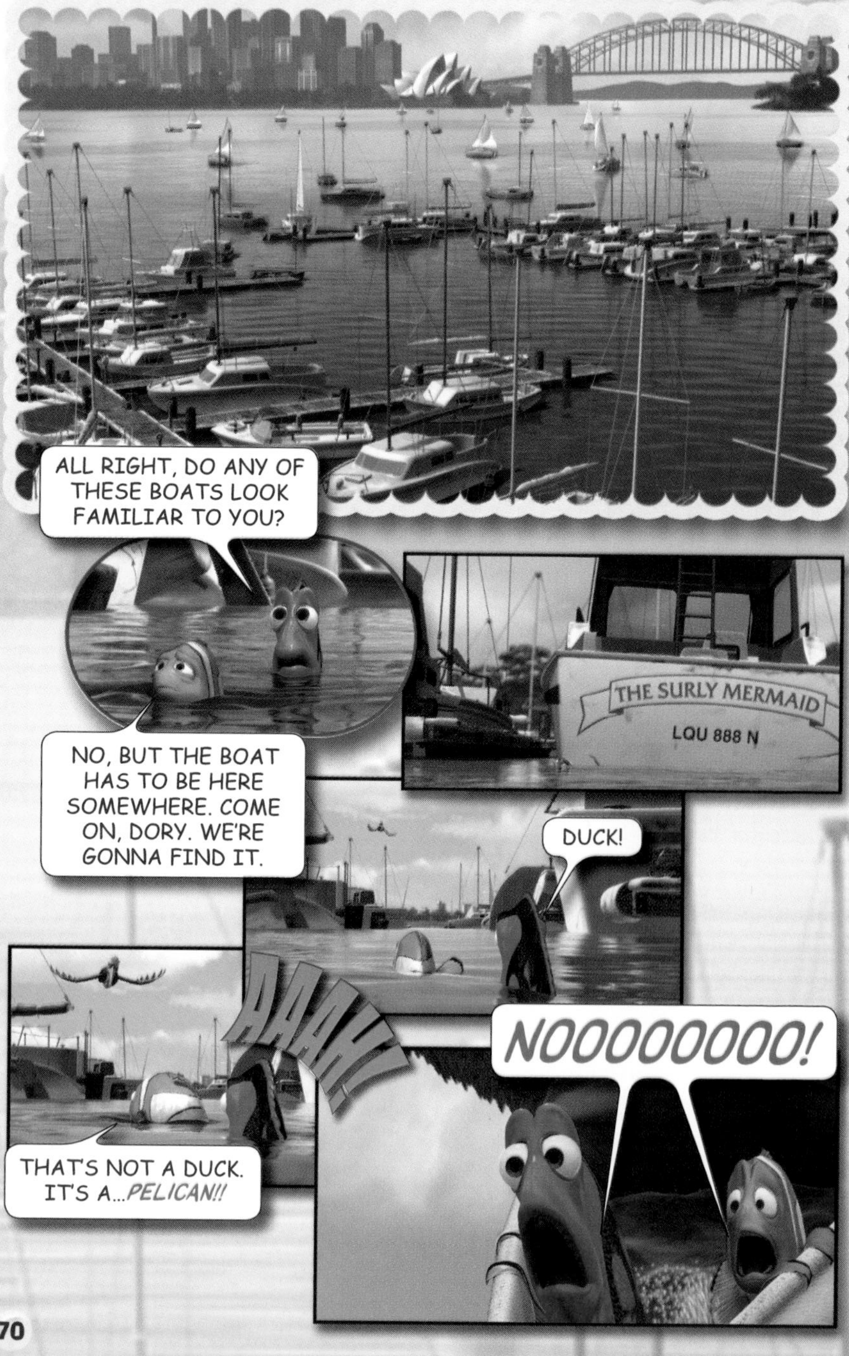
ALL RIGHT, DO ANY OF THESE BOATS LOOK FAMILIAR TO YOU?
NO, BUT THE BOAT HAS TO BE HERE SOMEWHERE. COME ON, DORY. WE'RE GONNA FIND IT.
THE SURLY MERMAID
LQU 888 N
DUCK!
THAT'S NOT A DUCK. IT'S A...PELICAN!!
AAAH!
NOOOOOOOO!

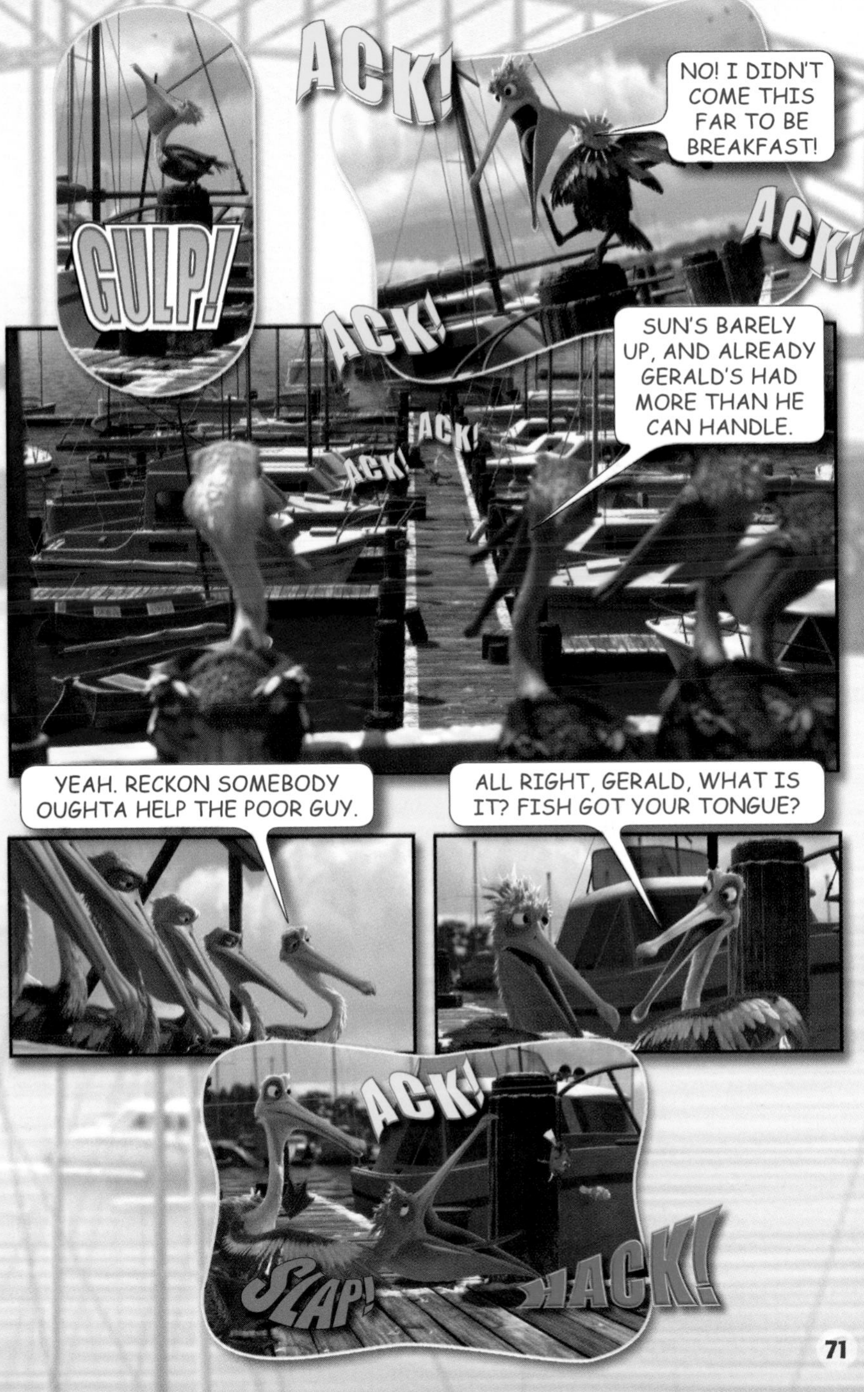
GULP!
ACK!
NO! I DIDN'T COME THIS FAR TO BE BREAKFAST!
ACK!
ACK!
ACK!
ACK!
SUN'S BARELY UP, AND ALREADY GERALD'S HAD MORE THAN HE CAN HANDLE.
YEAH. RECKON SOMEBODY OUGHTA HELP THE POOR GUY.
ALL RIGHT, GERALD, WHAT IS IT? FISH GOT YOUR TONGUE?
ACK!
SLAP!
HACK!

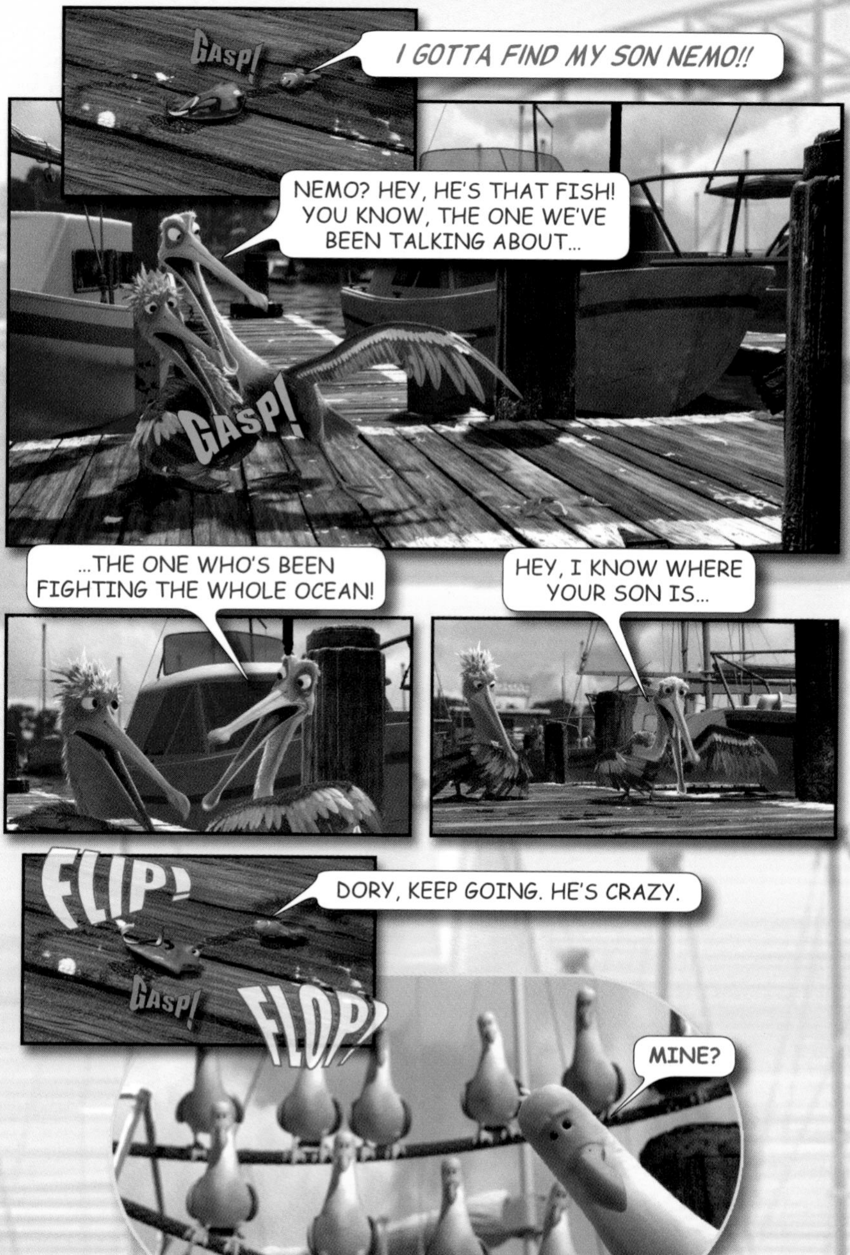
GASP!
I GOTTA FIND MY SON NEMO!!
NEMO? HEY, HE'S THAT FISH! YOU KNOW, THE ONE WE'VE BEEN TALKING ABOUT...
GASP!
...THE ONE WHO'S BEEN FIGHTING THE WHOLE OCEAN!
HEY, I KNOW WHERE YOUR SON IS...
FLIP!
DORY, KEEP GOING. HE'S CRAZY.
GASP!
FLOP!
MINE?

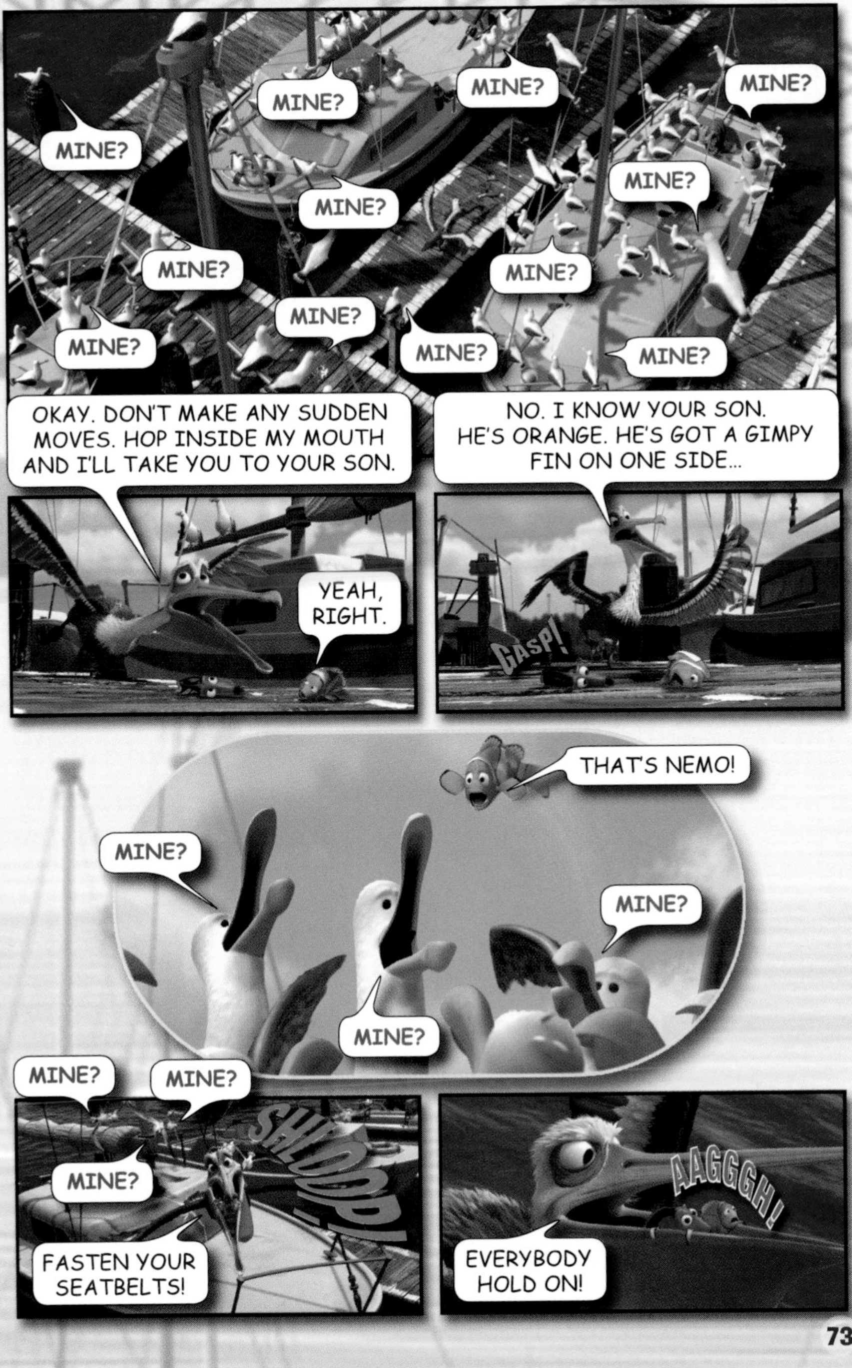

MINE?
MINE?
MINE?
MINE?
MINE?
MINE?
MINE?
MINE?
MINE?
MINE?
MINE?
MINE?
OKAY. DON'T MAKE ANY SUDDEN MOVES. HOP INSIDE MY MOUTH AND I'LL TAKE YOU TO YOUR SON.
YEAH, RIGHT.
NO. I KNOW YOUR SON. HE'S ORANGE. HE'S GOT A GIMPY FIN ON ONE SIDE...
GASP!
THAT'S NEMO!
MINE?
MINE?
MINE?
MINE?
MINE?
MINE?
SHLOOP!
FASTEN YOUR SEATBELTS!
AAGGGH!
EVERYBODY HOLD ON!

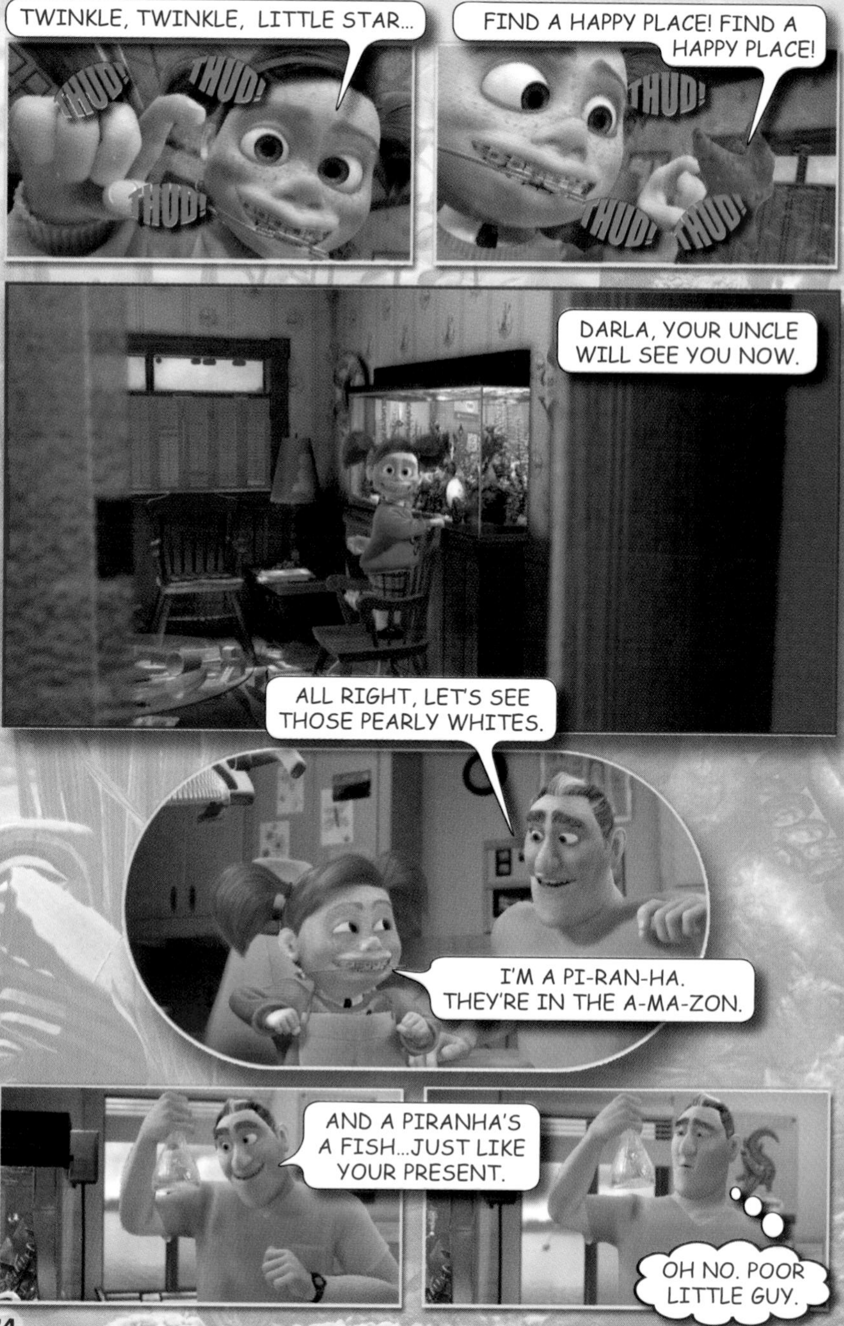
TWINKLE, TWINKLE, LITTLE STAR...
THUD!
THUD!
THUD!
FIND A HAPPY PLACE! FIND A HAPPY PLACE!
THUD!
THUD!
THUD!
DARLA, YOUR UNCLE WILL SEE YOU NOW.
ALL RIGHT, LET'S SEE THOSE PEARLY WHITES.
I'M A PI-RAN-HA. THEY'RE IN THE A-MA-ZON.
AND A PIRANHA'S A FISH...JUST LIKE YOUR PRESENT.
OH NO. POOR LITTLE GUY.

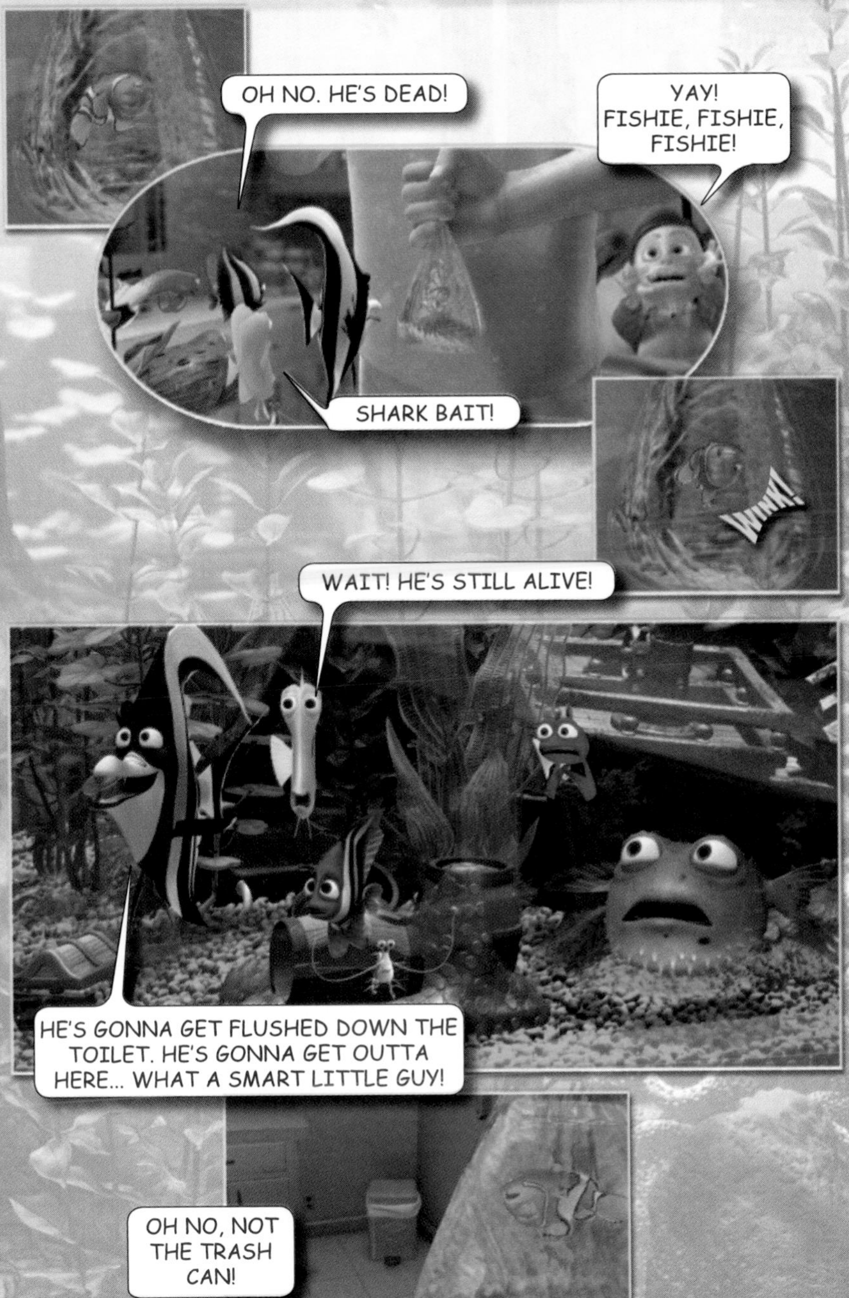
OH NO. HE'S DEAD!
YAY! FISHIE, FISHIE, FISHIE!
SHARK BAIT!
WINK!
WAIT! HE'S STILL ALIVE!
HE'S GONNA GET FLUSHED DOWN THE TOILET. HE'S GONNA GET OUTTA HERE... WHAT A SMART LITTLE GUY!
OH NO, NOT THE TRASH CAN!

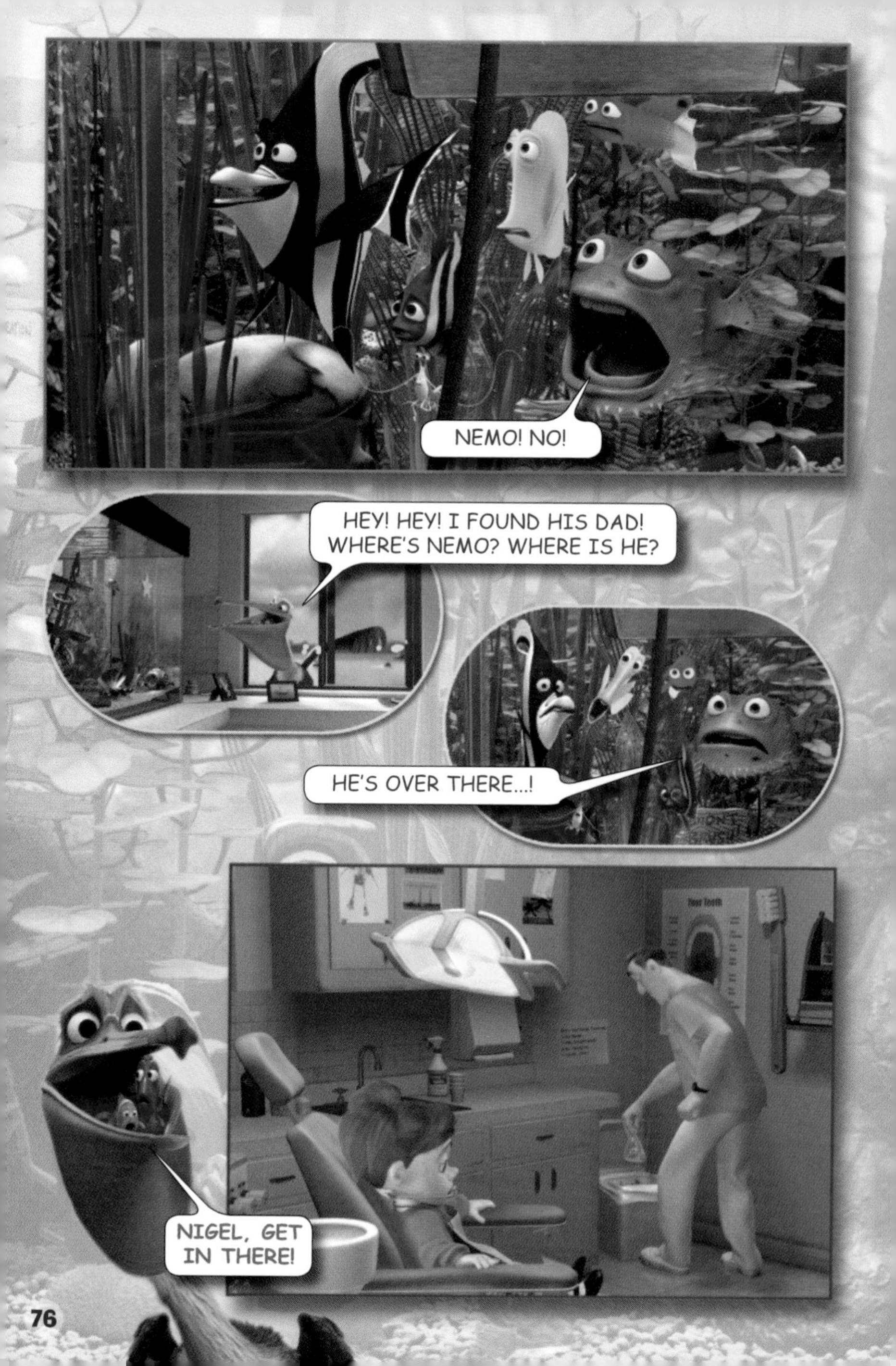
NEMO! NO!
HEY! HEY! I FOUND HIS DAD! WHERE'S NEMO? WHERE IS HE?
HE'S OVER THERE...!
NIGEL, GET IN THERE!

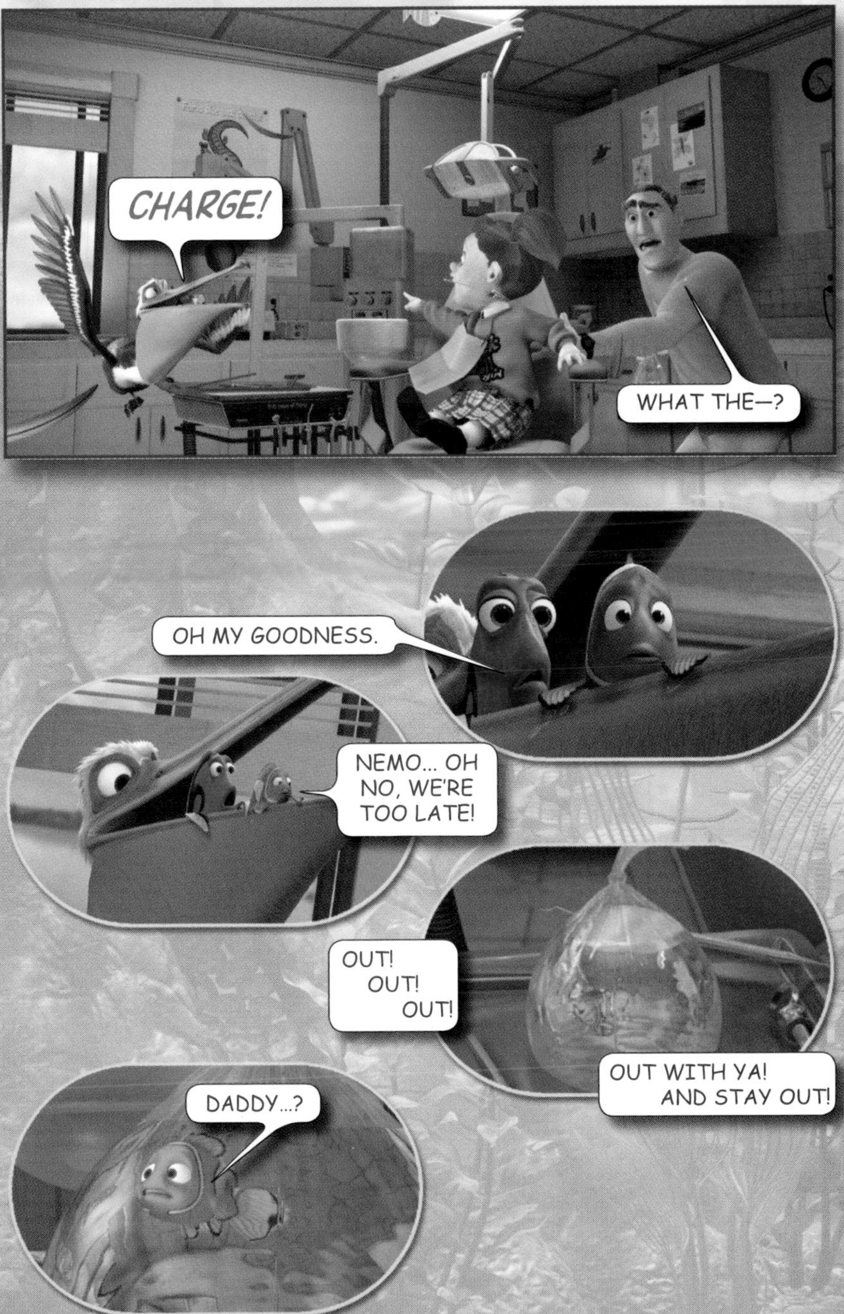
CHARGE!
WHAT THE—?
OH MY GOODNESS.
NEMO... OH NO, WE'RE TOO LATE!
OUT! OUT! OUT!
OUT WITH YA! AND STAY OUT!
DADDY...?

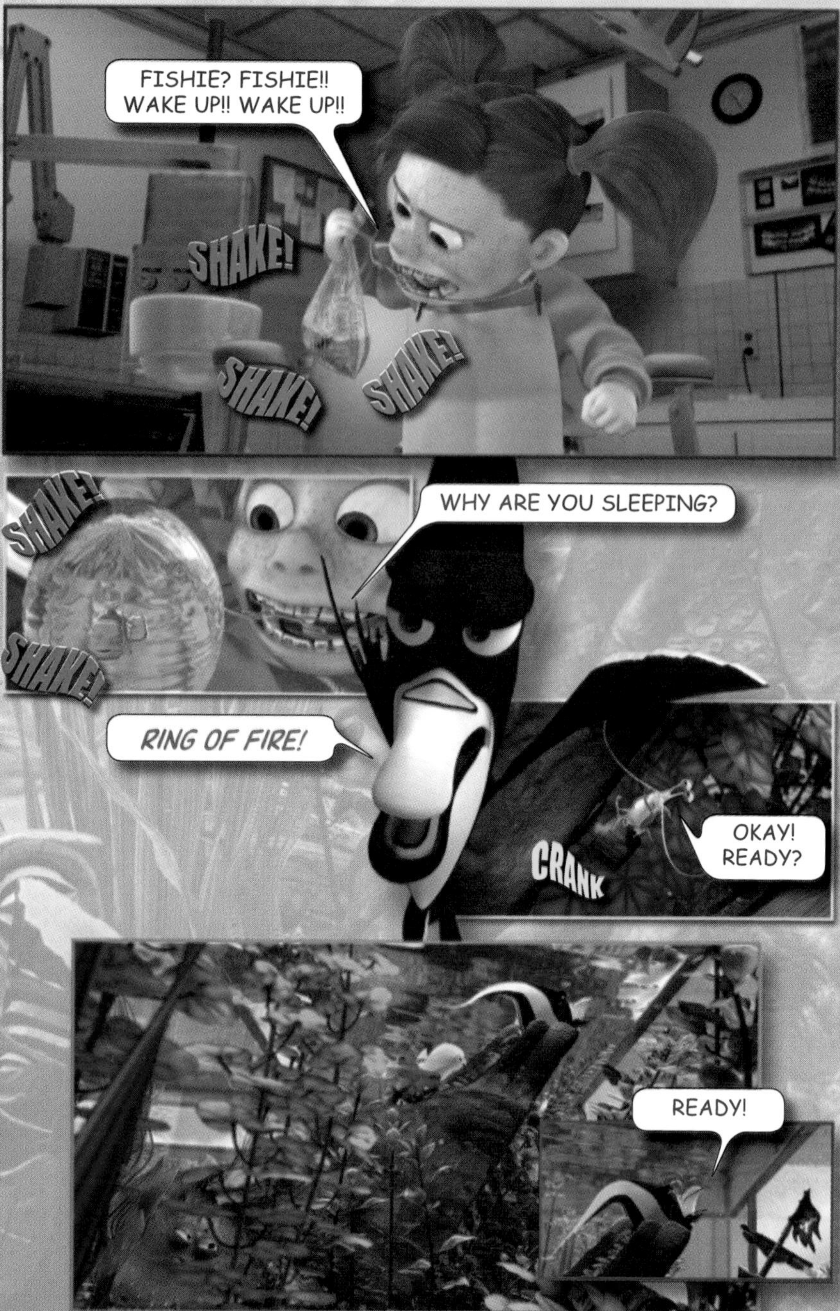
FISHIE? FISHIE!! WAKE UP!! WAKE UP!!
SHAKE!
SHAKE!
SHAKE!
SHAKE!
SHAKE!
WHY ARE YOU SLEEPING?
RING OF FIRE!
CRANK
OKAY! READY?
READY!

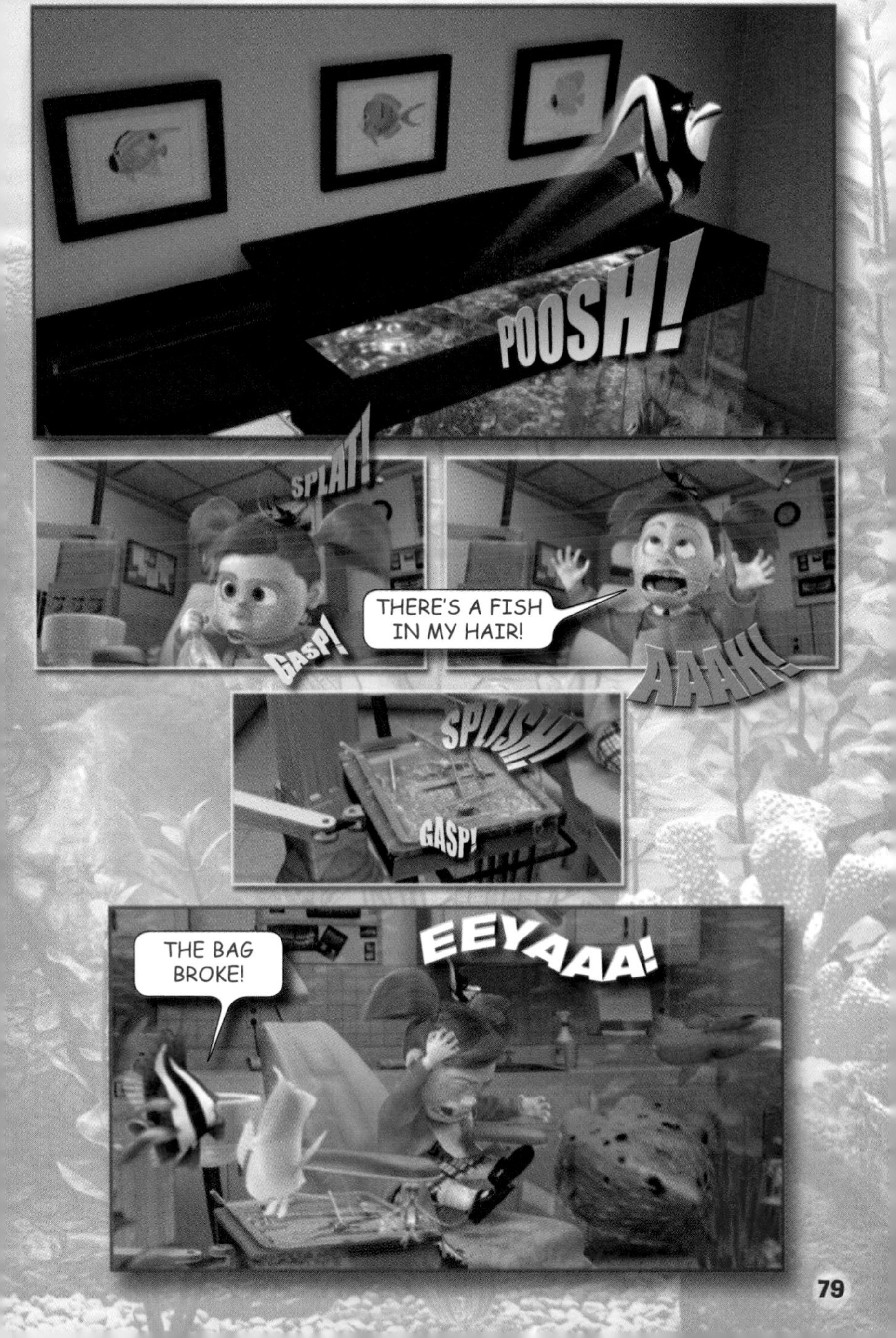
POOSH!
SPLAT!
GASP!
THERE'S A FISH IN MY HAIR!
AAAH!
SPLISH!
GASP!
THE BAG BROKE!
EEYAAA!

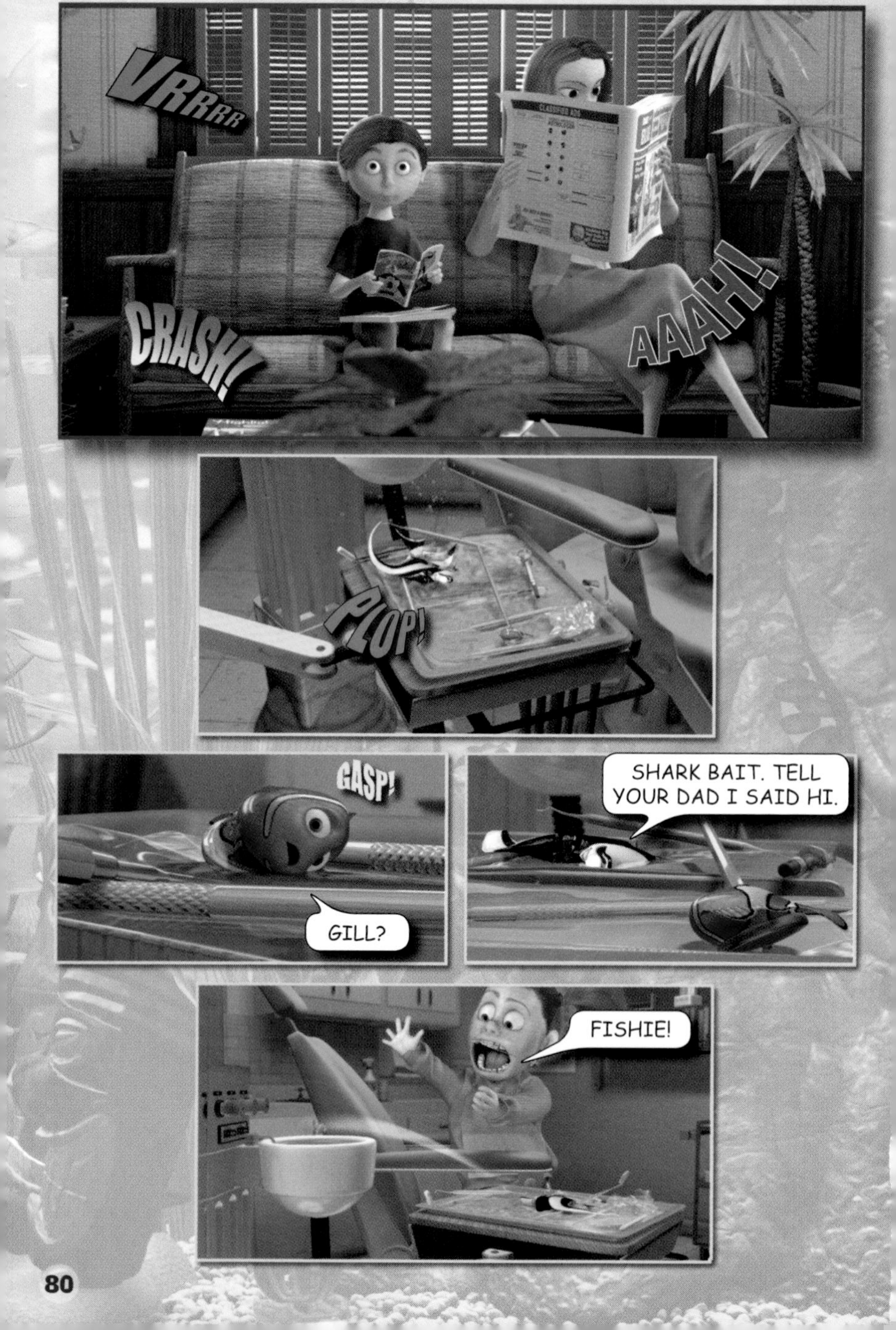
VRRRRR
CRASH!
AAAH!
PLOP!
GASP!
GILL?
SHARK BAIT. TELL YOUR DAD I SAID HI.
FISHIE!

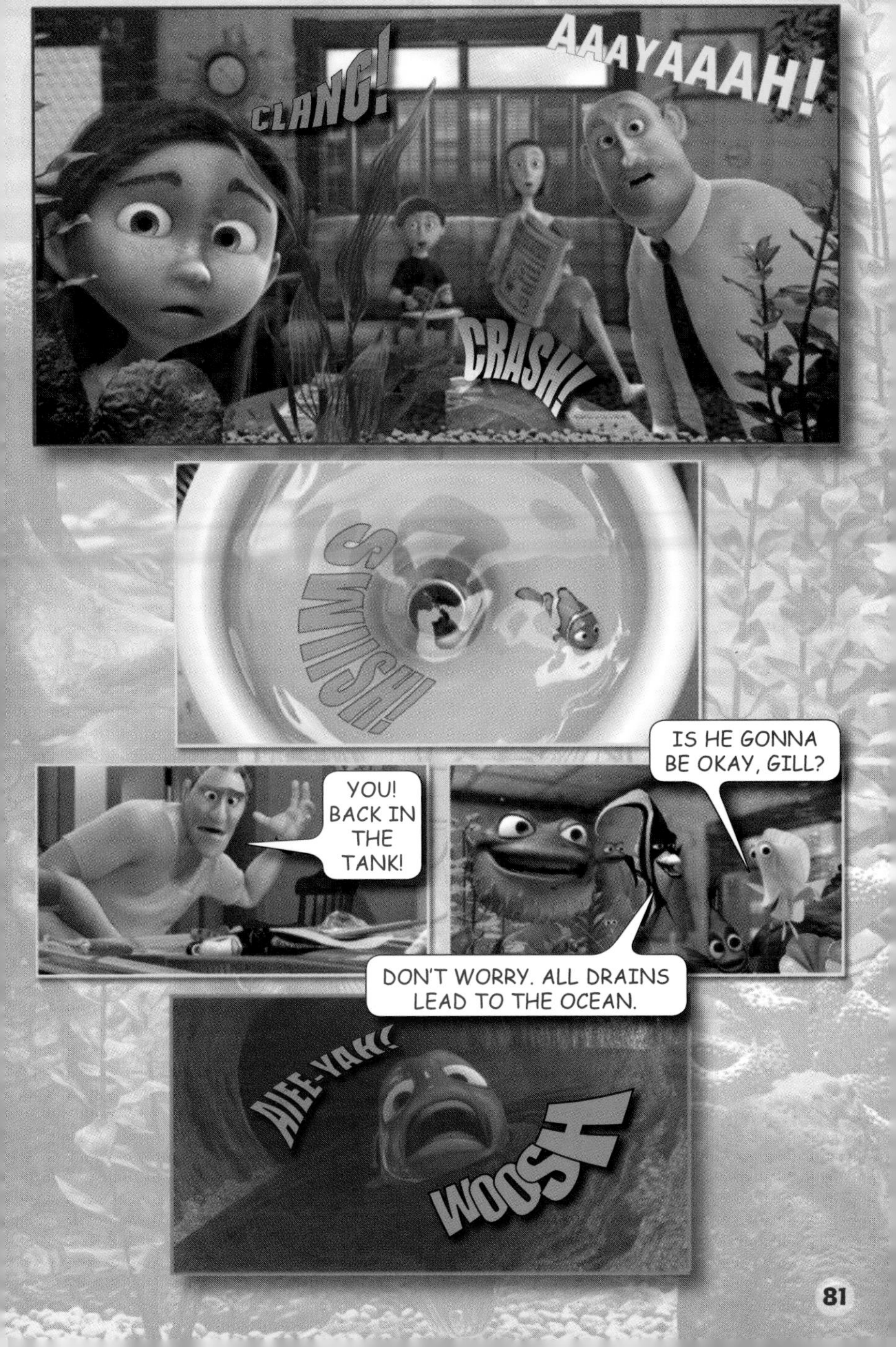
CLANG!
AAAYAAAH!
CRASH!
SWISH!
YOU! BACK IN THE TANK!
IS HE GONNA BE OKAY, GILL?
DON'T WORRY. ALL DRAINS LEAD TO THE OCEAN.
AIEE-YAH!
WOOSH

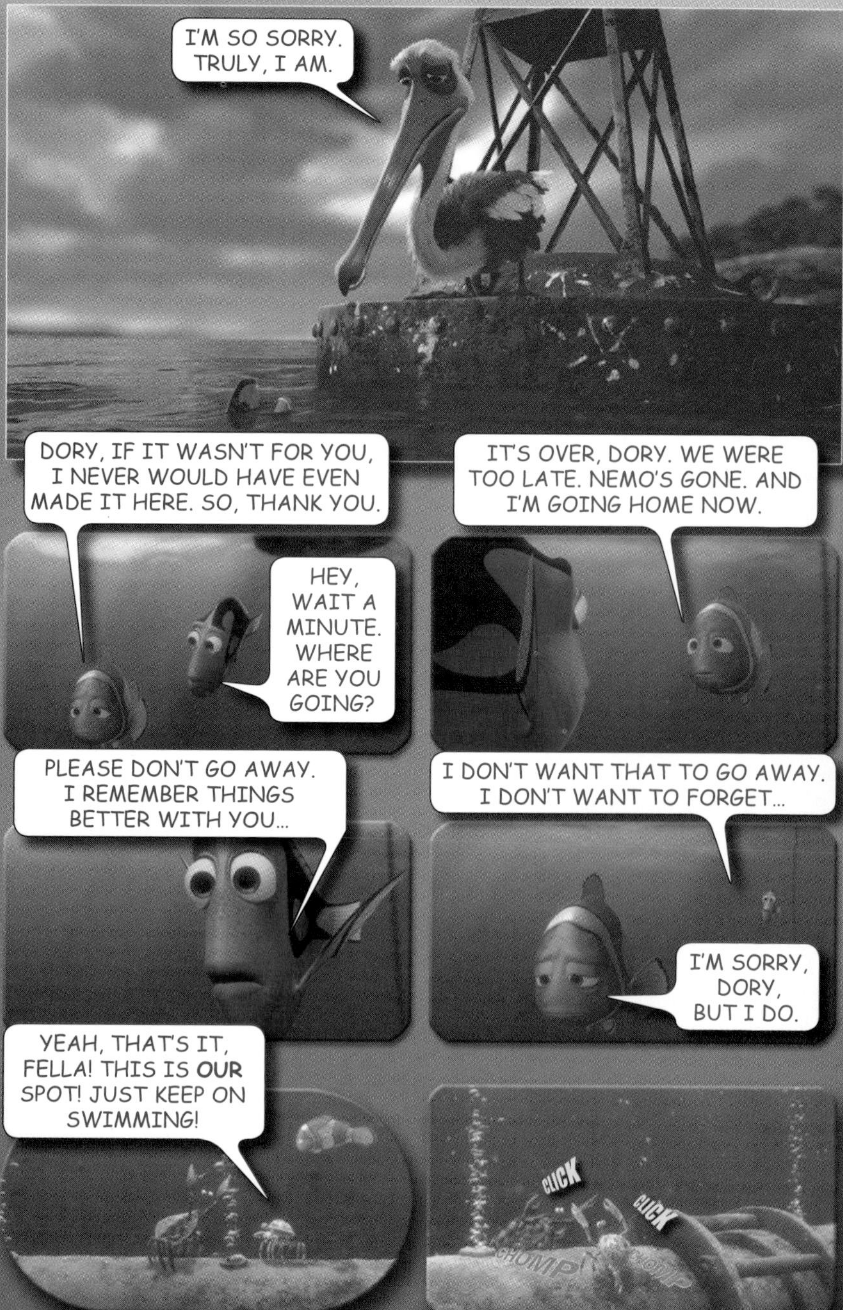
I'M SO SORRY. TRULY, I AM.
DORY, IF IT WASN'T FOR YOU, I NEVER WOULD HAVE EVEN MADE IT HERE. SO, THANK YOU.
HEY, WAIT A MINUTE. WHERE ARE YOU GOING?
IT'S OVER, DORY. WE WERE TOO LATE. NEMO'S GONE. AND I'M GOING HOME NOW.
PLEASE DON'T GO AWAY. I REMEMBER THINGS BETTER WITH YOU...
I DON'T WANT THAT TO GO AWAY. I DON'T WANT TO FORGET...
I'M SORRY, DORY, BUT I DO.
YEAH, THAT'S IT, FELLA! THIS IS **OUR** SPOT! JUST KEEP ON SWIMMING!
CLICK
CLICK
CHOMP!
CHOMP

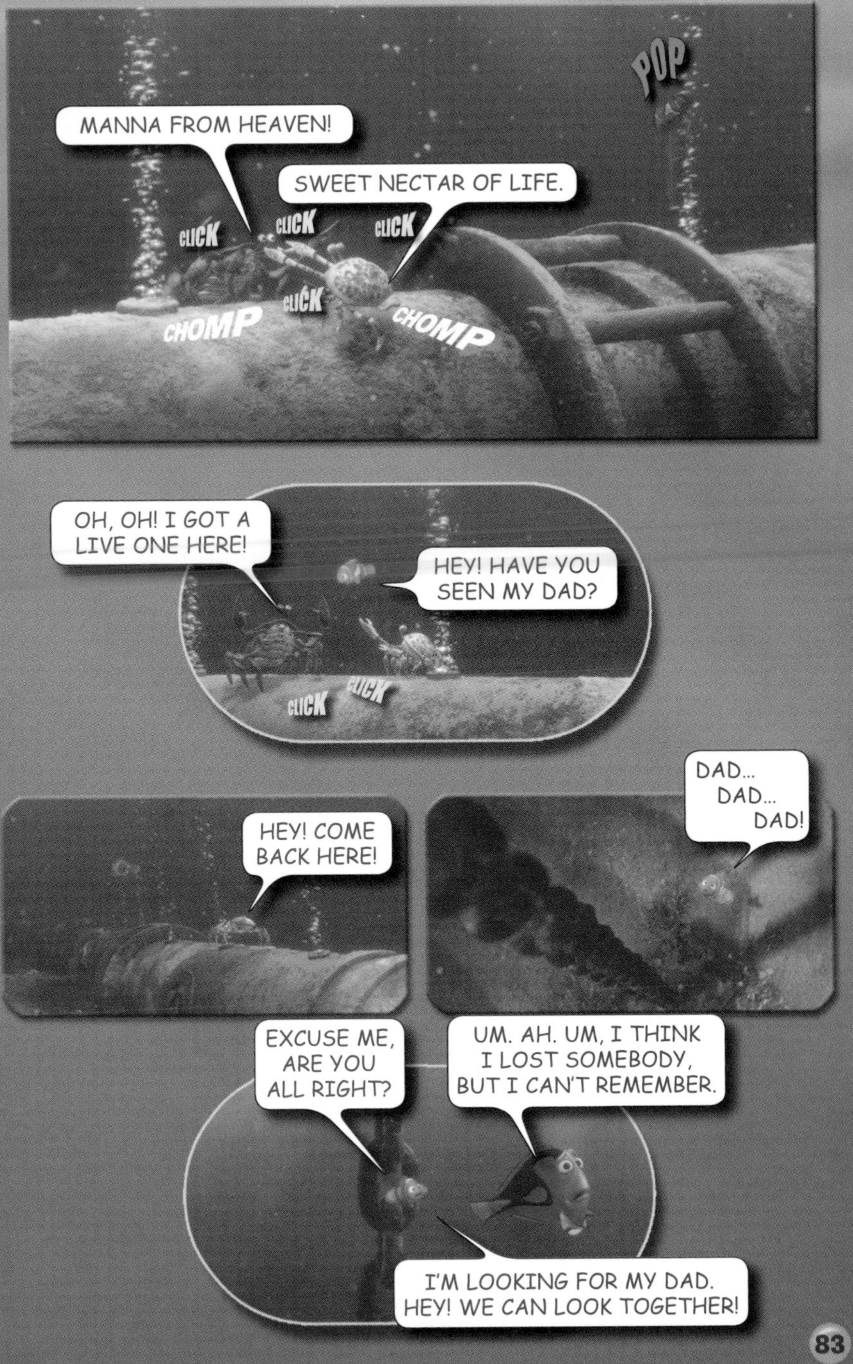
POP
MANNA FROM HEAVEN!
SWEET NECTAR OF LIFE.
CLICK
CLICK
CLICK
CLICK
CHOMP
CHOMP
OH, OH! I GOT A LIVE ONE HERE!
HEY! HAVE YOU SEEN MY DAD?
CLICK
CLICK
HEY! COME BACK HERE!
DAD... DAD... DAD!
EXCUSE ME, ARE YOU ALL RIGHT?
UM. AH. UM, I THINK I LOST SOMEBODY, BUT I CAN'T REMEMBER.
I'M LOOKING FOR MY DAD. HEY! WE CAN LOOK TOGETHER!

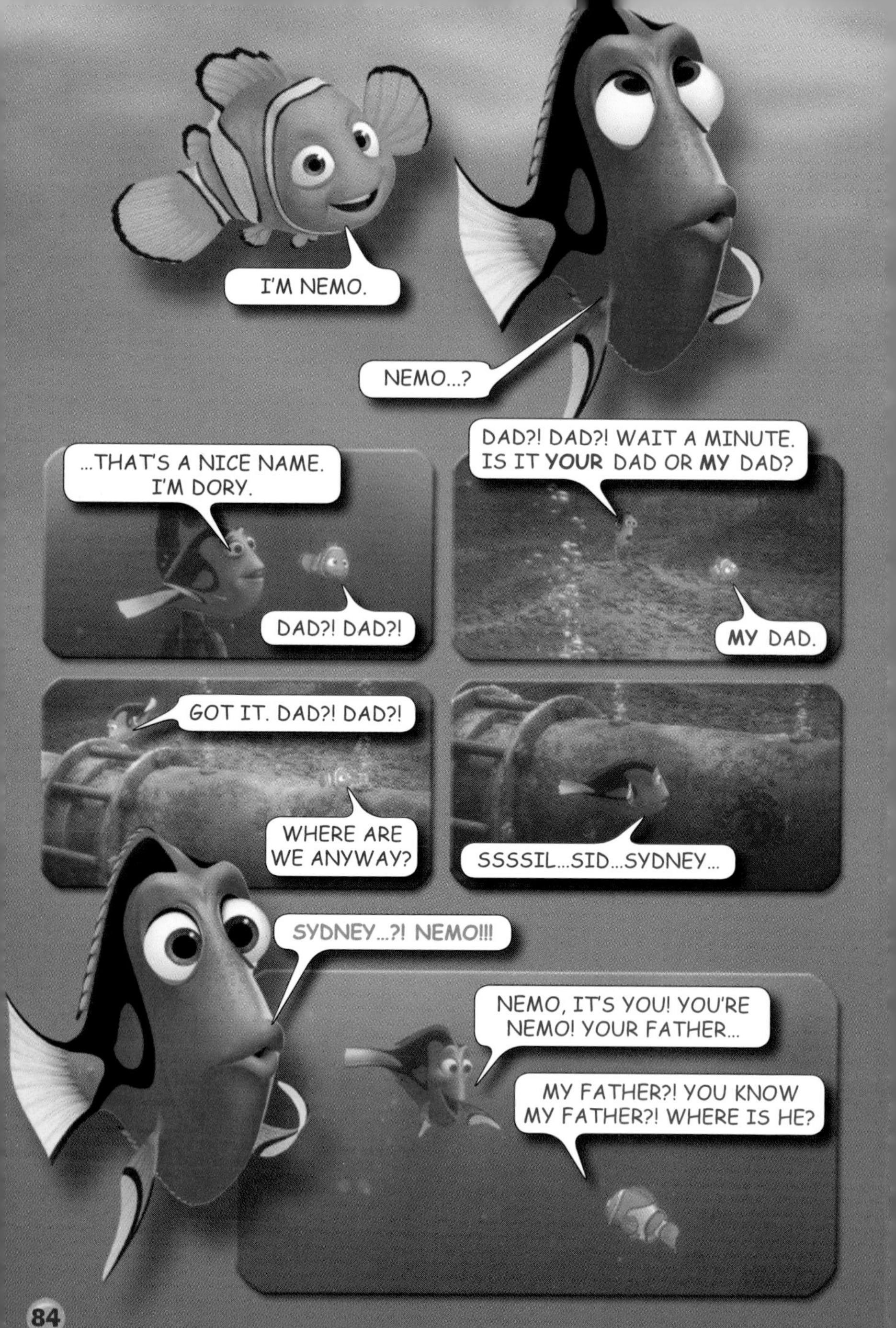
I'M NEMO.
NEMO...?
...THAT'S A NICE NAME. I'M DORY.
DAD?! DAD?!
DAD?! DAD?! WAIT A MINUTE. IS IT **YOUR** DAD OR **MY** DAD?
MY DAD.
GOT IT. DAD?! DAD?!
WHERE ARE WE ANYWAY?
SSSSIL...SID...SYDNEY...
SYDNEY...?! NEMO!!!
NEMO, IT'S YOU! YOU'RE NEMO! YOUR FATHER...
MY FATHER?! YOU KNOW MY FATHER?! WHERE IS HE?

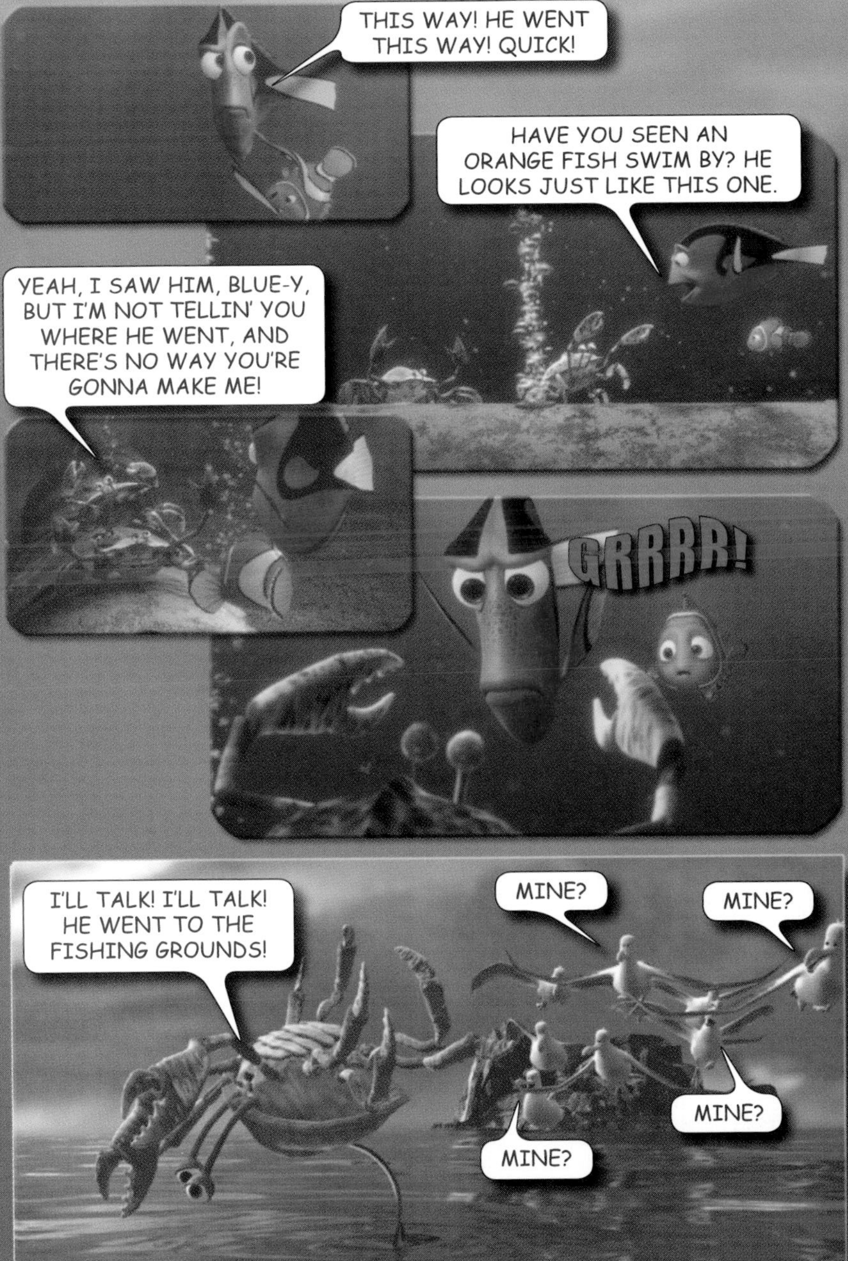
THIS WAY! HE WENT THIS WAY! QUICK!
HAVE YOU SEEN AN ORANGE FISH SWIM BY? HE LOOKS JUST LIKE THIS ONE.
YEAH, I SAW HIM, BLUE-Y, BUT I'M NOT TELLIN' YOU WHERE HE WENT, AND THERE'S NO WAY YOU'RE GONNA MAKE ME!
GRRRR!
I'LL TALK! I'LL TALK! HE WENT TO THE FISHING GROUNDS!
MINE?
MINE?
MINE?
MINE?

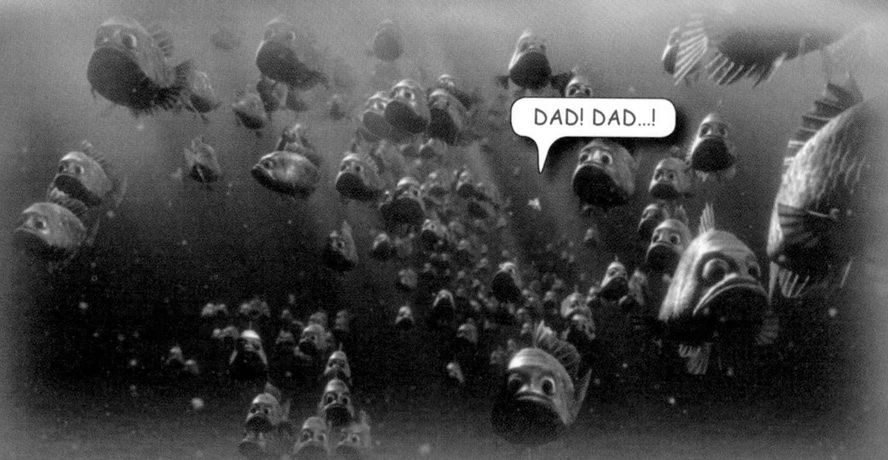
DAD! DAD...!

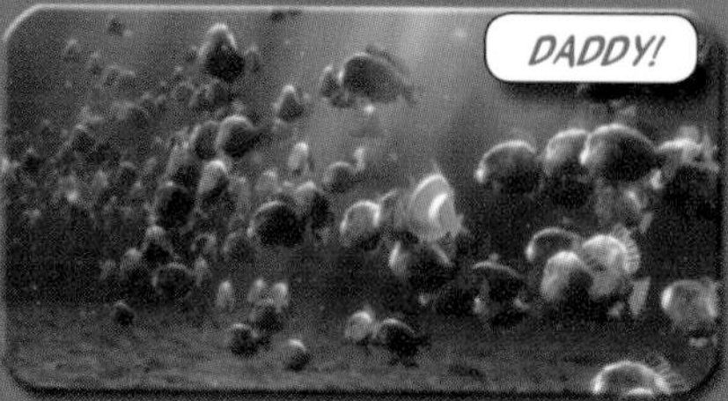
DADDY!

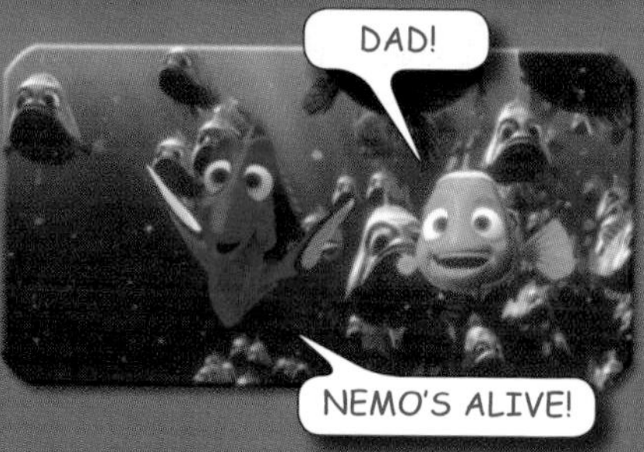
DAD!
NEMO'S ALIVE!

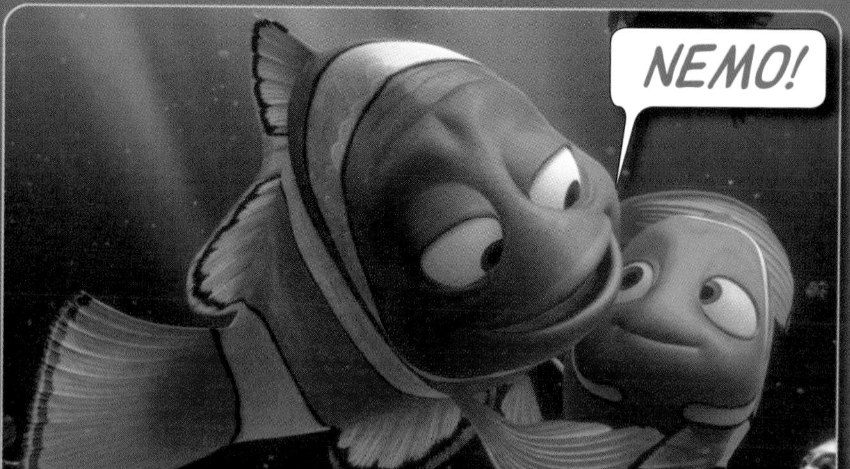
NEMO!

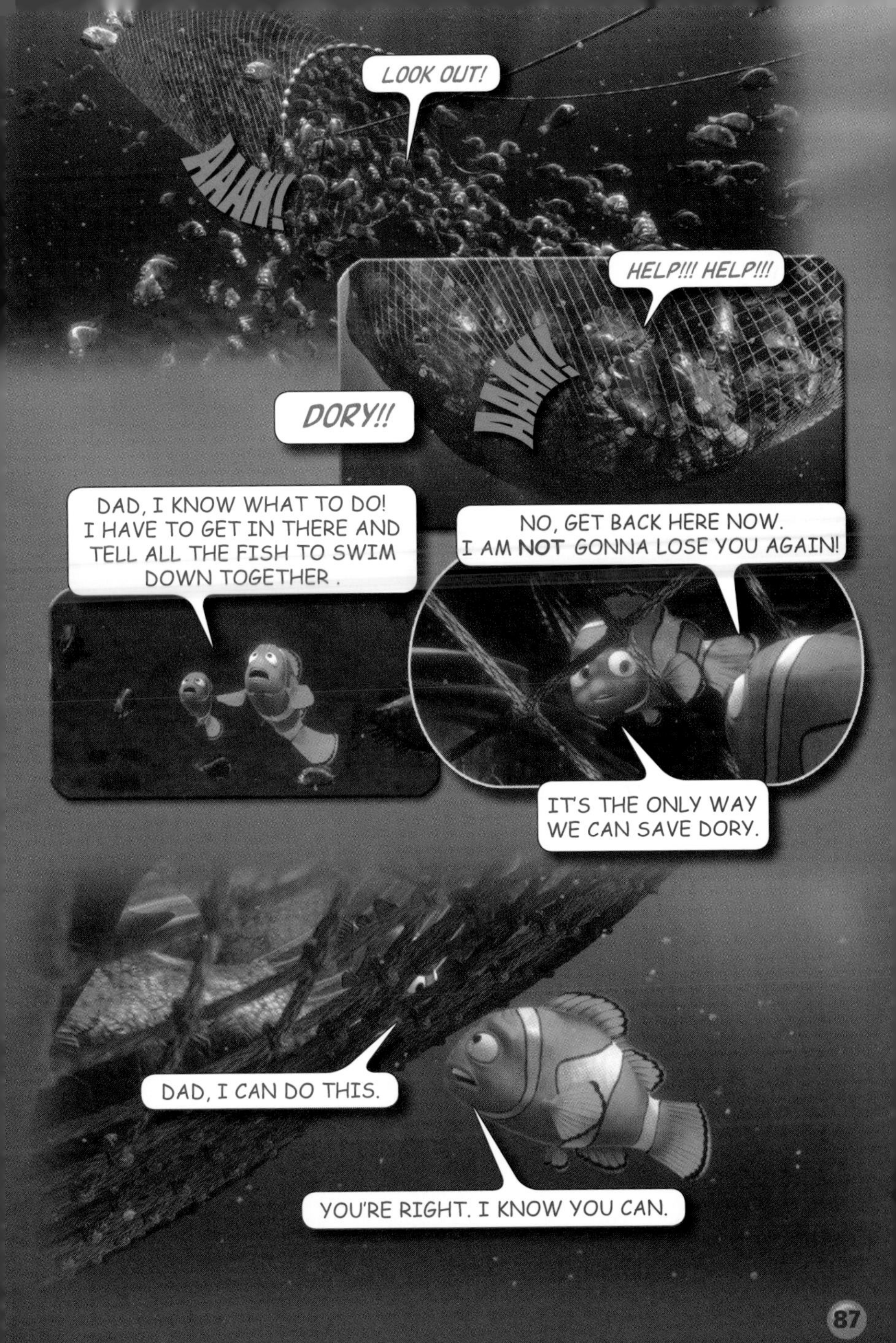
LOOK OUT!
AAAH!
HELP!!! HELP!!!
AAAH!
DORY!!
DAD, I KNOW WHAT TO DO! I HAVE TO GET IN THERE AND TELL ALL THE FISH TO SWIM DOWN TOGETHER .
NO, GET BACK HERE NOW. I AM **NOT** GONNA LOSE YOU AGAIN!
IT'S THE ONLY WAY WE CAN SAVE DORY.
DAD, I CAN DO THIS.
YOU'RE RIGHT. I KNOW YOU CAN.

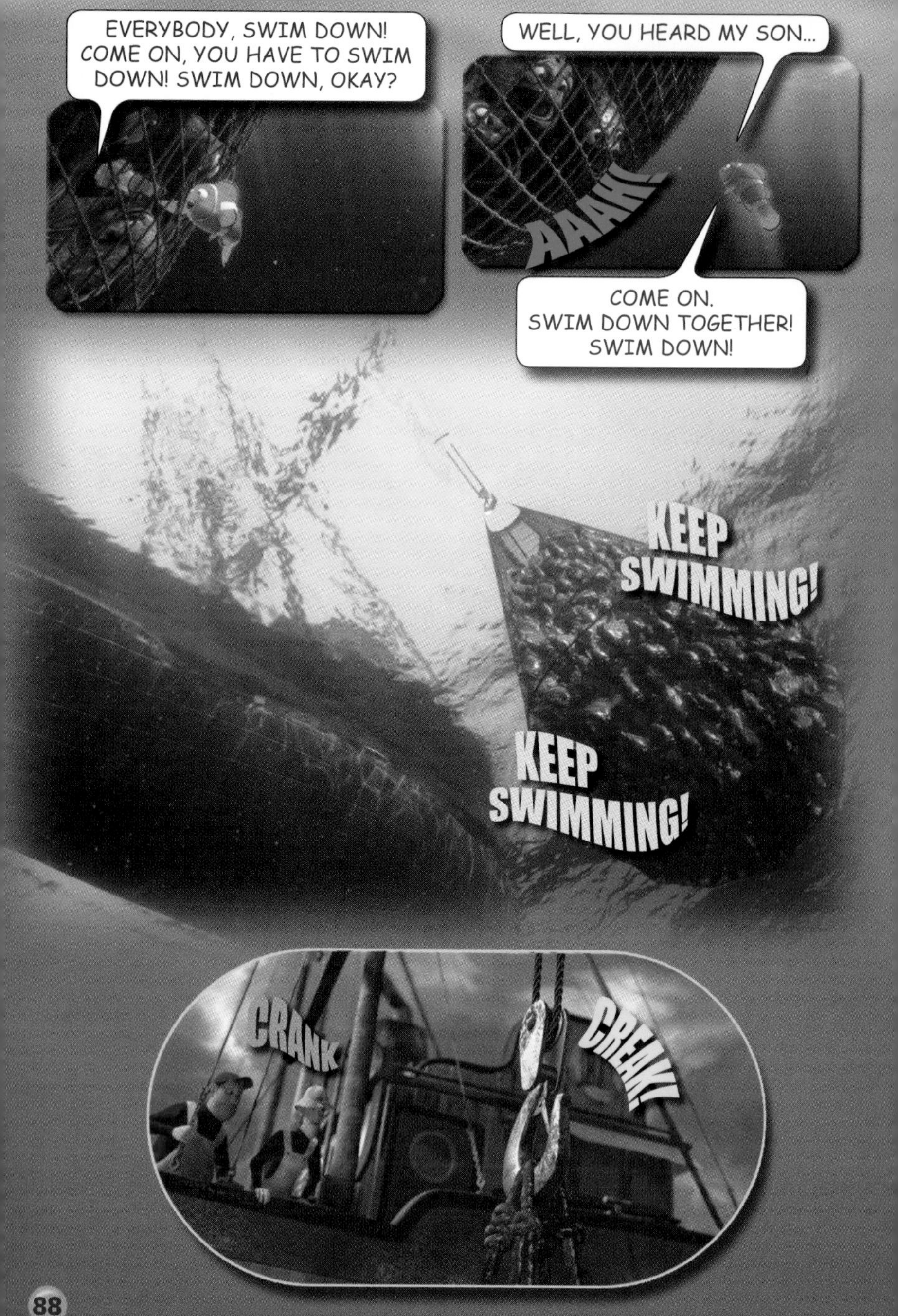
EVERYBODY, SWIM DOWN! COME ON, YOU HAVE TO SWIM DOWN! SWIM DOWN, OKAY?
WELL, YOU HEARD MY SON...
AAAH!
COME ON. SWIM DOWN TOGETHER! SWIM DOWN!
KEEP SWIMMING!
KEEP SWIMMING!
CRANK
CREAK!

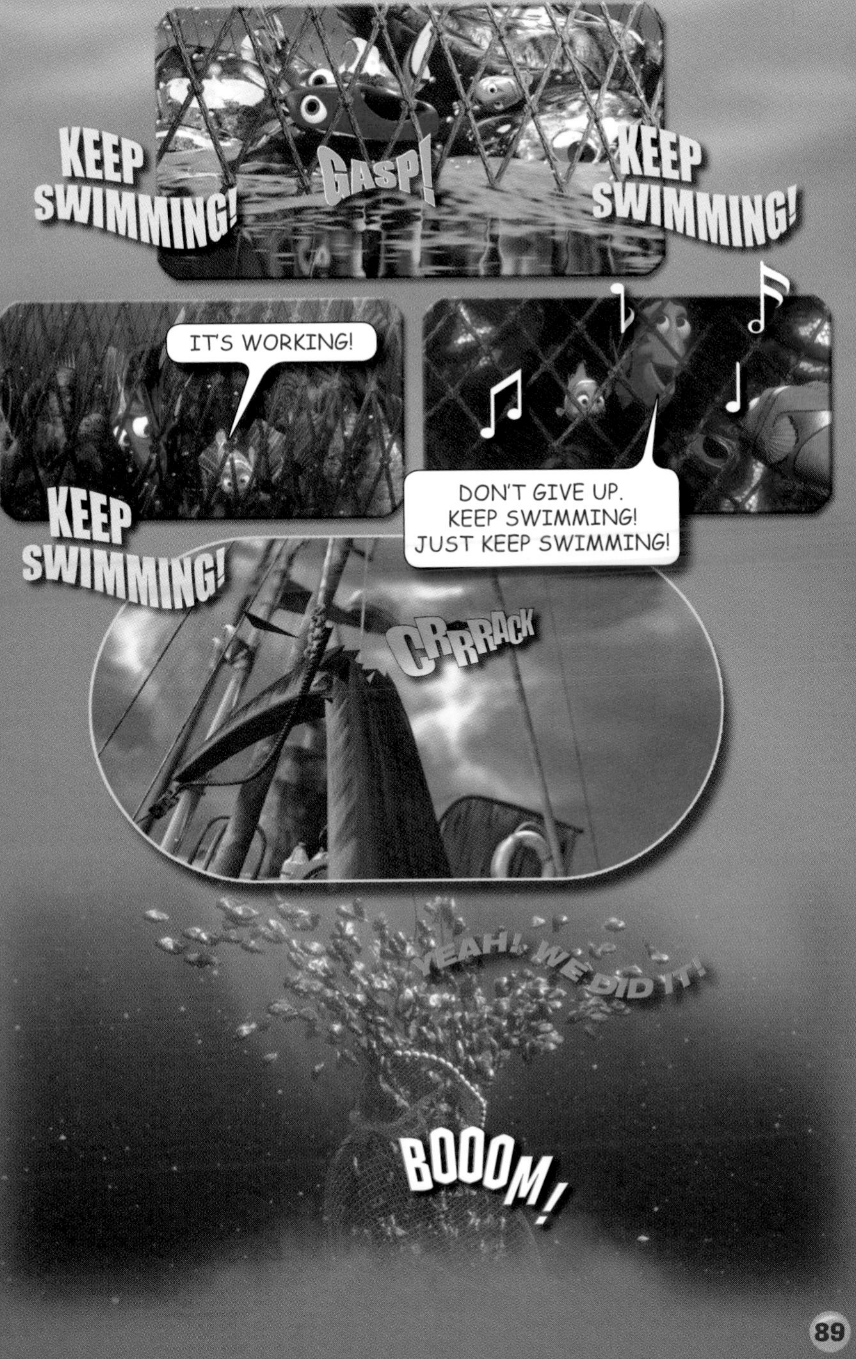
KEEP SWIMMING!
GASP!
KEEP SWIMMING!
IT'S WORKING!
KEEP SWIMMING!
DON'T GIVE UP. KEEP SWIMMING! JUST KEEP SWIMMING!
CRRRACK
YEAH! WE DID IT!
BOOOM!

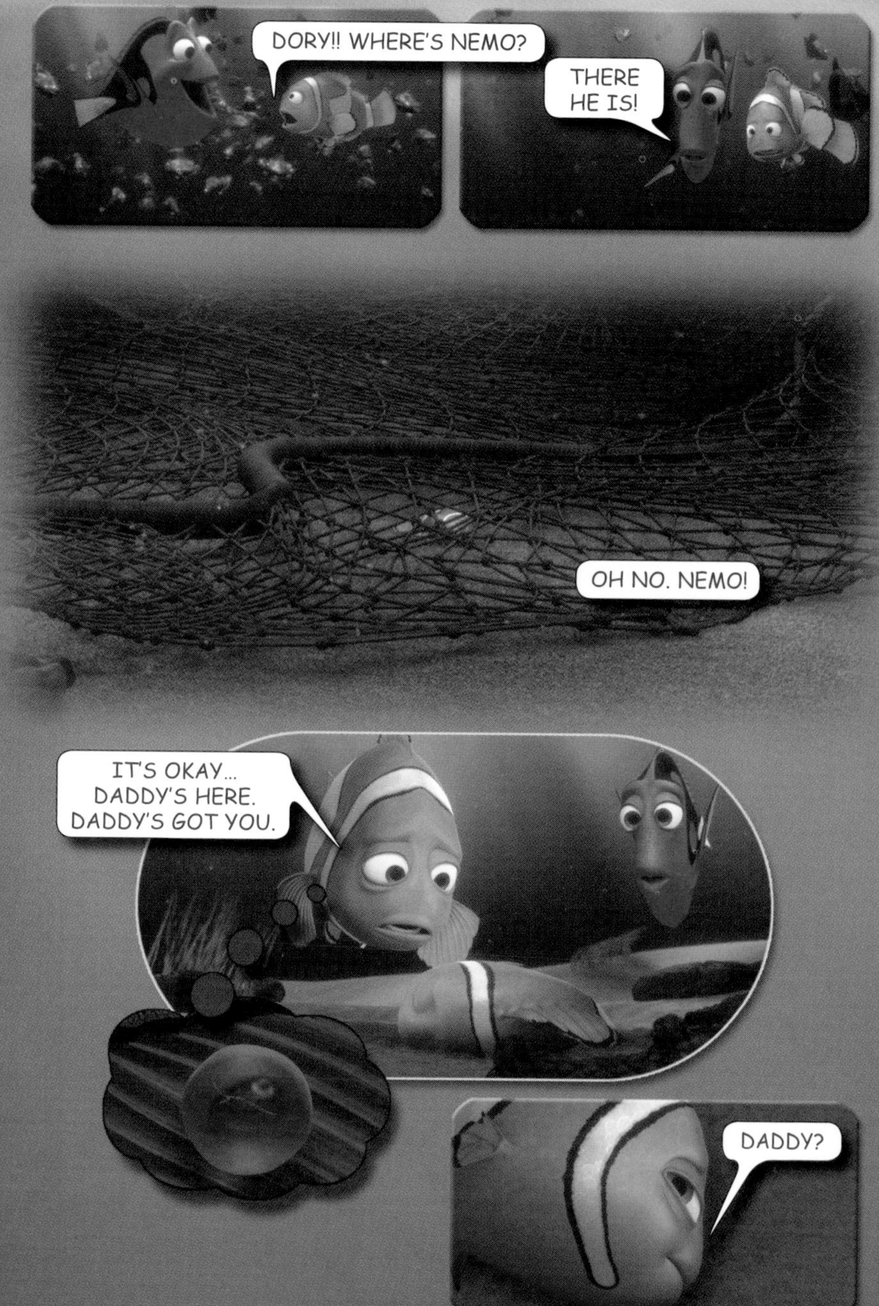
DORY!! WHERE'S NEMO?
THERE HE IS!
OH NO. NEMO!
IT'S OKAY... DADDY'S HERE. DADDY'S GOT YOU.
DADDY?

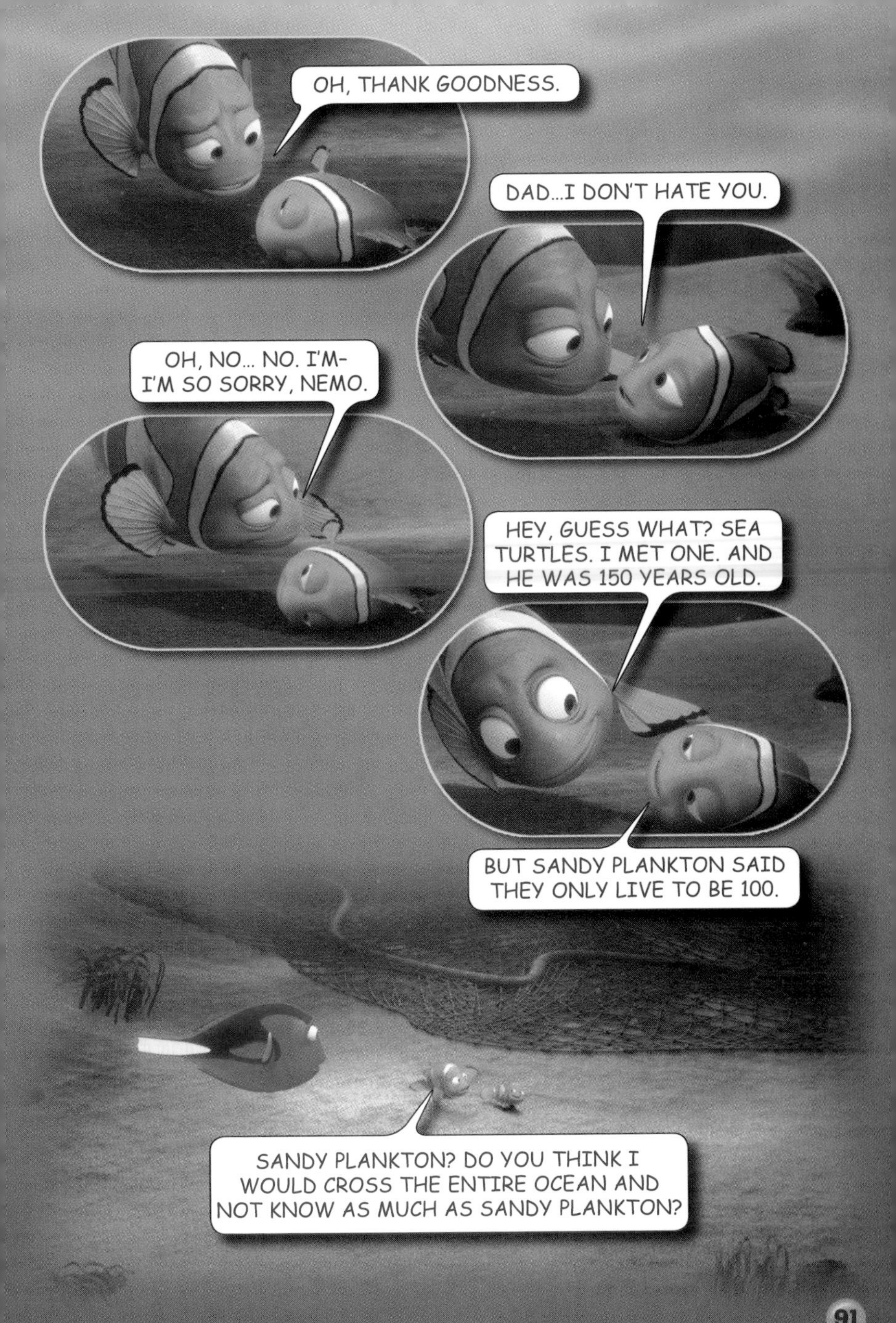
OH, THANK GOODNESS.
DAD...I DON'T HATE YOU.
OH, NO... NO. I'M-
I'M SO SORRY, NEMO.
HEY, GUESS WHAT? SEA
TURTLES. I MET ONE. AND
HE WAS 150 YEARS OLD.
BUT SANDY PLANKTON SAID
THEY ONLY LIVE TO BE 100.
SANDY PLANKTON? DO YOU THINK I
WOULD CROSS THE ENTIRE OCEAN AND
NOT KNOW AS MUCH AS SANDY PLANKTON?

A FEW WEEKS LATER...

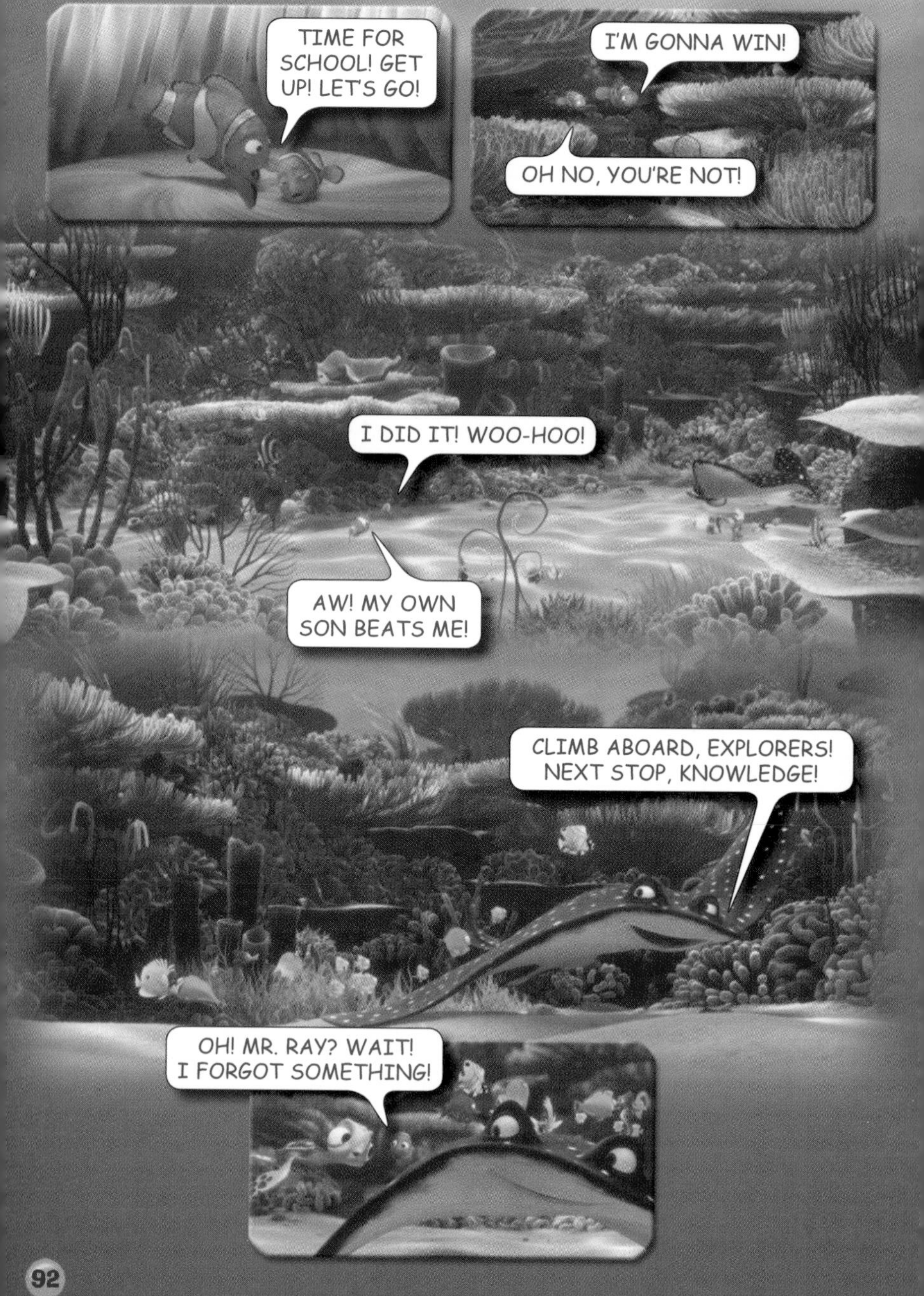
TIME FOR SCHOOL! GET UP! LET'S GO!
I'M GONNA WIN!
OH NO, YOU'RE NOT!
I DID IT! WOO-HOO!
AW! MY OWN SON BEATS ME!
CLIMB ABOARD, EXPLORERS! NEXT STOP, KNOWLEDGE!
OH! MR. RAY? WAIT! I FORGOT SOMETHING!

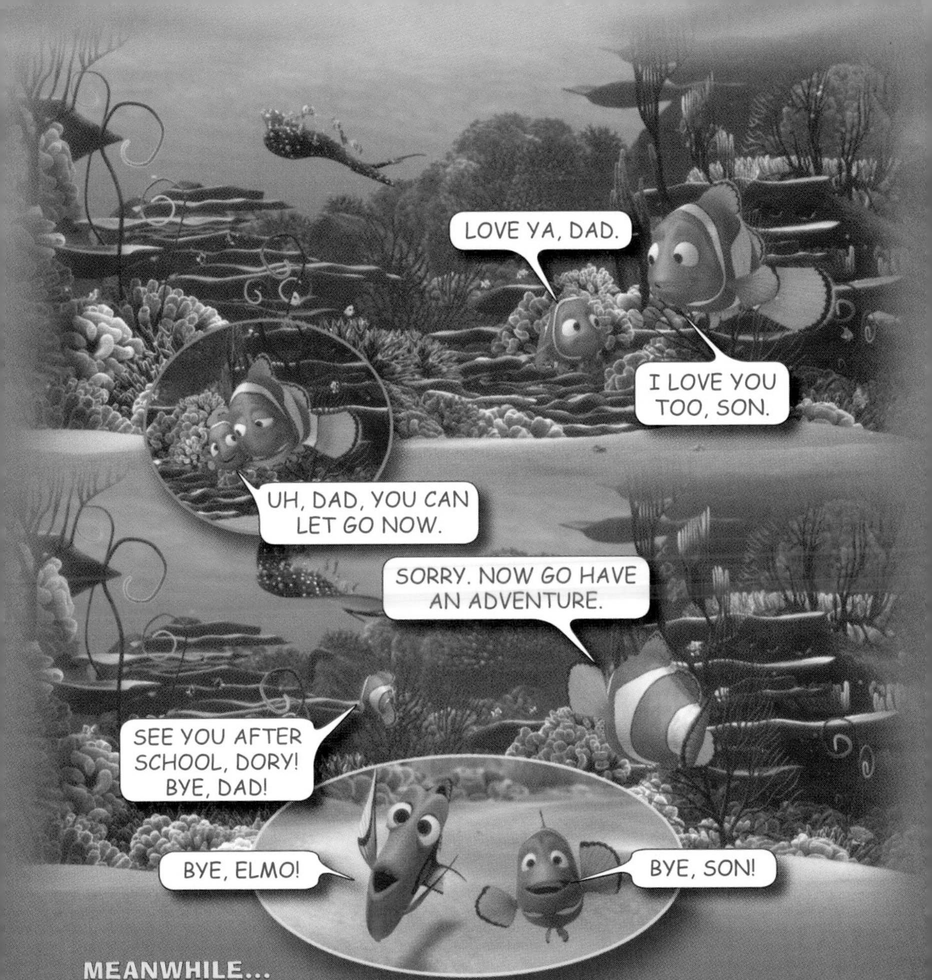
LOVE YA, DAD.
I LOVE YOU TOO, SON.
UH, DAD, YOU CAN LET GO NOW.
SORRY. NOW GO HAVE AN ADVENTURE.
SEE YOU AFTER SCHOOL, DORY! BYE, DAD!
BYE, ELMO!
BYE, SON!

MEANWHILE...

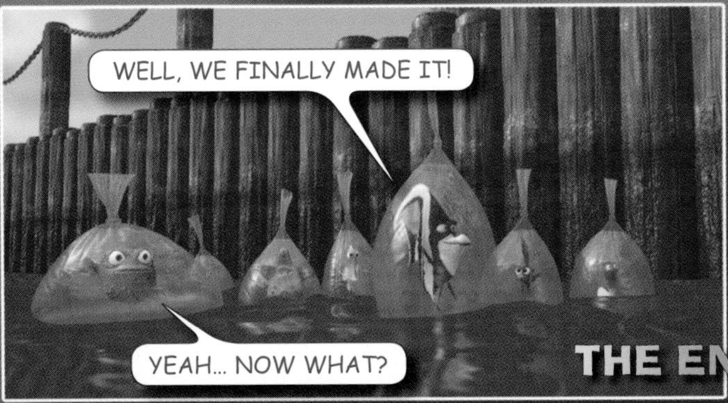
WELL, WE FINALLY MADE IT!
YEAH... NOW WHAT?

THE END

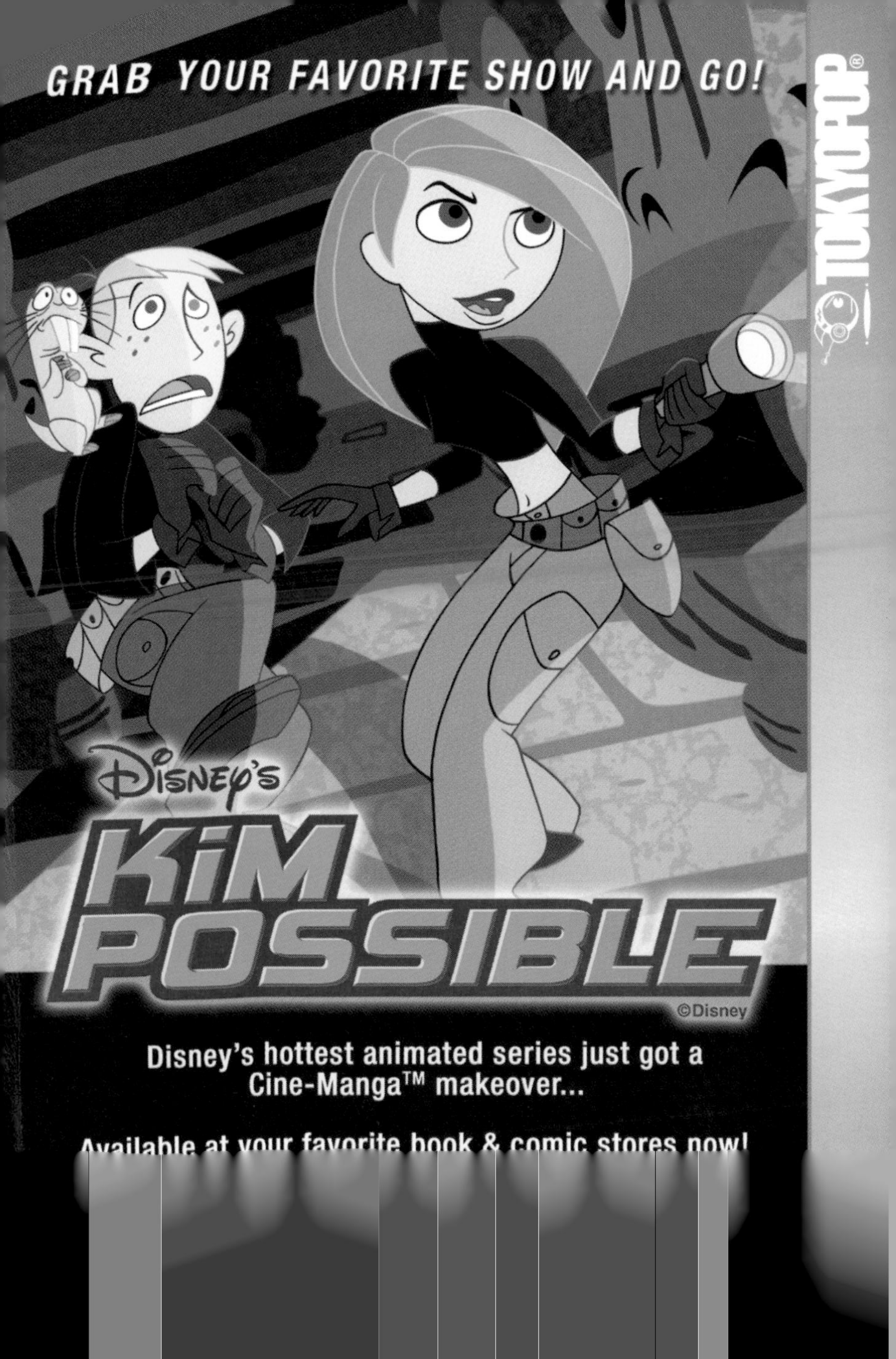

GRAB YOUR FAVORITE SHOW AND GO!
TOKYOPOP®
Disney's
KIM POSSIBLE
©Disney
Disney's hottest animated series just got a Cine-Manga™ makeover...
Available at your favorite book & comic stores now!

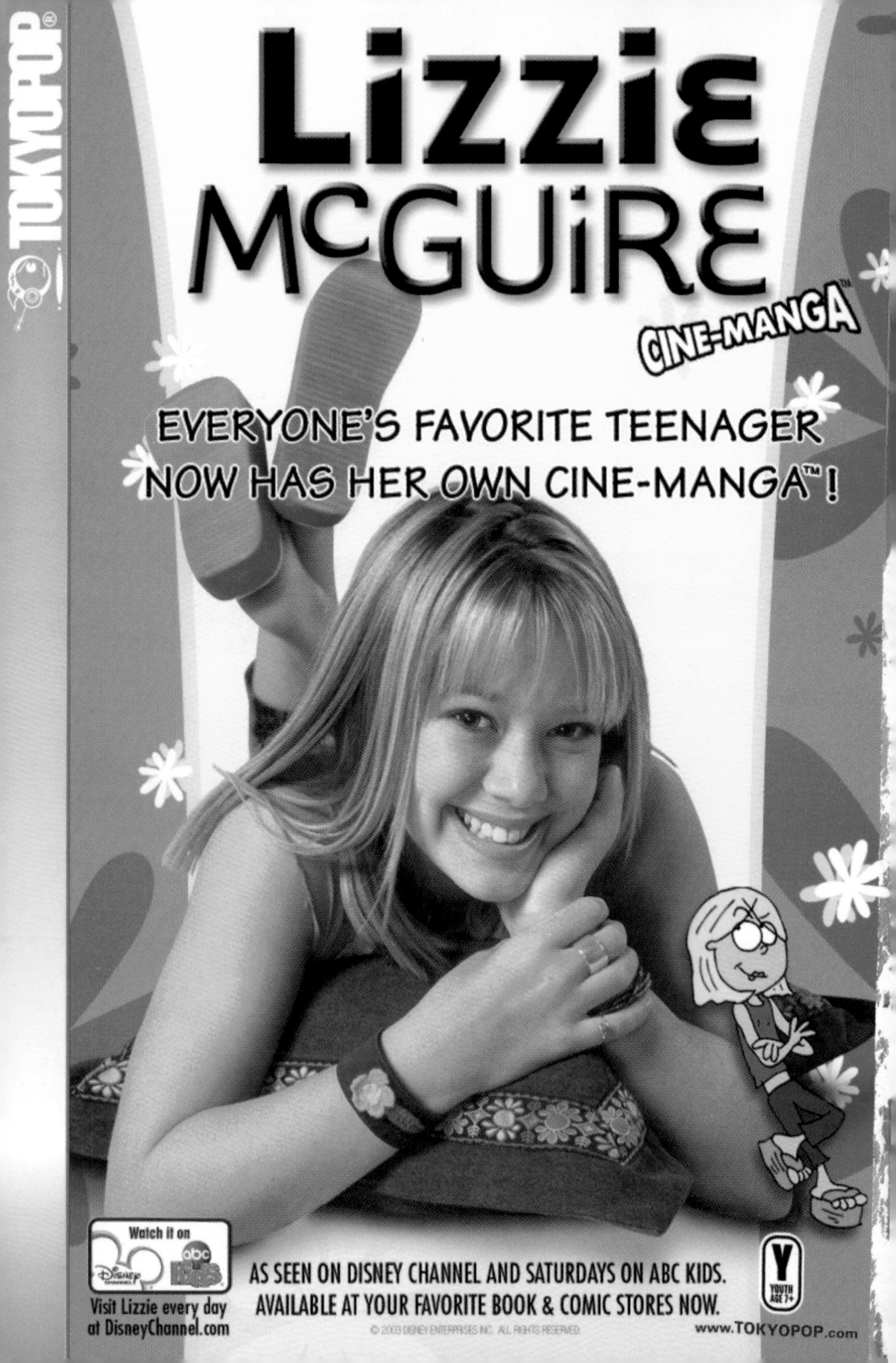
TOKYOPOP®
Lizzie McGUiRE
CINE-MANGA™
EVERYONE'S FAVORITE TEENAGER
NOW HAS HER OWN CINE-MANGA™!
Watch it on
DISNEY CHANNEL
abc KIDS
Visit Lizzie every day
at DisneyChannel.com
AS SEEN ON DISNEY CHANNEL AND SATURDAYS ON ABC KIDS.
AVAILABLE AT YOUR FAVORITE BOOK & COMIC STORES NOW.
© 2003 DISNEY ENTERPRISES INC. ALL RIGHTS RESERVED.
Y
YOUTH AGE 7+
www.TOKYOPOP.com